CONSENSUS AND COMPROMISE

Creating the First National Urban Policy under President Carter

Yvonne Scruggs-Leftwich

University Press of America,® Inc.
Lanham · Boulder · New York · Toronto · Oxford

4501 Forbes Boulevard
Suite 200
Lanham, Maryland 20706
UPA Acquisitions Department (301) 459-3366

PO Box 317
Oxford
OX2 9RU, UK

Printed in the United States of America
British Library Cataloging in Publication Information Available

Library of Congress Control Number: 2005934182
ISBN 0-7618-3355-2 (paperback : alk. ppr.)

™ The paper used in this publication meets the minimum requirements of American National Standard for Information Sciences—Permanence of Paper for Printed Library Materials, ANSI Z39.48—1984

Dedicated to the Memory of

The Honorable Patricia Roberts Harris, Esq.
May 31, 1924 - March 23, 1985

Contents

List of Tables and Figures

Tables

Figures

Preface

There are many good reasons, in 2005, for revisiting America's only official National Urban Policy. One is the need to reflect on a time in U.S. history when federal attitudes toward cities were not mere guises for serving the unbridled greed of the wealthy, but rather were constructive, sensibly creative, and intentionally protective of poor people's rights. That time culminated in the national public policy collaboration chronicled in this book.

The first official "National Urban Policy: A Partnership to Conserve America's Communities," was created during a time when Congress and federal agency appointees were actually troubled by the dim prospects for "cities in distress," in contrast to today's slash-and-burn, scorched-earth use of federal power. As a consequence, the Treasury Department's policies sought to provide public relief, not to the richest among us, but to identifiable distressed cities where most of the poorest among us lived. Public appointees consciously sought to meet the challenge of high-minded standards of personal and public performance:

> Please make sure that the urban policy statement leads off with a position on the poor and black of our cities, and how the first aim of an urban policy should be to transform this group into a stable community with dependable and adequate income, social equality and racial mobility.[1]

In 1977 and 1978, President Carter's National Urban Policy process sought to design strategies for cities that took into account the desirable interdependence of economic development, employment availability, gentrification, racial diversity, settlement density, shelter affordability, transit convenience, and the growth of private enterprise.

From Constructive to Toxic—A Reversal of the Federal Role

Few of these concerns for protecting the poor and transforming urban communities for the better are seen today in legislative proposals presented to Congress by the George W. Bush administration. For example, a coalition of city and housing watchdog organizations characterizes one recent initiative proposed by the Department of Housing and Urban Development (HUD) as:

> ... designed to deny protections to the poor, elderly and disabled, while it offers the nation's housing authorities enough flexibility to dump low-income households out of the program in exchange for higher income renters.[2]

The majority of HUD-regulated public housing units are located in urban areas. Previously, the agency was the primary advocate for survival of the cities and for a responsible national urban policy.

"The State and Local Housing Flexibility Act of 2005," a radical piece of legislation at odds with past initiatives, is strongly opposed by respected professionals in the field "on behalf of the 9.7 million extremely low income households with severe housing cost burdens who need housing assistance, and the 5 million families able to afford safe and decent housing today (only) through HUD's major housing subsidy programs."

It is projected that 75 percent of those low-income public housing beneficiaries soon will be either homeless or extremely vulnerable to homelessness. Today, homelessness is an intractable challenge to all major cities, where an estimated 3.5 million people, 39 percent of them children, have nowhere to live.[3]

Meanwhile, the historically powerful Senate Committee on Banking, Housing and Urban Affairs, the font since 1970 of deliberation, funding support and regulatory control over urban policies, including its 1978-mandated annual national urban policy report, was dismantled in April 2005. Its functions are to be distributed across several Senate committees, none of which has as its primary concern the condition of cities. Current federal policies and priorities have created a climate that is toxic for all urban communities.

An Uneven History

Looking back over the years since 1978, only the efforts by the Clinton administration approached any continuation of the Carter administration's spirit and focus on urban policy. Inspired in part by the 1996 global meeting of "Habitat II: City Summit," convened in Istanbul, Turkey, the Clinton administration was pushed and shoved--from within as well as without--to replicate the international dialogue in a White House summit on urban policy.

Under the leadership of then-Secretary Henry Cisneros, HUD had been a vigorous participant in "Habitat II," preparing and issuing a comprehensive report, *The Urban Challenge.* When pressed for a more pro-active role by the White House in helping cities, President Clinton responded as follows to Dr. Ramona H. Edelin, President of the National Urban Coalition:

> Thank you for ...suggesting a White House Conference on Urban Policy. My administration has worked hard to make urban policy a priority and to bring greater opportunity and individual empowerment to our nation's communities....I also agree that we have a great opportunity to strengthen and broaden our efforts through a high- profile discussion of urban issues and I have asked the Vice-President to explore...having such a meeting.[4]

Unfortunately, although some preliminary meetings took place, such a summit never occurred. To his credit, however, Clinton announced during the first ninety days of his presidency, that he was advancing an agenda to "Rebuild America's Cities." The agenda included:

- Investing in communities
- Empowerment through economic opportunity
- A national crime strategy
- Rebuilding the urban infrastructure
- New hope for affordable housing
- Fighting homelessness
- Empowerment through education, and
- Quality, affordable health care

The viable urban initiatives that followed were the Empowerment Zone/Enterprise Community Program and a Department of Transportation urban revitalization initiative centered around transit facilities, stations, and urban transit shelters. This more subtle, modest, and decentralized approach to urban policy characterized the eight years of the Clinton Presidency.

This was a vast improvement, however, over the Ronald Reagan/ George H.W. Bush tenure. Until the riots in Los Angeles in April 1992, urban policy had virtually disappeared from the federal lexicon as well as from popular journals and other mainstream media sources. A search of "Readers' Guide to Periodical Literature" in the late 1980s revealed no category at all for "national urban policy" and all "urban policy" citations were found in the category for "HUD." The city-sympathetic HUD Secretary at the time of the riots, former Senator Jack Kemp, obviously had been unable to advocate successfully for Executive Branch attention to his mandated area.

When Los Angeles went up in flames, programs that Secretary Kemp had been unsuccessfully promoting were hastily revived, dusted off, and presented by the Bush White House as solutions to the tinder of urban ills that had ignited the city's fires. One perceptive journalist for National Public Radio, reporting on President Bush's speedy resurrection of Jack Kemp's formerly dead-on-arrival urban proposals, wrote:

> Bush has finally discovered his urban policy. It has been hiding in Jack Kemp's desk drawer.[5]

In the twelve years of the Reagan and Bush I administrations, this was the only time when urban policy was advanced as a serious federal initiative. Quite literally, it took the burning of a city to light a fire under a federal urban policy discussion in the White House.

The Exercise in Conflict and Compromise

When President Carter and his HUD Secretary, the late Patricia Roberts Harris, undertook the development of a national urban policy in the early months of the administration, conditions in cities were deplorable, as this book documents. The national context, however, was essentially egalitarian, the commitment to an aggressive tide to lift all boats was strong, and the will to fulfill America's promise of improving life for all urban dwellers was determined. The policy process used this proactive climate to good advantage.

This study of the year-long path to a codified national urban policy analyzes the actions, processes, and incremental decisions that finally led to its creation rather than the substance of the policy itself. The focus is upon the dynamics of transactions among federal bureaucrats, public officials, private citizens, urban advocates, and scholars that characterized the policy's development. Records document how these transactions ultimately led to the ten urban policy components—a series of amended choices—that President Carter announced in March 1978.

The retrospective analysis examines the role of political stakeholders, vested institutional interests, and individual values in the policy development process. The President's ultimate decisions, on both policies and policy title, were guided by complex conflicts and compromises, negotiations and trade-offs, and finally, by his technical as well as his political concerns.

Carter's policy planning mechanism often was paralyzed by a number of power struggles over:

- Health Education and Welfare's (HEW) welfare reform;
- HUD's assisted housing and community development programs;
- Commerce's planned economic development expansion;
- Labor's push to preserve expensive concentrated employment initiatives;
- Treasury's Urban Bank; and
- A persistent political demand for the Urban Policy to concentrate on both large *and* small cities.

Issues of urban poverty, unemployment, and disinvestment contended with, and were neutralized by, managed growth concerns and sun-belt needs. Yet, in retrospect, it seems like it was a "walk in the park," even *with* that fractious group of basically humane sojourners.

Where Are The Key Actors Now?

President Jimmy Carter, like most of the other urban policy advocates who shepherded the first National Urban Policy through its creation, approval, and final Congressional enactment in 1978, has continued his work to improve human settlements and provide decent "shelter in the poorest ghetto areas in America."[6] His current status as a Nobel Peace Laureate overshadows somewhat his housing and urban policy credentials, not just for the first and only official National Urban Policy, but also for his profoundly effective leadership with Habitat for Humanity. These contributions have been burnished by time and by comparison with the dismal performance in these areas by his White House successors.

In celebrating the twenty-fifth anniversary of Habitat for Humanity in 2001, President Carter explained his continuing commitment to these issues:

> I would say that one of the greatest personal crises for (a family) would be not having a shelter for one's children, which would

> generate despair and a sense of hopelessness and isolation and abandonment.[7]

These are common emotions in the barren wasteland that is much of the urban core. The current threat from Congress and the Bush-2 administration of further dislocation and inevitable homelessness does nothing to assuage these anxieties.

HUD Secretary Patricia Roberts Harris subsequently became the first Secretary of the new (1979) Department of Health and Human Services (HHS, formerly HEW), the first African American and first woman to achieve this dual federal role. At the end of the Carter administration, she returned to the practice of law. She made an unsuccessful run for mayor of the District of Columbia in 1984 and died in 1985, at age 59, after a difficult illness. Her career of extraordinary accomplishments has been commemorated by the issuance of a United States postal stamp in her honor in 1999, more than twenty years after she led the successful creation of a codified National Urban Policy.

Robert C. Embry, Esq., President Carter's Assistant Secretary of Community Planning and Development, and Secretary Harris' deputy for the Urban Policy process, is president of the Abell Foundation. He currently lives and works again in his beloved Baltimore, Maryland.

Dr. Donna Shalala, appointed by President Carter as Assistant Secretary for HUD's Policy Development and Research office where much of the Urban Policy analysis was conducted, became the President of Hunter College in New York City and, later, Chancellor of the University of Wisconsin at Madison. In 1992, she became Secretary of the HHS Department in the Clinton administration where she served for the full eight years of the Clinton presidency.

Stuart Eizenstat, Esq., President Carter's Domestic Policy Advisor, is a partner with a Washington, DC, law firm. He served as Assistant Secretary in the U.S. Treasury Department in the Clinton Administration.

Congresswoman Marcy Kaptur, former Special Assistant to President Carter for the Urban and Regional Planning Group's community and neighborhoods' policy, left the White House at the end of that administration. After a short time as a city and regional planner, she ran for political office and has now served twelve terms (24 years) as representative from Ohio's 9th Congressional District.

The first URPG Executive Director, Dr. Lynn Alan Curtis, founded and, after twenty-five years, remains the President of the Milton S. Eisenhower Foundation. The Eisenhower Foundation continues many of the National Urban Policy traditions through its commitment to urban issues that affect those who are "locked in the cities' poorhouse." He also is the author of several books.

R. Joyce Whitley, my principal policy advisor while I was URPG's executive director, died suddenly in 1992. At that time, she was an urban planner/urban designer in her family's Architecture and Planning firm in Cleveland, Ohio.

Since the end of the Carter administration, I have continued working in the area of urban policy, first, with city and state governments, then with research and public policy institutions, and, immediately following URPG and most recently, in academia. I returned initially to my post of professor and chair of city and regional planning at Howard University. Then, I served as Deputy Mayor of Philadelphia and as Commissioner of Housing and Community Renewal in New York State Governor Mario Cuomo's Cabinet. I also directed the Urban Policy Institute for the Washington-based think tank, the Joint Center for Political and Economic Studies. For nearly a decade, I served as Executive Director/COO for the premier national civil rights advocacy confederation, the Black Leadership Forum. Recently, I returned to academia as a professor at the National Labor College—George Meany Campus, in Maryland.

Yvonne (Perry) Scruggs-Leftwich
Silver Springs, Maryland
May 2005

Notes

1. Robert C. Embry, Jr., memorandum to Yvonne Perry, September 1977.
2. Lynda Carson, "New Bill Would Kill Section 8 Housing Program," San Francisco Bay View, May 5, 2005. SFBayView.com.
3. Urban Institute, "A New Look at Homelessness in America," Fed. 2000," www.urban.org.
4. Letter dated September 9, 1996.
5. Leo E. Heagerty, ed., *Eyes on the President: George Bush: History in Essays and Cartoons* (Occidental, CA: Chronos Publishing, 1993), 107.
6. Celebration at Indianapolis, September 15, 2001.
7. Ibid.

Acknowledgments

When a book has taken as long in its completion as this one, the list of those who deserve recognition for their contributions, both intentional and unintentional, grows longer as well.

First, I owe a special debt of gratitude to the Ford Foundation for supporting my research during the initial phases, which enabled me to collect, review, and preserve all the URGP archival materials.

Then, there are those whose contributions have spanned the entire process. Drs. Thomas A. Reiner and Howard E. Mitchell were involved from the very beginning of my preparations and planning. To them I am deeply indebted. I also continue to benefit from the echoed advice and enduring pencilled marginal notes of the late Morton Lustig and the challenge issued by Dr. Morton J. Schussheim to undertake this study.

I am grateful, also, to Cathryn D. "Kate" Perry, my daughter and first research assistant on this project, who organized and catalogued the archival materials and the working bibliography at the beginning of the research. Dr. Anthony R. Tomazinis graciously agreed to serve as a reviewer after the process was underway and made valuable references available.

Wanda Green was indispensable in the transition from typed to word-processed text. Kitty Garber, my friend and editor, prepared the manuscript for publication and handled coordination with the publisher.

Finally, I wish to thank my entire family, and especially my husband, Edward V. Leftwich, Jr., my other daughters, Geneva-Rebecca S. Perry-Glickstein and Tienne D. Leftwich-Davis, and my son Edward Leftwich, III. They all have given individual encouragement and substantial support while enduring my obsession. They also helped to preserve the archives by personally carting many boxes of data and files during numerous office and household relocations and transitions.

I wish also to thank my long-time friends, Dr. Phillip E. Jones, Professor Sally A. Ross, Dr. Jewelle Taylor Gibbs, Dr. Jeffalyn Johnson, and the late R. Joyce Whitley, all of whom urged me to finish and publish the work.

Introduction

A Context for Urban Policy

One way in which people gain perspective on current events which are moving around them, indeed events which are moving in and through them since their choices and actions contribute to shaping the events, is to think of those events historically. What human needs, aspirations, and conflicts lent motivation to the events? What changes in life conditions gave them impetus and focus? And what ideas and ideals provided direction and justification for them?[1]

The context for an event, much like the history that precedes it, sets the tone and gives direction and shape to the event. It has been argued convincingly that human beings are uncomfortable with unprecedented and drastic changes and do not, in fact, adapt quickly or graciously to new ideas and circumstances. Thus, it is reasonable to assume that the greater number of indicators there are to herald an event's occurrence, the more likely people are to accept the event, internalize it, and claim it as their own with relatively little resistance.[2] The same is the case for new modes or ideas. If there are signs in the air, if there are warnings and false starts in the direction of changes, if there has been a stage set appropriately to receive the new idea or the visible change through a series of ritualized steps and stylized foreplay, then the new idea is more likely to survive.

If, however, the new mode or idea is perceived as a surprise, an innovation about which no one has thought very deeply, then its reception, as well as its survival, is unlikely. The new idea is destined to be discounted because nothing in the wind, no tremors in the environment, nothing in the context from which the idea emerged, telegraphed its arrival.

This condition, of course, runs counter to the constant public importuning for new ideas, for innovative solutions to difficult problems, and for approaches other than the familiar, warmed-over strategies of yesteryear. Unfortunately, that conflict between reality and ideal seems continually to characterize the human experience. Thus, even though the public demand is for novelty, imagination, and innovation, human beings do not encourage these as virtues. The tried, the familiar, the expected, that idea or notion that has been foretold or for which the receiving environment has already been prepared, usually will be granted acceptance.[3]

This book offers a discussion of the environment or context within which the codified national urban policy came to be developed. We will identify some of the factors that, by virtue of their presence, made the environment receptive to the Carter administration's intentions: first, to develop an urban policy at all; and, second to see that the policy was written, announced, and legislated so that everyone could at least agree on the policy's existence.

The political context created by the events associated with the presidential election, the dynamics of race and poverty in the American economy, and the evolution and maturing of cities, all converged to force the drafting of an urban policy. Achievements and efforts designed to attack urban problems during the preceding two decades created a historical context from which a national urban policy finally could emerge, in spite of cynics or cynosures. In a way, the national urban policy's hour had arrived.[4]

The writings of scholars and other experts generated a rich conceptual context within which the Carter administration reasonably could begin to think about an urban policy and about what it ought to address and seek to accomplish. Not only was the time right, but also, the elements in the total context made its creation inevitable.

The *National Urban Policy: A Partnership to Conserve America's Communities,* was announced by President Jimmy Carter on March 27, 1978. This federal commitment to cities had been prompted by public interest representatives and various urban scholars for nearly twenty years. Several national level programs—notably the Gray Areas' Projects, the Antipoverty Program, and the Model Cities Program, a sequence of urban efforts occurring between 1958 and 1978—have been classified retrospectively as attempts at making a national policy for cities.

Each of these programs, however, was directed at a shallow layer of the urban topography, focused more on people than on place remedies and addressed only a limited set of urban problems. None of the earlier programs took the city, along with its economic, fiscal, regional, *and* people dynamics, as its agenda. None attempted to produce a comprehensive policy context for guiding federal behavior toward cities, or for influencing cities' expectations about their own future—which is, in part, a good working definition for a national urban policy. Thus, the national urban policy achieved an objective unrealized by previous Democratic administrations. It was a written, presidentially endorsed set of standards against which behavior toward and by urban areas might be measured—which is the rest of the urban policy definition.

Relevance of the Research

What follows is an analysis of the process engaged in by the principal actors in urban policy development. The intent is to examine how and why compromise decisions were reached on selected critical policy issues, what procedures were followed in achieving consensus—for the first and final time—about a formal, written federal policy toward cities, and whether these processes appear to have been governed by known theory, either at the time of their occurrence or when considered retrospectively.

This effort is valuable for several reasons:

1) Practitioners in the public policy arena may find some guidance for future policy development efforts through testing and further refining procedures set out here.
2) Students of planned urban change may find the experiences of the policy development group helpful in designing alternatives to current urban remedies.
3) Those interested in relieving the distressed urban condition may find sobering the marginal and incremental potential for improvement that formal public policy realistically offers, given the character of the American administrative system and the constraints of American representative government.
4) More generally, the book shows how the introduction of a major policy initiative into the public arena worked in this case.
5) The book offers a detailed record of an important event in the history of urban planning and development.

The Author's Role

During the period under review, I served as the executive director of the President's Urban and Regional Policy Group (URPG). The URPG was created by President Jimmy Carter in March 1977, to produce the urban policy document and disbanded in March 1978, when its assignment was complete. Composed of the secretaries and principal assistant secretaries of the federal agencies having urban responsibilities, URPG represented an approach to solving the "urban problem" that differed from earlier attempts.

Simultaneously, I served as deputy assistant secretary, U.S. Department of Housing and Urban Development (HUD), for Metropolitan Planning and Areawide Concerns in HUD's division of Community Planning and Development (CPD). My appointment to this position occurred first, before my designation as the head of URPG. In spite of the momentous assignment of directing URPG, I always considered that role as derived from my HUD responsibilities.

I served at HUD for more than a year beyond the demise of URPG. In August 1979, I returned to my tenured positions as professor and chairperson of the department of city and regional planning, in the School of Architecture and Planning of Howard University in Washington, DC. This intense, unique two-year experience has supplied the data and perceptions about this period and about the urban policy development process that are presented in this book.

Approach to the Research Study

Different dimensions of the research invoke different research resources from the field of urban policy development, planning and policy analysis. One aspect of this study depended upon the author's role as active participant in the process, as observer of other participants' behavior and as creator of the archives that are largely unavailable elsewhere. This aspect required reference to the definitive studies by James Sundquist of the model cities and antipoverty programs.[5] In these cases, Sundquist conducted extensive interviews with actors, reviewed documents and archival materials, and recaptured the context and dynamics of the policy-making process.

Charles Harr, on the other hand, offered a highly personal account of the model cities experience, drawing on his own daily familiarity with the actors, the issues, and the bureaucratic system into which the policy-makers tried to intervene with their new policy approaches. Similarly, Peter Marris and Martin Rein reviewed the Gray Areas Program from the vantage of participant/observers who were not active in program and policy development, but who often were present as the events unfolded, and later reflected on the policy decision with the help of the actors. Further, Marris and Rein showed the connection between the precursor Gray Areas Program and the antipoverty program, adding another dimension and an historic value to the later work of Sundquist and Levitan.[6]

Even research of more recent vintage, for example, the works of George E. Peterson and Carol W. Lewis or of Marshall Kaplan and Peggy L. Cuciti, rely as well upon these earlier policy analysis efforts. However, these more recent materials are a compilation of multiple authors, rather than of one or two authors, into an edited anthology. Thus, the integration of co-existing perspectives, which characterizes the earlier work, tends to be more superimposed upon, than integral to, the analysis in the more recent works. Nonetheless, each of these research efforts provided guidance in sorting through weighty materials and in organizing my own psychological and experiential baggage in order to present the chronology of events that produced the national urban policy.[7]

A fundamental question, however, has been how to treat the rich body of existing and recognized research that addresses the substance of policies to relieve urban distress. While most of these materials were relevant to the content of the national urban policy, they have been considered as a part of the context within which the policy development process took place, rather than as primary source materials for discussing the product of that policy development process.

This distinction is subtle but important. To the extent that any of this recognized research was instrumental or influential in decision-making about the policies to be adopted, that role has been examined and explicated. There has been no attempt, however, to evaluate or assess the final product of the process using this research as a criterion, although some of the writers became integral and crucial participants in the policy process. Much of this existing research, therefore, is included in the bibliography and referred to in various endnotes because of its significant relationship to the policy development dynamic rather than because of its substance.[8]

Archival materials have been presented to show what issues were considered. They have formed the basis for the chronology of events that constitute the major narrative portion of the study. Where appropriate, documents have been analyzed to describe where the lines of battle were drawn on selected issues, such as targetting, place-versus-people, state involvement and incentives, or the prominence of a particular remedy or another in the strategies for policy implementation.

A limited number of interviews were conducted with a few of the key actors, notably former HUD officials, the late Secretary Patricia Roberts Harris, Assistant Secretary Robert C. Embry, Jr., Assistant Secretary Donna E. Shalala, Lynn Curtis, Wyndam Clarke, and Robert Duckworth. Where my recollections are key to understanding the process, these also have been included.

Finally, the research on the theory of policy development that served as the principal analytical tool for this study was the work of David Braybrooke and Charles Lindblom. Their concept of serial analysis, also known as the strategy of disjointed incrementalism, offered a relevant framework for ordering the events that occurred in developing the national urban policy and provided a model for organizing the decisions finally taken with regard to the policies themselves. The marginality of many of the policy choices reflected the caution that Braybrooke and Lindblom attribute to political behavior in the American system and to the security that is offered by narrow movement within the domain of the status quo.[9]

With regard to the relationship between the urban policy and previous urban-oriented programs such as the Great Society's set of programs, Linblomian incrementalism, defined by Enid Bok Schoettle as a "long chain of amended choices," accounted both for the failure of the earlier efforts to achieve what Robert Weiss and Martin Rein call "broad aim objectives" and also for the ability of the policy exercise under review to achieve codification. Further, the openness of the process and the highly interactive, transactive mode of consultation with interest groups and sundry constituents is best understood in the framework discussions of organizational behavior, organizational exchange, and sub-optimization to achieve instrumental ends by Herbert Simon, William Evan, Howard E. Mitchell, and Peter Blau.[10]

The relevance and appropriateness of this theoretical framework has been explored. Included in the discussion is the work of David Easton, John Friedmann, Paul Davidoff and Thomas A. Reiner, and Robert Warren.[11]

Notes

1. Warren G. Bennis, Kenneth D. Benne, Robert Chin, and Kenneth E. Corey, eds., *The Planning of Change*, Third Edition (New York: Holt Rinehart and Winston, 1976), 11.
2. Roland L. Warren, *Love, Truth and Social Change*, (Chicago: Rand, McNally and Company, 1971); Peter Marris, *Loss and Change* (New York: Pantheon Books, 1976).
3. Donna E. Shalala and Julia Vitullo-Martin, "Rethinking the Urban Crisis: Proposals for a National Urban Agenda," *Journal of the American Planning Association* 55(1, Winter 1989):3–13.
4. David Braybrooke and Charles Lindblom, *A Strategy of Decision* (New York: The Free Press, 1970).
5. James Sundquist, *Making Federalism Work* (Washington, DC: The Brookings Institution, 1969); James Sundquist, *Politics and Policy* (Washington, DC: The Brookings Institution, 1975).
6. Charles M. Haar, *Between the Idea and the Reality: A Study in the Origin, Fate and the Legacy of the Model Cities Program* (Boston: Little, Brown & Company, 1975); Peter Marris and Martin Rein, *Dilemmas of Social Reform: Poverty and Community Action in the United States* (New York: Atherton Press, 1967); Sundquist, *Making Federalism Work*, 1975; Sar A. Levitan, *The Great Society's Poor Law: A New Approach to Poverty* (Baltimore, MD: Johns Hopkins Press, 1969).
7. George E. Peterson and Carol W. Lewis, eds., *Reagan and the Cities* (Washington, DC: The Urban Institute Press, 1986); Marshall Kaplan and Peggy L. Cuciti, eds., *The Great Society and Its Legacy: Twenty Years of U.S. Social Policy* (Durham, NC: Duke University Press, 1986).
8. See, for example, the Advisory Commission on Intergovernmental Relations (ACIR), *American Federalism: Toward a More Effective Partnership* (Washington, DC: ACIR, August 1975); ACIR, *Improving Urban America: A Challenge to Federalism* (Washington, DC: ACIR, 1979); Herrington J. Bryce, ed., *Small Cities in Transition: The Dynamics of Growth and Decline* (Cambridge, MA: Ballinger Publishing Co., 1977); David A. Caputo, *Urban America: The Policy Alternatives* (San Francisco: W.H. Freeman & Co., 1976); William Gorham and Nathan Glazer, eds., *The Urban Predicament* (Washington, DC: The Urban Institute, 1976). Also, Robert L. Green, *The Urban Challenge: Poverty and Race* (Chicago: Follett Publishing Co., 1977); Hearings before the Subcommittee on the City of the Committee on Banking, Finance and Urban Affairs, *Successes Abroad: What Foreign Cities Can Teach American Cities*, U.S. House of Representatives, 95th Congress, First Session, April 4-6, 1977; Richard P. Nathan and Paul R. Dommel, "The Cities," in *Setting National Priorities: The 1978 Budget*, J. Pechman, ed. (Washington, DC: The Brookings Institution, 1977); National Urban League, *Population Policy and the Black Community* (New York: NUL, 1974); National League of Cities, *State of the Cities: 1975*, Washington, DC,

January 1976; National League of Cities, *National Municipal Policy,* Washington, DC, 1977; Morton J. Schussheim, *The Modest Commitment to Cities* (Lexington, MA: Lexington Books, 1974); Harold Wolman, *Politics of Federal Housing* (New York: Dodd, Mead & Co., 1971); Robert K. Yin, ed., *The City in the Seventies* (Itasca, IL: F.E. Peacock Publishers, Inc., 1972.)

9. Braybrooke and Lindblom, *A Strategy of Decision*, 1970; see also, Robert A. Dahl and Charles E. Lindblom, *Politics, Economics and Welfare: Planning and Politics: Economics Systems Resolved into Basic Social Processes* (New York: Harper & Row, 1953); Charles E. Lindblom, *The Policy-Making Process* (New Jersey: Prentice-Hall, Inc., 1968); Charles E. Lindblom, "The Science of Muddling Through," *Public Administration Review* 19 (1959):79-99.

10. Robert S. Weiss and Martin Rein, "The Evaluation of Broad-Aim Programs: Experimental Design, Its Difficulties, and an Alternative," *Administrative Science Quarterly* 15 (March 1970): 97-109; John Friedmann, *Retracking America: A Theory of Transactive Planning* (Garden City, NY: Anchor Press/Doubleday, 1973); Herbert Simon, "Decision-Making and Administrative Organization," *Public Administrative Review* IV (Winter 1944); Herbert Simon, "Theories of Decision-Making in Economic and Behavioral Science," *American Economic Review* X (June 1959): 255-257; James G. March and Herbert A. Simon, *Organizations* (New York: John Wiley & Sons, Inc., 1958); William M. Evan, "An Organization-Set Model of Interorganizational Relations," in *Organizational Decision Making*, edited by M.F. Tuite, M. Radnor, and R.K. Chishold (Chicago, IL: Aldine Publishing Co., 1972), 181-200; Howard E. Mitchell, Sr., *Paradigm of the Diffusion of Social Technology Process* (Philadelphia: Human Resources Center, University of Pennsylvania, 1974); Peter M. Blau, *Exchange and Power in Social Life* (New York: John Wiley & Sons, 1967); Peter M. Blau, *The Dynamics of Bureaucracy: A Study of Interpersonal Relations in Two Government Agencies*, 2nd ed. (Chicago: University of Chicago Press, 1963); Peter M. Blau and Marshall W. Meyer, *Bureaucracy in Modern Society*, 2nd ed. (New York: Random House, 1971).

11. David Easton, *A Systems Analysis of Political Life* (New York: John Wiley & Sons, Inc., 1965); John Friedmann, *Retracking America: A Theory of Transactive Planning* (Garden City, NY: Anchor Press/Doubleday, 1973); Paul Davidoff and Thomas A. Reiner, "A Choice Theory of Planning," *Journal of the American Institute of Planners* XXVIII (May 1962):103-115; Robert Warren, "National Urban Policy and the Local State: Paradoxes of Meanings, action, and Consequences," *Urban Affairs Quarterly* 25 (June 1990):541-561; Congressional Quarterly, Inc., "Urban America: Policies and Problems" (Washington, DC: Congressional Quarterly, August 1978.)

Chapter One

The Political Context

> *Critics of the series of reports in the Republican administration frequently charged that the collapse of the dream of a national urban...policy stemmed from a lack of presidential commitment.*[1]

In spite of frequent allegations of insensitivity to things urban, and the implied lack of priority accorded urban issues by "an administration with rural roots (which) now must address the cities,"[2] there were also good reasons to believe the Carter administration would commit to the production of a unified, written national policy for cities. Carter gave early notice in his presidential campaign that he intended to draft an "urban policy for the remainder of the twentieth century."[3]

A Friend in the White House

In a major address on urban policy to the United States Conference of Mayors in June 1976, Carter stated:

> Today, America's number one economic problem is our cities, and I want to work with (mayors) to meet the problems of Urban America just as Franklin Roosevelt worked to meet the problems of the rural South in the 1930s.
>
> ...I pledge to you an urban policy based on a new coalitionXrecognizing that the president, governors, and mayors represent the same urban constituency. I pledge to you that if I become president, you, the mayors of America, will have a friend, an ally, and a partner in the White House.
>
> ...It is time for our government leaders to recognize that the people who inhabit even the poorest and most deteriorated of our central cities are our fellow Americans, and that they want the same things we all want....

> Our goal must be to develop a coherent national urban policy that is consistent, compassionate, realistic, and that reflects the decency and good sense of the American people.[4]

In his campaign speeches, Carter described several avenues through which he would seek to establish a "balanced national partnership (to carry out) a mutual commitment to the future of the American city."[5] Citing the Republican administration's "indifference" and "divisiveness"[6] toward urban areas, Carter projected a position that was to serve, after his election, as the organizing context for urban policy development efforts, as well as a weapon with which the urban and poor people's lobbies were to badger his administration into greater sensitivity to their concerns:

> I think we stand at a turning point in history. If, a hundred years from now, this nation's experiment in democracy has failed, I suspect that historians will trace that failure to our own era, when a process of decay began in our inner cities and was allowed to spread unchecked throughout our society.
>
> But I do not believe that this must happen. I believe that, working together, we can turn the tide, stop the decay, and set in motion a process of growth that by the end of this century can give us cities worthy of the greatest nation on earth.[7]

Carter spoke to skeptical mayors, many of whom were hapless custodians of cities experiencing population shifts, an exodus of jobs and industries, erosion of municipal tax bases, an escalation of municipal costs, and rising crime. Most dramatic for the bulk of these cities was the continuing legacy of the Nixon-Ford administrations' announced policy of benign neglect of cities and their occupants. Almost three months before the Milwaukee address, Carter's campaign had circulated a separate position paper outlining his five-point agenda for cities and for the urban policy that he intended to pursue.[8]

Unlike many campaign working papers and speeches, both the city policy paper and the Milwaukee speech were to appear again and again in the hands and on the desks of the staff drafting the urban policy. In fact, one copy carried the admonition from a principal administration policy-maker to his urban policy executive director: "We should always...keep these ideas in our mind as we formulate an urban policy."[9]

The five-point agenda for an urban policy featured in the Carter campaign policy paper proposed implementation steps, some specific dollar figures, and the number of people to be served:

1) Human Needs and Unemployment: Through various devices to create 600,000—700,000 regular jobs; 800,000 summer youth jobs; undertake welfare reform; refine the categories of the near-poor, the working poor, and the fully dependent; and provide dollars to pay for these changes and increased services through "increased tax revenues generated by the reduction in unemployment from the (existing) jobs programs...assisted by the $5 billion to $8 billion streamlining of the defense budget...;[10]
2) Assisting the Fiscal Needs of the Cities: Restoration of counter-cyclical assistance; extension of the revenue-sharing program for five years, and exploring the creation of a federal Municipalities Securities Insurance Corporation;
3) Solving the Physical Needs of Cities: Meeting the two-and-a-half million housing units per year commitment; increasing federal subsidies and low-interest loans for a variety of existing housing programs; prohibiting red-lining; encouraging private-sector mortgages; and generally bolstering mass transit funding, revitalizing railroads, and experimenting with new transit utilization patterns and with regulatory flexibility;
4) Meeting the Total Needs of our Cities such as Crime Control, Parks, the Arts: Proposing reforms and statutory changes; reduced federal regulations; and unspecified funding assistance for software programs;
5) Partnership between the President and the Mayors: Lamenting the long dry spell of inaccessibility to the White House by mayors, Carter promised to recreate President Franklin Roosevelt's open access, in words that justify repeating verbatim:

> As President, I shall develop close, personal, and continuous working relationships with you. I will beef up the role and functions of the domestic policy council to serve as a direct link to you. Moreover, I will have a high-level assistant at the White House to help coordinate programs related to cities between the various government departments, and to serve as the President's direct link to the mayors and other city officials. Mayors need a person at the White House with the President's ear to whom they can relate directly about city problems.
>
> You are on the firing line every minute facing tough problems. I do not intend to let you stay there alone.
>
> You also have my assurance that the federal government itself will be pro-city. Too often the federal government has pursued policies which

> have encouraged urban decay, such as past procedures in the location of federal buildings and the construction of highways through urban neighborhoods. As President, I intend to put a halt to such counterproductive policies.[11]

Of course, a candidate's campaign rhetoric can often become that same candidate's broken record, and the rather colorful and expansive language just reviewed ultimately may not be exempt from that judgment. However, although history may indeed judge Carter to have promised more than he delivered, my purpose for recalling these promises and pre-presidential postures is to highlight them properly as a significant part of the context within which the national urban policy was produced.

There is a prevailing notion that national-level controversies best respond to ministrations directly from, or personally ordered by, a sitting president. This idea frequently is reinforced by a recurrent public nostalgia for the decisive, crisis-oriented leadership of Franklin Delano Roosevelt and Harry S. Truman, or for the moral leadership of John Fitzgerald Kennedy with regard to the civil rights movement. This perception can be characterized as a self-fulfilling prophecy; it is true because it is believed to be true.

Thus, those who most wanted a national urban policy developed had sufficient evidence that the President supported their position. Presidential staff who easily fell victim to the White House syndrome of attributing all manner of wishes to the President ("The President wants. .." or "The President would prefer...") did not lack authentic documentation and, therefore, a conducive context for formulating sentences and directives such as : "The President wants an urban policy without delay."

An Open Administration

The process by which the urban policy was developed has been characterized as an open, interactive process, welcoming the participation of people from all sectors of the American public and from all levels of elected leadership, national and local.[12] While this characteristic will be more fully explicated later and will be thoroughly documented by specific evidence of open and broad participation, the President's commitment to openness and participatory involvement served also as a part of the context for policy development as well as a dynamic of the process itself. Again, Carter's early public statements provided sufficient evidence to support aides' subsequent assertions about his desires. As a staff person once asserted: "We need to invite one hundred neighborhood groups to a meeting in the White House to discuss urban policy because the President wants this to be an open process." In July 1976, before the election, Carter promised that, if elected, his administration would address three themes:

> 1) The need for an open, responsive, honest government...
> 2) The need to restore a compassionate government in Washington, which cares about people and deals with their problems;
> 3) The need for a streamlined, efficient government, without the incredible red tape, duplication and overlapping of functions.... This government must become open. If we intend to rebuild confidence in the government process itself, policy must be shaped through the participation of Congress and the American people.[13]

The promises of openness were well received, especially by traditional liberals and Democrats. The stench of Watergate was still heavy in the air around the capital, and the prospect of no more closed doors was welcomed. Moreover, those whom Carter chose as his urban advocates, notably Housing and Urban Development (HUD) Secretary Patricia Roberts Harris and her principal urban policy staff were very unlikely candidates for carrying out clandestine, surreptitious urban policy planning. We welcomed the President's position and later used it like a crowbar or a sledge hammer on some of our more reluctant, less forthcoming colleagues.

Political Debts to Blacks, Minorities, and the Poor

The President's stated commitment to cities and to an open administration were only two elements of the context within which the national urban policy was developed. After the Carter administration had been in office for several months, those who viewed themselves as being primarily responsible for his victory at the polls began to agitate for some show of appreciation for their efforts. As Chuck Stone, of the *Philadelphia Daily News*, pointed out in his column:

> Jimmy Carter owes his election to black support, not only in yesterday's massive turnout, but from the beginning when Atlanta blacks wrapped their arms around him and proclaimed to the nation he was no Lester Maddox or George Wallace.
>
> Carter's election...does accomplish two things: It will move this country racially closer together and it will get the country moving again under a

> man who believes the President can take the lead in solving the awesome problem of unemployment.[14]

This view of the role of the black and urban vote in determining the election results was widespread and fairly well substantiated. According to a post-election analysis by the Joint Center for Political Studies in Washington, DC: "Black voters provided Carter with the crucial margin of victory in several closely contested states without which he could not have been elected."[15] Following a methodology that provided for the direct survey of a million black voters in areas that were at least 87 percent or more black, the Joint Center monitored results from 1,165 areas in twenty-three states. The results from the survey showed the black vote to have been the margin of victory in thirteen states: Alabama, Florida, Louisiana, Maryland, Mississippi, South Carolina, Texas, and Wisconsin.[16] Further, in these states, black voters gave Carter at least 86.0 percent of the vote, with an average of 91.6 percent in all thirteen states.

Commenting on the analysis of the survey results and on the post-election prospects, Joint Center President Eddie N. Williams summarized the views of the black constituency and their expectations:

> For the first time in history, black Americans this year played a major role in nominating a presidential candidate and in electing him to office.
>
> The question now is what do blacks expect from Carter and what can Carter deliver. There is a significant overlap of black pleas and Carter promises: increasing jobs and reducing crime; reforming tax laws and welfare programs; insuring health care and the vitality of our cities. There is little doubt that some of these concerns will be converted into programs in one form or another, sooner or later, for better or for worse. There is a question, however, about how they will be conceived and implemented and by whom.
>
> ...If Jimmy Carter wants to show black America that he is aware of the role they played in his election and of their high expectations, he could start by integrating the nation's policymaking apparatus and by requiring that all of his people, policies and programs be infused with a sensitivity to the special hurts of blacks and the poor. It is this sensitivity which Carter himself exhibited during his campaign for the presidency and which ultimately got him elected.[17]

Vernon Jordan, executive director of the National Urban League, commented on the symbiotic relationship between the Carter administration and the black community, and thus initiated his role as primary monitor of how well Carter was doing in paying off his debt to minorities. In the Urban League's annual assessment of black America's progress, delivered in January 1977, just before Carter's inauguration, Jordan stated:

> Of all the problems confronting black America in 1976, none was more critical than that of unemployment. Of all the events that occurred during the Bicentennial Year, none was more important in the eyes of black America than the Presidential election. Of all the disappointments experienced by black America over the past none was more disheartening than the widespread indifference of the American people to the plight of minorities and the poor.
>
> Judged by accepted indices of progress—income, educational attainment, family stability, etc.—there was little cause for rejoicing in black America as the nation marked its 200th birthday. But as the year drew to a close, something appeared in Black America that had not been there for almost a decade—the first faint sign of optimism about the future.
>
> Perhaps more accurately, it was more of a hope or a wish, than optimism. After eight years of a national administration that blacks—rightly or wrongly—regarded as hostile to their needs and aspirations, they now feel that 1977 might bring a change in direction and that possibly the same type of moral leadership that led the nation to accept the legitimacy of black demands for equality during the 60s, might once again be present in Washington.[18]

Jordan's allusion was only partially to the direct debt that Carter had incurred in exchange for the black and poor peoples' votes feeding his election victory. More specifically, Jordan's optimism alluded to a sense of the Democratic Party tradition: liberalism, advocacy for the poor and minorities, and federal governmental intervention—both symbolic and direct on behalf of the disenfranchised.

In the view of Jordan, the National Urban League, and most urban blacks, each of these traditions promised a better deal under Carter than had been forthcoming during the eight years of Nixon and Ford. This promise simply was reinforced through votes for Carter in the ballot boxes of the predominantly black and poor communities across the country. This debt continued to be an compelling element in the policy-making context, as well as in the policy-making process.

The Condition of Cities

Carter made his first ceremonial visit to HUD on February 10, 1977, twenty-one days following his inauguration. Newly appointed HUD Secretary Patricia Roberts Harris, who hosted the occasion, concluded her brief welcoming remarks with the comment:" We are glad that you share our concern for cities in distress."[19]

The characterization of cities as being "in distress" had by then become the euphemism for what was happening in and to urban communities across the country. The perspectives from different sectors altered the hierarchy within the litany of urban ills, but there was commonality among the items on everybody's list.

Arising from the "...accumulated discontent of millions of human beings, mistreated, discriminated against, ignored or dissatisfied with life in American cities,"[20] population decline, commercial and industrial disinvestment, attendant unemployment, social problems and anti-social behavior, housing and infrastructural deterioration, fiscal instability, and crisis and general abandonment plagued many cities. The American Center for Intergovernmental Research (ACIR) writing in 1976 on ways to improve urban America, listed the specific deficiencies suffered by the nation's urban areas, including decayed central city housing and poorly built suburbs; transportation troubles, including access and congestion; pollution of air, water, and land; paucity of urban recreational spaces; crime, safety, and delinquency profiles; urban educational standards; and racial unrest and civil disorder, "...rooted in long-standing and currently aggravating employment and other economic inequalities, making central cities pockets of poverty and disease."[21]

The Urban League listed the major concerns within black America, in order of priority: employment, housing, education, health and social welfare, politics and community planning, public safety, and crime,[22] offering a slightly different emphasis on behalf of the minority interest sector often identified with urban settlements. Released in January 1976, the National League of Cities' Annual Report was called the *State of the Cities: 1975—A New Urban Crisis?* and focused on fiscal distress paralleling the social distress of the 1960s. The report cited all of the problems chronicled by ACIR and the Urban League, adding energy along with insolvency to the list.

Convinced of the crisis proportions of the urban problem, but confounded by the inadequacy of the federal response, the House Committee on Banking, Currency and Housing held hearings on "The Rebirth of the

American City" during the autumn of 1976. The hearings were preceded by an editorial in the *Washington Post* stating, in part:

> With any luck, the ideas and proposals that will be aired at these hearings will find an echo and stimulate the debate in the political election campaign for the President as well as the lesser offices. The campaign discussions have, so far, been almost devoid of ideas and proposals on how to arrest the decline and promote the recovery of cities...[23]

In January of that same year, the *Los Angeles Times* offered an editorial opinion that carried the caption: "To hell with the Cities. Let >em Die: When they're Exhausted and Useless, Why Not move on to Better Places?"[24] These extreme and conflicting views in the press mirrored similar positions among lay people and experts alike, converging often only in agreement on the problem: cities were in serious trouble.

The prime example for those who felt that the cities were the architects of their own misfortune was the favorite prototype of all urban evils, New York City. The League of Cities documented repeatedly throughout the year the city's budgetary problems. By the end of 1975, New York's budget crises had attracted the attention of the public "to the generally strained state of urban finance."[25] Later, in time to influence the urban policy planners, New York's Senator Daniel Patrick Moynihan charged the federal government with having caused the fiscal crisis through "largely unintended, but nonetheless direct and palpable consequences of [its] policies."[26]

With sundry aches and pains being felt in the soft underbelly of urban America in general, and with the urban colossus itself on the brink of bankruptcy as a specific case in point, the stark outlines of urban distress already had shaped the context for urban policy as the Carter administration got underway. Little else was required to dramatize the immediacy of the cities' trauma or to finger the source of the solution. Two national events, one with international implications, served to intensify the drama. Energy scarcity, along with newly documented census evidence of urban population decline, heightened the cities' anxieties and strengthened many mayors' determination to hold Carter to his promises. Echoes from the 1960s urban unrest added to this anxiety.

Energy as Equalizer

> *What will be the impact of the president's energy program on the cities, and what other things can the cities do that will help on the energy question[?]In my view, the city is due for somewhat of a renaissance because of the energy shortage. The city is a marvelous way to save on commuting and travel. It is a marvelous way to save on heat by grouping housing together, row housing or clusters or whatever.*[27]
> *XRep. Henry Reuss (D-Wisc.)*

Clearly, the Organization of Petroleum Exporting Countries'(OPEC) embargo of 1973 had implications for cities. The lifestyle and settlement pattern at that time was characterized by expressways, sprawl, decentralization, and other instances of high energy use. This lifestyle was based on an economy of energy abundance and flexible settlements. The primary constraining factors, governing who exercised what preferences with regard to residential and work locations, were money and race. Inevitably, this meant that poor people and minorities usually could not afford to be "energy junkies."[28] In the main, they were concentrated in the cities and did not live in the suburbs. Within the urban region, they occupied the older, most densely settled parts.

As Cary pointed out, "Urban centers are being populated by blacks, Hispanics, and other powerless minorities while whites are seeking the illusion of sanctuary in suburbia."[29] Of most importance, by default minorities had claimed the portions of the urban region that, at first blush following the embargo, appeared to be the most energy efficient and economically attractive in an impending environment of scarcity.

President Carter announced finally in November of 1977: "We must face an unpleasant fact about energy prices... They are going to go up as fuel becomes scarcer and more expensive to produce."[30] Thus, the conclusion that some reached, based on these analyses, was reflected above by Congressman Henry Reuss: Energy conservation would be good for the cities. Others, however, saw a paradox inherent in the obvious solution.

Ellis Cose, a specialist in issues of the minority community and energy policy, expressed two levels of skepticism. First, a more substantive analysis of the assumptions about the cost-benefit relationship between suburban and urban residential conditions revealed that the costs of energy probably would not escalate at a pace sufficient to reverse settlement trends from suburban to urban. Thus, the cost of alternative modes of conservation, such as insulation and redesigned heating systems, could be very competitive with the cost of relocation to more concentrated urban sites. Since the cities evidently were not the preferred choice of residence for many who could afford to choose, the more urban locations were unlikely to enjoy instant revitalization in response to the energy crisis.

Second, the technologies associated with energy conservation might well prove to be incompatible with the perceived energy advantages of contemporary cities. The decentralized, renewable energy forms and the environmentally beneficial technologies of energy conservation and efficiency might not be consistent with the dense settlement patterns of cities as they exist. "In short, those who favor [these solutions] may find themselves on a collision course with city dwellers—largely black and poor—who are unable to pick up and go as they please, and who may therefore see such technologies as threatening an already difficult existence."[31]

I don't wish to convey the impression that these complex considerations found precise expression from the start in early urban policy planning. What did find expression was that the President had to complete the administration's energy package quickly to respond to the growing inconvenience and rising costs of energy. Therefore, pursuit of a viable energy policy probably would not benefit from inclusion in the complicated and controversial urban policy process. Instead, the President felt, energy policy development ought to continue on its own separate track.

Further, the fact of the crisis offered a window of opportunity for the city lobbies, not because careful analysis had shown a re-concentration in cities to be an optimum response to the energy shortage, but because the energy shortage might offer an excellent opportunity for attracting people back to cities, generating revitalization efforts, and increasing revenues from the tax-paying public. These energy considerations, however, led naturally to a fuller awareness of the urban policy context: the population had changed from urban to suburban, from central cities to the peripheries of metropolitan regions and to smaller cities, and from the industrial, northern, and midwestern "frost-belt" cities to the smaller southern and southwestern "sun-belt" communities. The interim census report bore out the decennial trends, reflecting alarming changes in regional populations and in the demographic characteristics of city dwellers.

People and Job Loss

The 1970 United States Census Report on Population reflected a change in the distribution of urban and metropolitan population that reversed a trend of almost two centuries.[32] In place of the historic pattern where people moved toward the urban core, or redistributed themselves within the urban region and nearer the cultural, social, and economic institutions traditionally associated with the amenities of cities, most urban regions showed significant losses of population. Furthermore, while there still is no consensus regarding whether people follow jobs to nonurban locations or vice-versa, both people and jobs moved out of cities in droves.

The Interim Year Population Report of the Bureau of the Census offered no reassurance to the pro-city forces that 1970 was an aberration. The trend of population and employment exodus not only continued, but accelerated between 1970 and 1975. "Twice as many people left central cities from 1970 to 1975 as left during the entire previous decade.[33] Thus, in 1977, as the urban policy development effort was begun, many experts, serious students, and casual observers agreed that a significant element of the policy development context was the dramatic exodus of jobs and people.

Public discussions about cities for several years preceding 1977 had included the population shift as an important factor in urban distress. Moreover, the obvious relationships among revenues, dependence, housing abandonment, population change, and level of unemployment stimulated charges of federal favoritism toward nonurban communities,[34] and led to rather substantial discussions among experts on the issue of regional disparities.[35] Also, the argument advanced by some as early as 1969—that the primary victims of job and population mobility, regardless of the causal relationship between these two, were certainly the poor and most probably also blacks[36]—gained substantial acceptance. As reports appeared listing the specific cities that were losing both jobs and people and describing the types of people remaining in the cities, the verdict was in, so to speak.

In addition to becoming less solvent, less densely populated, less self-supporting, cities were also becoming more black and more the home of the unemployed. Table 1.1 summarizes the jobs and people losses for the twenty largest Standard Metropolitan Statistical Areas (SMSAs) for the period from 1960 to 1977.[37] These and similar statistics appeared frequently in various tracts discussing the urban problem. Ten of the dozen cities having the greatest increases in unemployment and the largest decrease in population since 1960 had given Carter 50 percent or more of their votes in the 1976 election—a fact not lost on the President. The average percentage of Carter votes in those ten cities was 59.8 percent. (See Table 1.2.)[38]

Summary

Thus the argument comes full circle. Carter had promised to develop an urban policy during his campaign, and in large measure, he won his most critical election-day battles with the help of voters who had ample first-hand experience with problems that an urban policy could address. In fact, the most distressed cities, which supported Carter most generously in his election bid, had no difficulty dramatizing both the dimensions of their distress and of their political support with numbers and hard data.

Jimmy Carter's campaign speeches and position papers set the tone for an open, pro-city administration, committed to writing a national urban policy. Additionally, the incidence of cities' high rank on the distress index because of job loss, fiscal insolvency, population loss, and resource scarcities threatened to intensify the decline and crisis in urban communities.

Perhaps the most dynamic force in the environment surrounding the President's urban policy planners, however, were the poor people and minorities whose interest group leaders gave expression to their concerns. Blacks especially were determined to hold their Democratic political party, and Jimmy Carter whom they felt that they had elected, accountable for the promises of the campaign and the traditions of the party. An urban policy, formal and unprecedented, seemed to offer a mutually acceptable settlement of the political debt. These factors, also, helped to round out the political context for developing the urban policy document.

Finally, and probably of greatest importance, was the reality of a Democratic president following a Republican administration into the White House, with a zeal to take new initiatives that demonstrated that a changing of the guard had taken place. The specter of Nixon and Ford, viewed by urban and minority constituents as having shirked the responsibilities of national leadership by failing to correct social ills and right equity wrongs, could best be vanquished by bold federal intervention—as HUD Secretary Patricia Roberts Harris said frequently—on behalf of the neediest, not of the greediest.

Table 1.1
Change in Central City Jobs and Population for the Twenty Largest SMSAs Between 1960 and 1977

City	Change in Population (%)	Change in Jobs (%)
New York	1.4	-1.9
Los Angeles	12.4	5.4
Chicago	-5.1	-12.1
Philadelphia	-2.6	-4.1
Detroit	-9.4	-18.8
San Francisco	-2.7	5.6
Washington, DC	-0.9	8.2
Boston	-8.0	-14.2
St. Louis	-17.0	-14.2
Pittsburgh	-13.9	6.1
Dallas	24.2	41.2
Baltimore	-3.5	-4.6
Cleveland	-14.2	-12.9
Newark	-5.6	-12.5
Houston	31.2	51.4
Minneapolis	-6.5	1.9
Atlanta	1.9	19.5
Seattle	-4.7	15.5
Anaheim	54.3	51.4
Milwaukee	-4.1	10.2

Source: Council on Economic Development (CED), "An Approach to Federal Urban Policy,"December 1977, Figures 1 and 2, 30–31.

Table 1.2
Vote for Carter in Cities Showing High Unemployment and Population Loss, Rank Ordered

City	Vote for Carter (%)
New York	75
Los Angeles	50
Philadelphia	66
Detroit	60
Baltimore	70
Washington, DC	70
Milwaukee	55
San Francisco	52
Cleveland	56
Boston	61
New Orleans	55
St. Louis	55
Total	59.8

Source: Council on Economic Development (CED), "An Approach to Federal Urban Policy," December 1977, Figures 1 and 2, 30–31.

Notes

1. Seymour J. Mandelbaum, "Urban Pasts and Urban Policies," mimeo (Philadelphia: Department of City and Regional Planning, University of Pennsylvania, October 1979), 7.
2. Robert Reinhold, "An Administration with Rural Roots Now Must Address the City," *New York Times*, November 1977.
3. Jimmy Carter's Presidential Campaign, "Cities: Urban Policy for the Remainder of the Twentieth Century," mimeo, Atlanta, Georgia, April 1, 1976.
4. Jimmy Carter's Presidential Campaign, "Urban Policy," address to United States Conference of Mayors, Milwaukee, WI, June 29, 1976.
5. Carter Campaign, "Urban Policy," 1.
6. Carter Campaign, "Urban Policy," 1.
7. Carter Campaign, "Urban Policy," 4.
8. Carter Campaign, "Cities."
9. Robert C. Embry, handwritten note to Yvonne S. Perry, on face of Carter Campaign, "Cities,"August 1977.
10. Carter Campaign, "Cities," 3.
11. Carter Campaign, "Cities," 4.
12. Congressional Quarterly, "How Carter Urban Policy was Developed," *Urban America: Policies and Problems* (Washington, DC: CQ, August 1978), 19.
13. Carter Campaign, "A New Beginning," paper presented by Jimmy Carter to the platform Committee of the Democratic Party, June 16, 1976, 1.
14. Chuck Stone, "Black Vote Did It Up Brown for J.C.," *Philadelphia Daily News,* Wednesday, November 3, 1976, 2.
15. Joint Center for Political Studies, *FOCUS* (November 1976), 4.
16. Ibid, see pages 3B6 for analyses and data.
17. Ibid, 2.
18. Vernon Jordan, *The State of Black America 1977* (New York: National Urban League, January 11, 1977), i.
19. In Perry archival materials.
20. Luther Gulick, *Problems of U.S. Economic Development* (New York: Committee for Economic Development, 1958), 317B318.
21. *Improving Urban America: A Challenge to Federalism* (Washington, DC: ACIR, September 1976), 3.
22. Jordan, *The State of Black America 1977*, ii.
23. *The Washington Post*, September 1976, Editorial Page.
24. J. L. Johnson, *Los Angeles Times*, Friday, January 7, 1977, Part II, 7.
25. "National League of Cities, State of the Cities: 1975, A New Urban Crisis?" mimeo, Washington, DC: National League of Cities, January 1976), 1.
26. Lee Lescaze, "Moynihan Hits Feds for NYC's Decline," *The Washington Post*, June 28, 1977.
27. "What is Henry Reuss Up To?" *Nation's Cities* (Washington, DC: National

League of Cities, September 1977), 12.
28. Ellis Cose and Milton Morris, *Energy Policy and the Poor*, (Washington, DC: Joint Center for Political Studies) 1977.
29. W. Sterling Cary, in Morris Milgram, *Good Neighborhood: The Challenge of Open Housing* (New York: W.W. Norton & Company) 1977, 1.
30. Jimmy Carter, transcript in *The Washington Post*, November 9, 1977.
31. Ellis Cose, *Energy and the Urban Crisis* (Washington, DC: Joint Center for Political Studies) 1978, 2; also see, Cose and Morris, *Energy Policy and the Poor*; Alvin J. Scheinider, "Blacks, Cities and the Energy Crisis," *Urban Affairs Quarterly* (September 1974).
32. Alonzo, in "What is Henry Reuss Up To?" 12.
33. Patricia Roberts Harris, Stuart Eizenstat, and Robert McIntyre, decision memorandum to President Carter, March 21,1978.
34. Barro, in Herrington J. Bryce, ed., *Small Cities in Transition: The Dynamics of Growth and Decline* (Cambridge, MA: Ballinger Publishing Co., 1977) for example; also, Kettering Foundation, "Whatever Happened to River City?"
35. Elaine Morgan, "Are Cities Really Worth Saving?" *Washington Star*, April 3, 1977.
36. John Kain, "Coping with Ghetto Unemployment," *AIP Journal* (Chicago, Ill: American Institute of Planning) Marc, 1969. B. William Austin, "Population Policy of the Black Community" (New York: National Urban League, July 1974).
37. Urban and Regional Policy Group, staff briefing, March 1978, based on analyses in Council on Economic Development (CED) "An Approach to Fed-eral Urban Policy," December 1977, Figures 1 and 2, 30B31.
38. Deborah Norelli, *The Current Fiscal Condition of Cities: Survey of 67 of the 75 Largest Cities* (Washington, DC: U.S. Government Printing Office, 1977); 1975 population figures from the Economic Development Administration, U.S. Department of Commerce, Washington, DC; Richard M. Scammon and Alice V. McGillivray, *America Votes 12 (1976): A Handbook of Contemporary American Election Statistics* (Washington, DC: Congressional Quarterly, 1977).

Chapter Two

The Historic Context

There has always been a federal urban policy. Unfortunately, no one has ever known what it was.[1]

—*Roy Bahl*

There is a difference between the federal urban policy[2] to which Roy Bahl referred in his testimony before the Reuss[3] Subcommittee on the City and the Carter administration's national urban policy. This difference is a matter of perception, definition, and codification.

The perceptual difference lies in whether the earlier efforts were intended, in fact, to address the range and domain of urban America or only a narrow slice of the urban geography and a limited dimension of the urban problem. The definitional difference is related to whether the earlier efforts were viewed publicly as overarching policy, as limited policy, or simply as problem-solving programs and projects. The difference involving codification is the rather straightforward matter of how the earlier efforts were labeled; that is, whether or not they were presented as federal (or national) urban policy and accepted by Congress as such.

The Great Society and Other Legacies

The more obvious and influential past experiences, also a part of the urban policy development context, were a series of public and public/private joint ventures designed to respond to serious, distressing urban phenomena as though they were discrete, generally independent functions within otherwise healthy urban environments. The earlier efforts often are seen retrospectively as federal policy responses to the urban condition and were the initial steps, without which the Carter effort could not have begun. They also were the classroom for educating most of those actors who sought to fulfill Carter's commitment to develop a national urban policy.

Finally, these early urban-oriented efforts developed the institutional history that sensitized the public and public servants to the range and constraints that were to define the limits of the most recent policy development process and that defined the extent of the policy proposals themselves.

Urban Renewal

Any discussion of precedents addressing the urban condition necessarily begins with the early housing and urban renewal efforts, representing the federal responses to the changing and aging urban environment.[4] Much has been written about these programs,[5] and it is redundant to review in great detail the policies supported by the early efforts. A summary, however, is helpful.

The Housing Act of 1949, and subsequent amendments up to and including those in 1954, provided for slum clearance, urban redevelopment, residential renewal, and subsequently, downtown CBD (Central Business District) revitalization. The early 1950s policies especially provided for a variety of community development approaches with much of the emphasis on housing and tools to create new shelter space and reclaim existing stock. Between 1950 and 1954, beginning with the Housing Act of 1950, at least fifty-four separate pieces of legislation, executive orders, and governmental committee reports augmented, changed, or refined renewal policy, particularly with regard to housing.[6]

The Housing Act of 1954 broadened the slum clearance and urban redevelopment programs of the Housing Act of 1949. The 1954 act authorized federal assistance to local communities, not only in the clearance and redevelopment of slum areas, but also in prevention of the spread of slums and urban blight, through the rehabilitation and conservation of blighted and deteriorating areas.[7] It also provided support for local planning and, subsequently, for metropolitan and regional planning. An illuminating view of the legacy of urban renewal and the inspiration that experience provided for a more comprehensive approach to the revitalization of cities has been recorded by Peter Marris and Martin Rein:

> The Housing Act of 1949, amended in 1954, provided through urban renewal a means to tackle at least one aspect of social and racial inequality. Slum clearance, with Federal subsidy, was to revitalize the declining finances of the central city. New houses would retrieve the well-to-do from the suburbs, offering the harassed suburban commuter once again the diversity of city life ... Meanwhile, as the slum dwellers were relocated, their welfare could be tackled afresh in new surround-

> ings, released from the demoralizing culture of the ghetto. Urban renewal dealt at once with the fiscal, social, and racial problems of the city, restoring a mutually supportive diversity of race and income.
>
> But it was crucially flawed. Where were the slum dwellers to be relocated? Unable to afford decent housing in the real estate market, excluded from the suburbs, reluctant to submit to the humiliating conditions of a public housing project, *they crowded into the marginal neighborhoods near their old homes—no better housed, and at higher rents. (Emphasis added)* Urban renewal became, for the city's poor, a cynical expropriation in the interests of business, real estate, and the tax base.[8]

The larger context for federal intervention in the economy of cities was the doctrine that economic growth would produce a filtering or trickle-down process that, ultimately, would include most of the marginal and nonparticipating members of society in its benefits.[9] In other words, the poor and the racial minorities in the cities, whose numbers were augmented by "the most massive migration in our history,"[10] from the South and West to the North in the 1950s, would benefit eventually from the increase in economic activity. The return to the city by the more affluent, white population, in turn, would increase the business and commercial enterprises located there. Thus, the number of jobs available in the transitional, post-war urban economy would increase.

With the progression of the decade, however, the results of this doctrine became increasingly discouraging. While absolute income rose, relative quality of life declined for the poor and for minorities. The CBD prospered somewhat, but the insistent patterns of segregation produced increasing racial concentration in the cities, while larger numbers of whites moved to the suburbs. Further, the commercial CBD did not compare favorably with suburban shopping areas. "Between 1950 and 1960...the central cities of the twelve largest metropolitan areas lost over two million white residents and gained just under two million non-whites, who [by the end of the decade] accounted for more than a quarter of their citizens. Meanwhile the suburbs had added only marginally to their meager colored residents."[11]

Morton J. Schussheim writes that the urban renewal program promised too much, delivered too little too slowly, and probably was empowered to use tools, especially in the form of land write-downs for commercial and industrial development, which were unnecessary and excessive subsidies for accomplishing the task at hand.[12] Others, reflecting on the predominant image of the renewal program, dubbed it "Negro Removal,"[13] characterizing it by one of its consequences.

In the mid-1950s, the Ford Foundation, the philanthropic bank roll for innovation and research, had focused the energies of its Public Affairs Program, one of the operating and funding divisions within the foundation, on supporting and studying urban renewal—along with metropolitan government—as possible solutions to the growing problems of cities. As urban renewal began to produce results, however, Ford, along with others, found these results most distressing.[14]

The Gray Area Projects

Many believe Ford's Public Affairs Program was the cutting edge of change. Its staff has been characterized as reformers and technicians to whom the guidance of social change was a career.[15] The program's director, Paul Ylvisaker, was experienced in the problems of local government and thoughtful about equality and other similar concerns of the liberal establishment.[16] He led his staff of reformers in a search for alternatives—especially for the socially and politically disenfranchised—to the physical orientation of urban renewal.

> The movement of reform...arose out of disappointment with urban renewal, seeking a form of social planning that would complement physical redevelopment.... (I)t reflected all the concerns which had become explicit in the previous decade—the assimilation of migrants, of young people, the relief of depressed areas, education, unemployment—and it faced the same political and administrative tangle which frustrated government action. These issues converged in the "gray" area projects of the Ford Foundation.[17]

The Gray Area Project took its name from that penumbra immediately surrounding the urban core and the CBD, into which the displaced, the relocateds, migrants, racial minorities, and generally economically and socially marginal people faded. The project was intended to devise a new formula for equalizing the competitive disadvantage of those who lived in this literal and figurative shadow of urban prosperity. "The Ford Foundation projects set out to show how the city might redeem its broken promise"[18] to those who still waited for renewal benefits to filter down to them.

Ylvisaker felt that "...the lengthening shadow of the Gray Area, even now blotting out the security of distinction between central city and suburb, should be reminder enough that this process of economic growth, as it expresses itself in the City, is not without its imperfections. What to do with and for this Area is one of the City's and the world's most difficult public questions."[19]

The Gray Area was described as the intersection of those who had failed to cope with the urban process and those who were just entering upon that process, seeking their place. Paul Ylvisaker envisioned an approach that would make urban adjustment less dehumanizing for the disadvantaged, sentenced to a dreary existence in the decayed and hopeless neighborhoods:

> The most important means of accomplishing this are not in the realm of the material, certainly not in the single field of real estate, essential as good housing may be. The problem of the Gray Area is first of all a human problem, and the principal job ahead of us is one of constructively developing and unleashing human energies and spirit. The tools will be many and varied...: education tailored to the needs of the newcomer, not ground out by some distant and universal formula; extension services of the kind long provided the American farmer as a matter of course, but only now beginning to appear as an experiment on the urban scene; careful calculation of the pace and form of urban renewal to preserve what tenuous hold the newcomers may have on the stabilizing process of family and neighborhood life; careful assessment of the damage to family life done by the disparities in employment opportunities of immigrant and low-income men and women; the development, encouragement, and employment of youth; occupational training, especially to raise the level of skills against the coming automation. And above all, an environment of respect.[20]

The Ford Foundation provided funds to a total of seventeen urban communities to help them develop plans and projects that would serve these cities' Gray Areas. These funds often augmented resources being provided to these communities by the National Institute of Mental Health's (NIMH) ongoing research and action program against juvenile delinquency.[21] Often, also, the Ford grants were made to communities already participating in the foundation's existing Great City Schools Program.[22] Manpower Development and Training Administration (MDTA) funds for training the unemployed youth also were made available to Gray Area projects on a selected basis by the U.S. Department of Labor. However, the most significant partner with the Ford Foundation in this experimental, "most imaginative and ambitious attempt to manipulate deliberate social change," was the President's Committee on Juvenile Delinquency and Youth Crime (PCJD).

The significance of PCJD's involvement was partially in the volume of money awarded to Gray Area organizations. PCJD grants during 1965, the last year of full program activity, were over $10 million and exceeded those of any of the other participants. But PCJD's great contribution lay in its position within the Kennedy White House and in the direct involvement of Ford Foundation principals in PCJD's design and development. For example, Lloyd Ohlin, joint author with Richard Cloward of the "opportunity theory"—the concept of wide-ranging social intervention—helped to structure the PCJD focus and methodology. Ohlin was tapped for this assignment by David Hackett, friend and campaign associate of the Kennedys and architect of the administration's efforts against juvenile delinquency.[23] David Hunter and Richard Boone, both Ford Foundation staff who were instrumental in organizing and advising Gray Area projects, consulted on the PCJD program. Boone later became a full-time PCJD staff member.

Thus, when PCJD was formally established by Executive Order on May 11, 1961, with Attorney General Robert F. Kennedy as its chair, its philosophy and mandate had been greatly influenced by the experiences and philosophy of the Gray Area effort. The PCJD grants began in 1961, at about the same time as Ford's Gray Area Project grants. Other aspects of the consolidated program had begun earlier, as indicated, with the Great City Schools grants beginning in 1959, and NIMH delinquency research grants in 1958 and again in 1960. All funds fed into the same local umbrella organization and contributed to the comprehensive planning and action activities.

Both Gray Area Program and PCJD-funded activities emphasized:

> Educational innovations, both in and out of the classroom, on the lines of the earlier great cities schools programme; vocational training and employment services for young people; legal aid and community service centers... Both placed emphasis upon changing the environment, rather than the individual and both recognized education and vocational opportunities as crucial aspects of the environment. Reform, they both believed, must grow out of a much more coherent integration of relevant institutions. They both concentrated their resources in a few projects for which they claimed wide relevance as demonstrations... Both too, were concerned to create a local constituency for their approach - not only by securing a commitment from the leadership of the communities but by drawing the people to be helped into the planning of their own welfare.[24]

The Gray Area Program was the smallest, most limited in scope, and the most narrowly focused of the major predecessors to Carter's national urban policy. At its zenith, it functioned only in seventeen cities, with direct funding support from the Ford Foundation. Although federal funds joined with the private philanthropic and sometimes local matching dollars to support the innovative, experimental projects of the Gray Area, the scope of the program itself was not public, not government-wide, and was not announced nationally as any kind of "new" federal policy to attack the problems of the cities. Furthermore, from the perspective of the total urban environment, the Gray Area Program focused narrowly on the most troubled "gray area" around the urban core, intentionally avoiding, especially so far as the Ford Foundation's motives were concerned, a broad-gauge urban renewal or metropolitan range in its activities.

Yet, the Gray Area Program was perhaps the most significant predecessor to the national urban policy. It broke through an intellectual barrier that confined treatment of urban problems to their physical dimensions as reflected in the public policy orientation toward housing, slum clearance, and downtown renewal. It introduced the concepts of institutional change, social engineering, client intervention and participation, and comprehensive action-planning as legitimate companion strategies to the hardware renewal techniques. Gray Area programs in a number of the cities brought together the resources of the renewal institutions—which had responsibility for planning housing and redevelopment projects—with the expertise of social analysts, citizens, and service delivery practitioners. Together, they designed plans for community action that would change the way that communities felt and behaved, as well as the way that they looked physically and worked economically.

A great long-term value of the Gray Area Programs was that it served as an incubator for a generation of social-change agents whose orientation continued to be toward activity in the public sector and who subsequently emerged as architects of increasingly more comprehensive attempts to forge and influence national policy toward cities. The possibilities of substantive social and physical change suggested by the Gray Area Program have yet to be realized. However, the ideas and ideals of the Great Society programs that followed had their genesis in Gray Area projects across the country.[25]

Criticisms of the program's limited numbers, scope, and narrowness of focus mask other contributions. In addition to the seventeen cities originally funded by Ford, PCJD, NIMH, and MDTA, a number of other cities were attempting to emulate the social-community change model on their own, using PCJD grants, local resources, and long-distance Gray Areas inspiration. Thus, even though the program was not officially national, it had national impact.

The benefits of operating a community change program with primary reliance on a coalition of private-sector, service-delivery, educational, and research institutions seemed attractive to the Gray Areas and to their would-be emulators. The notion that the best way to change public governmental agencies and their policies was through establishing parallel outside planning and action organizations began to pale toward the end of the Gray Area phase in the mid-1960s but was not publicly discredited until the concept had been transferred, almost unchanged, into the structure of the antipoverty program—where it also did not work. (This is discussed in greater detail in the following chapter.)

The "unique administrative arrangement"[26] between Washington and the local communities, as Frances Fox Piven and Richard Cloward characterized the direct funding pattern of the federal government to the Gray Area organizations, was transplanted in the antipoverty program's procedure in the form of the federal-community coalition. Coordination and citizen participation, both products of the Gray Areas experiences, also became legacies to the antipoverty Program.

The War on Poverty and "Community Action"

> *Now, look! I want to go beyond the things that have already been accomplished. Give me facts and figures on the things we still have to do. For example, what about the poverty problem in the United States?*
>
> —*President John F. Kennedy*[27]

If the Gray Area Project had developed essentially outside the federal bureaucracy—although with strong connections to White House and presidential staff structures—the war on poverty and its ensuing Office of Economic Opportunity (OEO) had just the opposite genesis. It was a federal program with presidential origins. Influenced by Michael Harrington's popular book about poverty in the United States,[28] by friend John Kenneth Galbraith's book contrasting American poverty and affluence[29] and by Leon Keyserling's definitive study on poverty and deprivation,[30] President John F. Kennedy initiated his efforts to do something about poverty. His interest coincided fortuitously with—and perhaps was further stimulated by—a growing enthusiasm for expanding and replicating the Gray Area experience.

James Sundquist argues that the "new strategic and tactical concepts for what became the war on poverty"[31] were suggested by four mutually reinforcing streams in the intellectual climate that converged to provide most of the new program components, giving the "war" its substance. These streams—identifying and treating the mental health of the community rather than that of the deviant individual, redirecting the focus of urban renewal from structures to people, rehabilitating welfare dependents through work to make them contributing members of the community, and retraining for the illiterate unemployed—emerged during the Kennedy administration's early legislative and executive initiatives. They were, therefore, the foundation for Kennedy's planning with his staff advisors for subsequent administration efforts in 1962 and 1963, that would, in Kennedy's words, "go beyond" what had already been undertaken.

The search for new initiatives could have been "the normal yearning of an idealist for ideas and of an activist for action—or the accustomed search of a politician facing a re-election campaign for a measure that will dramatize his principles and bear his name."[32] In any event, since it is axiomatic that man is both constrained and liberated by his experiences, those to which Kennedy was exposed—both the ideas and the individuals—influenced the direction of the search.

I share Sundquist's view that the streams of thought and action had begun to flow together at about the same time as Kennedy's search began. "Words and concepts determine programs; once the target was reduced to a single word (poverty), the timing became right for a unified program."[33] Responding to President Kennedy's charge to pursue an investigation of poverty, Walter Heller organized an informal interagency staff group.[34] By November 1963, their work generated a conceptual approach to an assault on poverty that President Kennedy asserted "would be the centerpiece of his 1964 legislative recommendations."[35] When the events in Dallas, Texas, on November 22, 1963, brought about the succession of Lyndon Baines Johnson to the presidency, the new President was quoted as saying that the poverty initiative "...is my kind of program... Move full speed ahead."[36]

President Johnson's immediate support of the poverty initiative is likely attributable to his need to demonstrate continuity of the Kennedy philosophy to the country and offer a dramatic example of his own commitment to the principles associated with Kennedy's "New Frontier" to those liberal Democrats who had reservations about how his Southern background would influence his policies. His own roots in a poverty-stricken region and first-hand childhood knowledge of what it is like to be poor most likely were equally compelling reasons.[37]

As the earlier streams of thought and actions were translated into legislative language through the executive and congressional process, the influence of the Gray Area veterans intensified. Paul Ylvisaker, Michael Harrington, Richard Boone, David Hunter, along with mayors and top staff from the most innovative Gray Areas programs, especially those in New Haven, Connecticut; Boston, Massachusetts; Oakland, California; and Chicago, Illinois, consulted with the task force created by Johnson's antipoverty chief, Kennedy brother-in-law, Sargent Shriver. Terry Sanford, the Governor of North Carolina, which was the only state to have a state-level "Gray Area" project, made a special plea for replication of the experimental, research, and planning effort.[38]

The Economic Opportunity Act, the antipoverty legislation that emerged from the interagency task force and subsequent legislative processes, had something for almost every dimension of the poverty problem. Of the eight titles in the act,[39] however, Title II, providing for community action to plan and implement a comprehensive, coordinated approach to improving the quality of life in the "pockets of poverty" in cities, which was the same as or similar to Gray Areas, was the title most oriented toward urban affairs.[40]

Evaluation of the community action program (CAP) depends on one's perspective. Kenneth Clark viewed it as a natural extension of the HARYOU (Harlem Youth Opportunities, Inc.) experience,[41] striving to redirect the traditional welfare/social worker approach into a comprehensive, government-endorsed local social service delivery mechanism, better able to "ameliorate the conditions of the poor."[42] Daniel Patrick Moynihan has elaborated his view of the CAP as hyperbole that its designers neither understood fully nor, ultimately, were able to guide properly and that was essentially planned by a group of nonblack reformers to serve a predominantly black urban client group.[43] This view contrasts somewhat with that of Piven and Cloward, who attribute the existence of the antipoverty legislation, as well as the CAP component, to the survival instincts of politicians, who needed "service programs" to placate the restless "inner cities," "slums," and "urban core," all terms that were euphemisms for the black ghetto.[44]

Whatever the original image and expectations of the CAP effort, the thrust, focus, and emphasis were adjusted in most cities by the impact of urban riots that began primarily in 1964, notwithstanding Edward

Banfield's characterization of the riots as "fun and games."[45] The preeminence of the local CAP agency increased as local citizens gained sophistication and a sense of accomplishment in effecting institutional change through citizen participation. Concurrent with this development, the federal monitor of the program, the OEO headed by Shriver, strengthened the direct relationship between the CAP communities and Washington by circumventing city halls and the patronage system. This led increasingly skittish local elected officials and their Congressmen to question the "direct relationship between the national government and the ghettos, a relationship in which both state and local governments were undercut."[46]

OEO achieved this direct relationship through a number of devices, not the least of which was the designation of consultants from a nationwide network with whom OEO had indefinite quantity contracts (IQC) to work directly with the local CAPs. The consultants had little or no contact with the local government. They assisted the CAP staff and often also neighborhood residents in developing programs, strategies, and whatever else appeared appropriate to strengthening the CAP. OEO frequently selected the consultants from the staffs of operating Gray Area projects, primarily because these people were thought to be knowledgeable about program development and planned change, were thought to have had experience in designing programs to relieve specific unhealthy social conditions, and were more than willing for the opportunity to proselytize on behalf of the Gray Area way of bringing about urban reform. For many of these consultants, avoidance of both local bureaucrats and local bureaucratic interference while assisting a CAP in designing projects was a standard approach to consultation.[47]

By the time that President Johnson began the process of formulating a program in 1965 and 1966 to dramatize the mission of the newly formed urban advocate, HUD, local political antennae already were a-quiver. The administration's urban programs had become a threat:

> Giving blacks control over some new service agencies did not turn out to be the chief consequence of federal intervention in the cities, nor was it the main source of the controversy that ensued. The new programs progressively became the instrument with which the federal government attempted to prod municipal agencies (and the private social welfare establishment) into responding to blacks. If local white politicians were agitated at the outset because a great deal of patronage escaped their control, they became hysterical when the federal government permitted, and often encouraged, its new apparatus of local agencies to put pressure on municipal services themselves—pressure to get more for blacks. And that was no small reason for anguish, because services are

> the grist of contemporary municipal politics... By interfering with the allocation of these services, with who got what, the...programs shook up established relations among constituent groups in the city. That urban politicians and bureaucrats reacted with indignation is hardly startling.[48]

Additionally, there were concerns in Washington that the war on poverty was falling short of the desired goals, while extracting the high political price described by Piven and Cloward. Sundquist summarizes the intellectual attitude in the White House:

> If the national decision was for such a unified "war on poverty," what resulted (was) something less. Under the pressure of program operations, the movement (was) almost steadily from the broader to the narrower conception, from the "war on poverty" to the "poverty program"—threatening ultimately only to add to the "series of uncoordinated and unrelated efforts" that the President had decried. And by 1967 the President and the administration appeared to be looking to a new program and a new device—the model cities program and the "city demonstration agency"—to fill the unifying and coordinating role for which the poverty program and community action agencies had proved unsuited.[49]

Model Cities: Rhetoric and Reality[50]

In a May 1965 memorandum to President Johnson, Walter P. Reuther—resident intellectual of the labor movement, President of the United Auto Workers Union, and dreamer of an "urban TVA"—set forth proposals for large-scale, in-depth demonstrations to show how progress might be achieved in fulfilling his dream. "It was this dream of Reuther's laid before the President on May 15, 1965 that can be taken to mark the genesis of the program that would bear the name 'model cities'."[51]

In characteristic Johnson style, the President, who held a special preference for private, nongovernmental task groups to provide him with guidance and recommendations, appointed such a task force to review the Reuther suggestion in greater depth.[52] The Reuther memo had called for a demonstration, in "six of the larger urban centers of America...(that) architecturally beautiful and socially meaningful communities of the twentieth century" could be created.[53] The task force agreed, after much deliberation, that a demonstration program was desirable because, in part, "the urban crisis was not only serious but, particularly in the central cities, was becoming explosive."[54] They did not agree, however, to confine the demonstration cities to the small number which Reuther proposed as the "research laboratories for the war against poverty and ugliness in the urban environment, the Gray Areas which are more and more tending to become ghettos for the poor and the racially discriminated—housed in 'hand me downs'."[55] Rather, the task force recommended that sixty-six cities be chosen, "representing communities of different sizes and from different regions of the country."[56]

Ultimately, the total of one hundred fifty cities chosen to participate in the Model Cities Program followed rules and procedures developed by an Advisory Committee in Demonstration Program Development. This committee was composed of seven people, including two Ford Foundation staff members, one Gray Area project board member, the national director of the Community Action Program, and the late President Kennedy's director of the Bureau of the Budget and co-architect of the CAP concept of local development corporations.[57]

In many respects, the Model Cities Program represented an aggregation of learning and experience from the predecessor Gray Area Project and CAP. This was partially a function of the experiences of those who designed the program, the advisory committee, and partially a function of the prototype that the earlier programs had generated in the public's perception of what the Great Society ought to be like. The Model Cities Program guide acknowledged the importance of antecedent efforts in instructing cities:

> There is no single program prototype. Each city should plan and develop its own distinctive demonstration program tailored to its particular problems and resources, and building on projects and activities already being carried out in the area.[58]

Given the seventeen original Gray Area cities, the additional PCJD grantees, and the 1,045 local Community Action Agencies that CAP had funded by 1966[59] when Congress passed the model cities legislation, most if not all Model Cities programs had sufficient local "projects and activities" upon which to build.

Sundquist, Haar, Schussheim, and others have reviewed and discussed the implementation of model cities from various perspectives.[60] Most agree that this complex effort to assist cities in improving living conditions met with uneven and generally ephemeral success at best. In general, a city participated in the program by the choice of its elected leadership. Each participating city was to receive federal funds for planning and implementation, in exchange for the mayor's promise that citizen participation would be widespread, that the plans would be comprehensive, and that coordination of federal, state, local, and private resources would take place. The goal of the demonstration was to "test whether we have the capacity to understand the causes of human and physical blight, and the skills and the commitment to restore quality to older neighborhoods, and hope and dignity to their people."[61]

In an earlier analysis, I summarized the more obvious conflicts that were a part of the model cities reality.[62] The early selection of rural and small towns such as Pikesville, Kentucky; Waco, Texas; and Winooski, Vermont, to receive some of the first grants seemed to defy the concept of creating an urban demonstration required by the guidelines. The disappointing level of congressional appropriations weakened the federal funding commitment.

Citizen participation took either a unicameral or a bicameral form[63] in the City Demonstration Agency (CDA) structure,[64] depending upon how troublesome local elected officials felt the CAP citizens' participation experience had been. In either case, the mood was more one of compliance than of participation. Coordination, which Sundquist viewed as the core of the Model Cities Program, never ascended above the level of "voluntary bargaining"[65] at the federal level, and coaptation at the local level, with the help of direct categorical funding.

> The vision of the Great Society, which entailed redistribution of resources and of local political power and emphasized equity as the performance test for judging government interventions and for orienting national policy, was the banner raised in the mid-1960's. Model Cities—a product of the national mood—embodies that vision, based as it was on the premise that the program would have an impact on the larger social institutions that spawned it.

The Model Cities Program was not permitted to survive long enough to work through the complexities of local-federal coordination and to build a comprehensive approach to program operation. After Richard M. Nixon was inaugurated as President in 1969, he began to dismantle the program, leaving cities feeling like Dorothy in Frank Baum's legendary book, the *Wizard of Oz*, wondering how she and her traveling companions were to find the Emerald (Model) City on their own. Figures 2.1 and 2.2 allegorically capture my view of the two-and-one-half year trek toward the ideal of a model city, from late 1967, when the first model cities grants were announced, until early 1970, when the Nixon administration began dismantling them.[66] The process that guided the conclusion of model cities was called "The New Federalism." The tool of the process was revenue-sharing.

The New Federalism: Benign Neglect of Cities

The Nixon administration did not move into its urban policy posture without thoughtful guidance. A task force on model cities, chaired by Edward C. Banfield, reported a set of recommendations to the President on December 16, 1969. The report stated that the model cities program had made a useful contribution, that "the Model Cities proposals, although they do not open new vistas, compare very favorably with the general run of the proposals" receiving federal support; and, that "the Model Cities Program is better than what went before."[67]

Nonetheless, the task force recommended decentralization of program administration.[68] "In the view of the task force, most city governments can be trusted to use federal funds in the manner Congress intends (and) it is necessary to allow them much more latitude because the alternative is waste and frustration and/or their replacement by vastly expanded federal-state bureaucracy."[69] The "over-regulated and under-funded" program thus was refocused toward greater local control, although not without dissension by several task force members.[70]

HUD Secretary George Romney issued new directives for model cities' administration that were more consistent with the laissez-faire, decentralization philosophy of the New Federalism. Greater discretion was given mayors in deciding where and how (i.e., in which neighborhoods and on which projects) they would spend the money, and federal review and monitoring were reduced. Although some apologists for the new policy have described the changes as a defense of the "central concepts of Model Cities: more money for needy cities, better coordination of federal programs, and greater authority and flexibility for mayors in managing federal dollars"[71]—there was the suspicion among reform-minded model cities staff that the motive for the changes was to suppress the very spirit of resource and power redistribution and institutional change that made the program unique.

The advent of the New Federalism significantly altered the decade-long trend of urban policy leadership from the central government and participation at the local level by the neediest sectors of the urban population. Indeed, the Kerner Commission Report on urban riots had called for both horizontal planning—among local public and private organizations—and vertical planning—among federal, state, and local units of government to achieve coordinated urban reform.[72] Yet, as Richard Bolan points out:

> New Federalism, in short, (was) intended to change the behavioral norms and decision latitude of the territorially diverse units of government in their efforts to solve their locally distinctive problems with unfettered financial assistance from the center. It, in effect, denie(d) common patterns in local problems and assert(ed) only a benign national interest in them.... The 'power' that New Federalism return(ed) (was) less significant when a great deal that really influences... urban life is increasingly beyond the control of state and local governments.[73]

Although President Nixon's first message to Congress in January 1970 identified housing, transportation, open space and pollution control, and "more generally, building new cities and rebuilding old ones,"[74] as priorities of his administration, the record seems clear that the priority was low, at least for cities. As his "first gambit in urban policies,"[75] he created an urban affairs council with membership from the secretaries of principal domestic departments and made conservative Democrat Daniel Patrick Moynihan its chairman.

The urban affairs council was short lived; on July 1970, the President terminated its activities. Instead, the functions the council had performed, whatever these were since the council was seen primarily as "window dressing for tightly controlled policy machinery in the White House,"[76] were to be performed by the domestic council in the Executive Office of the President. John Erlichman, the domestic policy advisor to the President, was put in charge.[77]

In March 1971, the President proposed a new Department of Community Development that was to absorb HUD, the vestiges of CAP, and other urban-oriented federal programs from the Departments of Transportation and Commerce. These activities were to be administered by a division within the new department to be called the Urban and Rural Development Administration.[78] "But the Nixon proposals were so radical and challenged so many powerful interests that they simply were not taken seriously."[79]

Various reductions in scale and funding ensued, initially affecting CAP most heavily. However, on January 8, 1973, the Nixon administration announced, through a speech by HUD Secretary Romney to the National Association of Home Builders, the impoundment of housing subsidy and community development funds, including low-rent public housing, water and sewer facility grants, open space land grants, and public facility loans. The declared intention was to freeze new commitments until existing programs had been reevaluated. Further, the HUD secretary announced that at the end of the fiscal year (as of June 30,

1973) "similar action would be taken with respect to urban renewal and model cities programs.... The secretary said that the...ban on the listed community development activities would continue until they were included in the community development special revenue sharing program."[80] The President subsequently presented his proposals and budget in support of revenue-sharing to Congress at the end of January 1973. The Community Development Block Grant Program, which was created by Congress with the Housing and community Development Act of 1974, formalized the fundamental change in the federal government's financial assistance to communities for their physical development and fully replaced any remaining urban renewal, neighborhood development, and model cities programs.[81] One hundred percent grants, distributed on the basis of a formula,[82] funded a city's development of its own plans and the programs that it carried out. This gave broad authority and flexibility to mayors in determining the operations to be undertaken by communities.[83]

The Watergate scandal and its attendant distractions increasingly absorbed White House and public attention through much of 1974. In 1976, after Nixon had finally resigned, Gerald Ford created a committee on urban development and neighborhood revitalization, chaired by HUD Secretary Carla A. Hills. The committee operated out of HUD, although with White House staff membership. During the four months of its existence before the 1976 election, it prepared a fifty-page interim report that summarized findings from visits by its members to a dozen major cities to confer with local officials.[84] It also made a series of recommendations for formulating an urban policy. However, the changing of the White House guard following the 1976 election precluded further refinement of the committee's short-term work.

Contrary to my views, the Ford urban policy has been described as advocating "a national commitment to preserving and restoring central cities and neighborhoods...targeting of federal resources to the neediest areas and more incentives for housing rehabilitation and central city economic development." Charles Orlebeke allows, however, that it did not provide "significant new money for the cities."[85] Furthermore, even the National Growth Reports, issued in 1972, 1974, and 1976 (discussed in the next section), which might have offered substantive policy directions, failed to go beyond the research and analysis phase. Thus, this nascent urban policy was not widely publicized—partially, no doubt, because it *was* nascent and preliminary.

Because a new Democratic administration understandably would be disinclined to use much of the erstwhile Republican administration's policy as a point of departure, there was never any public reference to the Ford administration's urban policy development effort by the Carter administration. Furthermore, partisan motives aside, it seemed much more exciting and responsive to cities for the Carter initiative to hark back to a time when Presidents cared publicly about the plight of urban communities, and expressed this concern through dramatic—though ephemeral—public policies. The New Frontier and the Great Society offered such inspirational points of reference—and a context for continuity—to the new Democratic administration.

Summary

Urban renewal introduced an era of national direction and federal standard-setting for local action against blight and urban decline. Criticisms of the program are legion, and many are justified. However, in addition to the gains in physical renewal that resulted, the effort also began the process of isolating the most malignant urban conditions for which more unconventional responses were required, namely, racial separation, poverty, and the neglect of human resources. Urban renewal represented the first attempt at a concerted national-level policy for urban areas. But its basic assumption was that by concentrating on physical deterioration and focusing primarily on the economy of the central business district, urban deterioration would be reversed. This assumption proved to be faulty. Thus, the policy was too narrow and proved unequal to the urban challenge.

Without the urban renewal program, however, the Gray Area Project probably would not have been initiated. The very successes of urban renewal served to emphasize its failures by contrast, because bad conditions in the Gray Areas worsened. Routine patterns of social adjustment for the poor and for immigrants were disrupted by clearance. Consequently, supportive social systems for the disadvantaged were destroyed.

It would be simplistic and untrue to imply that the entire country—or even most of the country—suddenly began observing and simulating the experimentation that was taking place in seventeen Gray Area communities. At best, any replication in nonfunded communities resulted from contacts between citizens who were beginning to experience limited success with changing the system, with other citizens who were frustrated by their separation from their own local systems. Bureaucrats, too, who were administering the Gray Area community grants—those from the Department of Labor's MDTA program and from the NIMH research program staff—spoke of the experiences to their colleagues and to local staff members in other cities that were receiving MDTA and NIMH funds but not participating in the Gray Area demonstration.

Pleased with the enthusiasm of Gray Area Program participants and with the possibility that this demonstration might succeed where their earlier urban renewal and metropolitan planning projects had failed, the Ford Foundation Public Affairs Program staff were probably the best grapevine, greatly assisted by PCJD staff, who shared this enthusiasm. The PCJD and Ford Foundation staffs, in fact, were the critical "pneumatic tube" through which flowed the ideas and the case examples—cannon-fodder for the embryonic war against poverty being planned in the Kennedy White House. As was stated earlier, although the Gray Area program was not official national policy, its impact was in fact national.

There are two perspectives from which observations can be made about the legacy of the war on poverty's CAP to its successor, the model cities program, and thus ultimately to the development of the national urban policy. The first perspective views CAP in terms of what it achieved relative to what it attempted. This can be called "the view from the top." The Gray Area's objectives of a coordinated, comprehensively planned attack on poverty generally survived the legislative negotiations to find expression in the language of the Economic Opportunity Act and in the implementation of the CAP.

The CAP was certainly a federal policy and federally operated. And while it was not intended for urban communities alone, its focus became increasingly urban, particularly after the urban riots of the mid-1960s. The Gray Area reformers' expectations also were met through the replication—in hundreds of cities—of the nongovernmental, local coalitions represented by the community-based organizations that sometimes complemented, but often conflicted with, the local CAP policy boards, whose membership included people outside the poverty community.

In his assessment of the war on poverty, Sundquist states:

> The distinctive contribution of the "war on poverty," as an idea, lay less in what it added to the battery of governmental programs than in the unifying theme it provided for the activities of many governmental and private agencies and the coordinating devices that were created—OEO in the Executive Office of the President, and the community action agency in each community.[86]

It should be added that the concept of coordination, introduced in the Gray Area Project and unilaterally attempted at the local level in the CAP, found full expression as a program objective in model cities. Further, in many cities, the local CAP, which had sometimes originated as an embryonic Gray Area umbrella organization or replica, became the model neighborhood organization in the community.

The second perspective can be called "the view from the bottom," and is an assessment of the unintentional consequences of CAP activity. In addition to creating a base for black political aspirations and participation, which Piven and Cloward see as a major CAP contribution, Clark feels that the program led to "various attempts to protect the interests of the poor" by the poor.[87] For example, CAP offered the poor the experience of addressing both the problems of social structure as well as of physical conditions and of experimenting with alternative service modes as well as pressuring local government to improve and provide requisite services. The process of considering alternatives and attempting to order these in a priority hierarchy, all contributed to poor communities' ability and readiness to participate in subsequent model cities efforts. Additionally, while attempting to change public institutions through the medium of parallel, nonpublic organizations proved unworkable, the opportunity that this model provided for ventilating grievances against "the system" was an invaluable educational dividend for community folk and a sobering baptism-by-fire for bureaucrats and politicians.

The beginning of the Model Cities Program differed little from the beginning of the program that preceded it. The war on poverty had been designed by an inside elite task force; the model cities program was designed by a task force of outside experts. This distinction had been noted elsewhere before and probably is somewhat forced. However, whether inside or outside, the task forces had an interlocking directorate—and both had strong representation from the Gray Area experience and from the Ford Foundation, the midwife to urban reform of the 1960s.

Nipped in the bud by a change in presidential leadership, the model cities program operated under its original mandate for only one year beyond the planning year. With the shift in focus from close federal monitoring to local discretion in 1969, the program limped along until it was officially terminated in 1973. Although some cities retained their commitment to the model neighborhoods originally selected, national policy was "hands off" with regard to program priorities and the enforcement of comprehensive planning.

Most important was the change in presidential posture with regard to the problems of cities under the Nixon/Ford administrations. Both Presidents launched abortive efforts to design a national urban policy based on the experiences and lessons from the past. Nixon quickly shifted to a broader urban/rural design. Ford's effort was too little and too late in his administration to produce results. As was noted earlier, in both cases there was "a lack of Presidential commitment."[88] Sundquist writes:

> In a democratic, pluralistic society, no system of intergovernmental relations can be established through a single action, or even a series of actions; it evolves. But the evolution, if the result is to be a series of relationships rather than a jumble, must be guided according to a consistent set of principles and governing doctrine.... The guidance, however, can come from but a single source of authority—the President. It is he who must apply the principles and the doctrine in proposing legislation to the Congress and in directing the execution of the laws.[89]

If this is true, then the Carter presidency was challenged not only to provide leadership for an assault on the urban crisis in 1976, but the President himself was destined to be held answerable for improving on the legacies of past urban policy attempts and for articulating a philosophy to guide further efforts. This accountability holds then despite the reality that when Carter took office:

> Those working to revitalize the inner cities...find themselves with their backs pressed even closer to the wall than they did in 1966 (when Model Cities began). The most intractable problems remain. And our present urban programs exist with neither consensus nor conviction to support them.[90]

Figure 2.1
Follow the Yellow Brick Road!

"Then you must go to the City of Emeralds...You must walk. It is a long journey, through a country that is sometimes pleasant and sometimes dark and terrible...The road to the City of Emeralds is paved with Yellow Brick..."

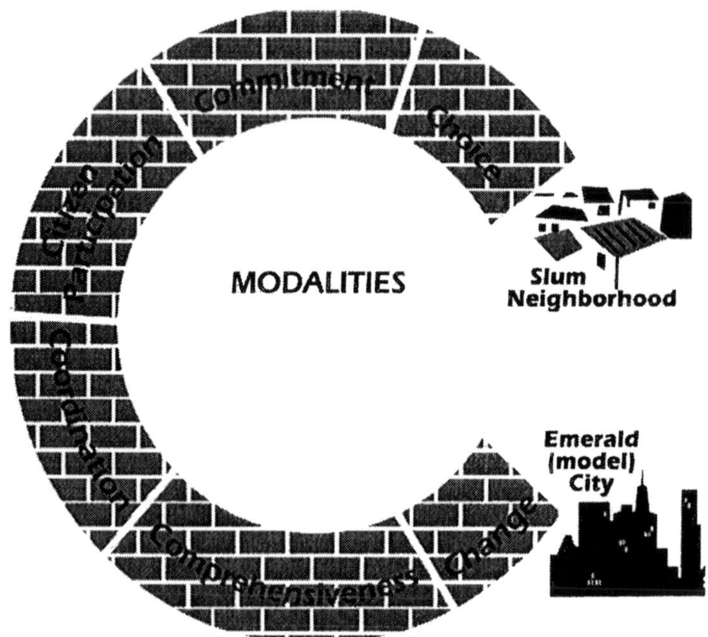

Figure 2.2
Follow the Yellow Brick Road?

"After a few hours the road began to be rough, and the walking grew so difficult that [they] often stumbled over the yellow bricks, which here were very uneven. Sometimes, indeed, they were broken or missing altogether, leaving holes..."

Notes

1. Roy Bahl, "Perspectives on a National Urban Policy," in *How Cities Can Grow Old Gracefully*, Subcommittee on the City, Committee on Banking, Finance and Urban Affairs, House of Representatives (Washington, D.C.: U.S. Government Printing Office, 1977), 149.
2. Bahl, "Perspectives on a National Urban Policy," 149. Bahl had an additional concern about a series of so-called inadvertent public policies, not intended to address any aspect of the urban condition directly or indirectly, and implemented with no conscious regard for urban impact. See, for example, Stephen M. Barrow, "The Urban Impact of Federal Policies: Their Direct and Indirect Effects on the Local Public Sector" in Herrington J. Bryce, *Small Cities in Transition: The Dynamics of Growth and Decline* (Cambridge, MA: Ballinger Publishing Company, 1977), 241ff. This concern, however, is of less importance for purposes of the present discussion and will be treated more fully later, where it will be placed in its proper perspective relative to the urban policy development process.
3. Congressman Henry S. Reuss, Chairman, Committee on Banking, Finance and Urban Affairs, House of Representatives, United States Congress, convened two hearings on the problems of the cities.
4. Of course, these programs had their own historic links, both to earlier New Deal responses to the needs of cities, and to the original "covert and indirect recognition given to cities as members of the federal system" prior to the transitions of the New Deal period in the 1930s. Roscoe C. Martin, *The Cities and The Federal System* (New York: Atherton Press, 1965), 111–114. See also Brooke Graves, *Federal Grant-in-Aid Programs, 1803–1958* (Washington, D.C.: The Library of Congress, Legislative Reference Service, June, 1958); Coleman Woodbury, ed., *Urban Redevelopment: Problems and Practices* (Chicago, IL: University of Chicago Press, 1953).
5. Studies of this period include the following: Leonard J. Duhl, ed., *The Urban Condition: People and Policy in the Metropolis* (New York: Basic Books, Inc., 1963); Lawrence M. Friedman, *Government and Slum Housing: A Century of Frustration* (Chicago: Rand McNally & Co., 1968); Scott Green, *Urban Renewal and American Cities: The Dilemma of Democratic Intervention* (Indianapolis: Bobbs-Merrill Company, Inc., 1965); Martin Anderson, *The Federal Bulldozer* (New York: McGraw-Hill, 1967); James Q. Wilson, *Urban Renewal: The Record and the Controversy* (Cambridge: The M.I.T. Press, 1966); Peter H. Rossi and Robert A. Dentler, *The Politics of Urban Renewal: The Chicago Findings* (New York: The Free Press of Glenco, Inc., 1961).
6. Subcommittee on Housing and Community Development of the Committee on Banking, Currency and Housing, House of Representatives, *Evolution of Role of The Federal Government in Housing and Community Development: A Chronology of Legislative and Selected Executive Actions, 1892-1974* (Washington, D.C.: U.S. Government Printing Office, October 1975), 28-43.

7. Subcommittee on Housing and Community Development, *Evolution of the Role of the Federal Government*, 46.
8. Peter Marris and Martin Rein, *Dilemmas of Social Reform: Poverty and Community Action in the United States* (New York: Atherton Press, 1967), 13–14.
9. Marris and Rein, *Dilemmas of Social Reform*, 10.
10. Mark J. Kasoff, "The Urban Impact of Federal Policies: A Preview of a New Rand Study," *Nation's Cities* (National League of Cities, November 1977).
11. Kasoff, "The Urban Impact"; Marris and Rein, *Dilemmas of Social Reform*, 12.
12. Morton J. Schussheim, *A Modest Commitment to Cities* (Lexington, Mass.: D.C. Heath & Co., 1974), 107–121.
13. See, among many others, Edward C. Smith, "The Coming of the Black Ghetto State," *The Yale Review* 61 (2, December 1971):176; James L. Sundquist, *Making Federalism Work* (Washington, D.C.: The Brookings Institution, 1969), 80.
14. See Paul N. Ylvisaker, "The Deserted City," *Journal of The American Institute of Planners* 24 (1, February 1959).
15. Marris and Rein, *Dilemmas of Social Reform*, 1.
16. Ylvisaker, "The Deserted City," 1–6.
17. Marris and Rein, *Dilemmas of Social Reform*, 14.
18. Marris and Rein, *Dilemmas of Social Reform*, 14.
19. Paul N. Ylvisaker, "Opening Minds and Expanding Cities," in *Ends and Means of Urban Renewal, Papers from the Fiftieth Anniversary Forum* (Philadelphia: Philadelphia Housing Association, 1961), 14.
20. Ylvisaker, "Opening Minds and Expanding Cities," 19–20.
21. NIMH made a preliminary research grant to Richard Cloward and Lloyd Ohlin of the Columbia School of Social Work to develop a research design to address the problems of gang delinquency. Begun in 1958, in conjunction with the established Henry Street Settlement on New York City's lower East Side, the project that finally emerged, Mobilization for Youth, was to serve as a prototype both for the President's Committee on Juvenile Delinquency and Youth Crime and for family and youth components of Gray Area projects in other cities. Mobilization demonstrated how universities could work with community-based institutions to bring research to the service of planned action. In Philadelphia, this model served to inspire the participation of Temple University, located in North Philadelphia, to take leadership in developing the structure and research design, under the direction of psychologist Herman Niebuhr and later with assistance from Howard E. Mitchell, a psychologist from the University of Pennsylvania, for Philadelphia's Gray Area Project, the Philadelphia Council for Community Advancement. For a full discussion of the mobilization experience and its subsequent action program, see Harlem Youth Opportunities Unlimited, Inc.

(HARYOU), *Youth in the Ghetto: A Study of the Consequences of Powerlessness and a Blueprint for Change,* prepared under the direction of Kenneth B. Clark (New York: HARYOU, 1964).

22. Seven urban school districts received total grants of one and one quarter million dollars ($1.25M) to demonstrate how schools could expand their programs to serve the entire community in which they were located and thereby improve the quality of education for children by bringing the home into the school and vice-versa. The initial grantees where Chicago, Cleveland, Detroit, Milwaukee, Philadelphia, Pittsburgh, and St. Louis. For fuller discussion, see Marris and Rein, *Dilemmas of Social Reform*, 16 ff. Later, Washington, San Francisco, and Buffalo, New York were added to the list.
23. James L. Sundquist, *Politics and Policy: The Eisenhower, Kennedy and Johnson Years* (Washington, D.C.: The Brookings Institution, 1968), 120.
24. Marris and Rein, *Dilemmas of Social Reform*, 24.
25. Some examples of these included the Greater Chester Movement, Chester, Pennsylvania; Action Housing in Pittsburgh, Pennsylvania, which received limited Ford support in 1964; Kansas City Association of Trusts and Foundations, Kansas City, Missouri; Hyde Park-Kenwood and The Woodlawn Organization (TWO), Chicago, Illinois, which altered existing renewal-oriented programs; the Lower East Side Neighborhood Association, New York City. Still others have been rumored to have had their beginnings between 1960 and1964, ostensibly following variations on the Gray Area Project's model.
26. Frances Fox Piven and Richard A. Cloward, *Regulating the Poor: The Functions of Public Welfare* (New York: Random House, 1971), 261.
27. Sundquist, *Politics and Policy,* 112.
28. Michael Harrington, *The Other America: Poverty in the United States* (New York: The Macmillan Company, 1964). Arthur M. Schlesinger, Jr., in *A Thousand Days* (New York: Houghton Mifflin, 1965), 1009, makes the claim of Harrington's influence. It must be assumed, therefore, that he referred either to a draft of Harrington's book or to conversation that Kennedy and Harrington had.
29. John Kenneth Galbraith, *The Affluent Society* (Boston: Houghton Mifflin Company, 1958).
30. Leon H. Keyserling, *Poverty and Deprivation in the United States* (Washington, D.C.: Conference on Economic Progress, April 1962).
31. Sundquist, *Politics and Policy,* 114.
32. Sundquist, *Politics and Policy,* 113.
33. James Sundquist writes: "No one can say how much of the new (Gray Area's) thought and experimentation had made an impression directly upon President Kennedy by 1962 or 1963, but some of it had been sponsored or subsidized by the Federal Government, and as a senator and as chief executive he had undoubtedly encountered it. Certainly, many of his close advisors

had—including his brother, Attorney General Robert F. Kennedy, who was chairman of the President's Committee on Juvenile Delinquency and Youth Crime (PCJD)." See Sundquist, *Politics and Policy*, 115.

34. Sundquist, *Politics and Policy*, 114.
35. Sundquist, *Politics and Policy*, 136.
36. Sundquist, *Politics and Policy*, 137, statement from November 23, 1963, the day after the assassination.
37. Sundquist, *Politics and Policy*, 145.
38. For details of activities and their sequence in formulating the final antipoverty legislation, see Sundquist, *Politics and Policy*, 143–154.
39. Generally, the titles addressed the following: Title I: Youth Unemployment; Title II: Community Action; Title III: Rural Action; Title IV: Adult Basic Education; Title V: Small Business Development; Title VI: Work Incentive; Title VII: VISTA (Volunteers in Service to America); Title VIII: Administration.
    For a definitive review of the content, the bureaucratic dynamics of drafting the legislation, and the compromises and negotiations in Congress, see, for example, Sundquist, *Politics and Policy;* Marris and Rein, *Dilemmas of Social Reform*; Daniel P. Moynihan, *Maximum Feasible Misunderstanding: Community Action in the War on Poverty* (New York, NY: Free Press, 1979); Piven and Cloward, *Regulating the Poor*; Sar A. Levitan, *The Great Society's Poor Law: A New Approach to Poverty* (Baltimore, MD: Johns Hopkins Press, 1969), Elinor Graham, "The Politics of Poverty," [PUB FACTS] and S.M. Miller and Martin Rein, "The War on Poverty: Perspectives and Prospects," in Ben B. Seligman (ed.), *Poverty as a Public Issue* (New York, NY: Free Press, 1965).
40. To appeal to the non-urban lobby and constituencies, the Rural Action section of the Act, Title III, offered a similar comprehensive approach to planned action for rural communities.
41. Harlem Youth Opportunities Unlimited, Inc., the New York City Gray Area Project.
42. Kenneth B. Clark and Jeanette Hopkins, *A Relevant War Against Poverty: A Study of Community Action Programs and Observable Change* (New York: Harper & Rowe, 1968), 7.
43. Moynihan, *Maximum Feasible Misunderstanding*, 75–100.
44. Piven and Cloward, *Regulating the Poor*, 256–272.
45. Banfield advances a somewhat prosaic argument, supporting a more generous sampling of conflict situations, including earlier black-white confrontations, beginning at least in 1961, in any analysis of the "urban crisis." See Edward C. Banfield, *The Unheavenly City: The Nature and Future of Urban Crisis* (Boston, MA: Little, Brown, and Company, 1970) and *The Unheavenly City Revisited: A Revision of the Unheavenly City* (Boston, MA: Little, Brown and Company, 1974), especially the chapter, "Rioting Mainly for Fun and Profit."

46. This knowledge about the cross-fertilization between some of the CAPs and the Gray Area projects, and about the missionary zeal of consultants with whom the local CAPs worked is first-hand. For several years, from 1964 until 1967, I served as an OEO consultant, receiving my assignments directly from the Washington CAP Office, often by telegram or weekend telephone calls, requiring immediate travel. One assignment was with a team of five other Gray Area veterans, to help the Chicago CAP develop $5 million worth of projects in a five-day period before their planning grant expired. I was told that President Johnson had promised Mayor Daley that Chicago would receive this amount of OEO funds for implementation and the CAP had been unable to produce fundable projects. For another assignment, I was detailed for one month by the Philadelphia Gray Area project, the Philadelphia Council for Community Advancement, to the Chester, Pennsylvania CAP to develop its Youth Employment package for the next funding cycle.
47. Based on personal experience, described in note 46, above.
48. Piven and Cloward, *Regulating the Poor*, 263.
49. Sundquist, *Power and Politics*, 154.
50. The official name of the Model Cities enabling legislation was "The Demonstration Cities and Metropolitan Development Act of 1966."
51. Charles M. Haar, *Between the Idea and the Reality: A Study of the Origin, Fate and Legacy of the Model Cities Program* (Boston: Little, Brown and Company, 1975) is a general source for many of the first-hand perspectives cited in this chapter on Model Cities. Haar was an advisor to President Johnson, chaired the President's Task Force on Natural Beauty, served on the task force to define the scope of the Department of Housing and Urban Development, and later served as HUD's Assistant Secretary for Metropolitan Development (p. 36).
52. Charles Haar writes: "Johnson...relied heavily on private task forces, cloaked in the secrecy he both enjoyed and regarded as indispensable for receiving unbiased and unvarnished judgments." Haar, *Between the Idea and the Reality*, 37.
53. Walter P. Reuther, memorandum of May 15, 1965 to President Lyndon B. Johnson, in Haar, *Between the Idea and the Reality*, Appendix I., p. 289.
54. Haar, *Between the Idea and the Reality*, 40.
55. Haar, *Between the Idea and the Reality*, 290.
56. Haar, *Between the Idea and the Reality* 45.
57. The Advisory Committee membership was: William L. Rafsky, Chairman, Philadelphia's Development Coordinator and member of the Board of Directors of the Philadelphia Council for Community Advancement, the Gray Area Project; Jack Conway, Director of the National Office, Community Action Program, OEO; Kermit Gordon, Bureau of the Budget Director under President Kennedy and President, The Brookings Institution; Clifford Campbell, senior project advisor, Gray Area Projects, the Ford Foundation; Edward Eichler, consultant, the Ford Foundation; Harvey Perloff, Professor,

Harvard University; and Fred Kramer, OEO advisor. See Advisory Committee on Demonstration Program Development, "Report to the Secretary on the Demonstration Cities Program," October 1966. See also Haar, *Between the Idea and the Reality* and Sundquist, *Making Federalism Work*, for detailed review of the task force deliberations and legislative chronology.

58. U.S. Department of Housing and Urban Development, *Improving the Quality of Urban Life: A Program Guide to Model Neighborhoods in Demonstration Cities* (Washington, D.C.: Government Printing Office, December 1966), 8.
59. Sundquist, *Making Federalism Work*, 39.
60. See also Frieden and Kaplan, *The Politics of Neglect* (Cambridge, MA: The MIT Press, 1975).
61. Robert C. Weaver, Secretary of HUD, in HUD "Improving the Quality of Urban Life," ii.
62. Yvonne S. Perry, "Follow the Yellow Brick Road: An Overview of the Model Cities Program," unpublished paper presented at Orientation Conference for Model Neighborhood Residents, March 16, 1970.
63. Sundquist, *Making Federalism Work*, 86–90.
64. The CDA was the local administrative unit for the Model Cities Program. Directives and guidelines to be used by the local government were developed in the Central Office of the Model Cities Administration in Washington, D.C. and were known as "CDA Letters." See The Areawide Council with Sherry L. Arnstein, "Maximum Feasible Manipulation," *The City*, June/July, 1970.
65. Sundquist, *Making Federalism Work*, 245.
66. Perry, "Follow the Yellow Brick Road." A *New York Times* article on April 26, 1970, captioned, "Nixon May Divert Model Cities Aid for Schools' Use," stated in part: "Administrative sources said today that a memorandum had gone from John D. Ehrlichman, the President's chief advisor on domestic affairs, to the Department of Housing and Urban Development asking about the feasibility of taking $500 million from Model Cities for the next fiscal year for the Education effort." The budget allocation for that same period for Model Cities was only $575 million.
67. Edward C. Banfield, Chairman, Model Cities Task Force, letter to the President, December 16, 1969, Harvard University, Department of Government, 15. Task Force members included: Edward C. Banfield, Joseph Barr, Charles Hill, James M. Buchanan, Bernard Frieden, Ralph Lazarus, Richard Lugar, William Robinson, David Rowlands, and James Q. Wilson.
68. Banfield, letter to the President.
69. Banfield, Model Cities Task Force, 3.
70. Banfield, letter to the President, 4.
71. Banfield, letter to the President., 4.
72. Report of the National Advisory Commission on Civil Disorders, March 1, 1968 (Bound Volume) (Washington, DC: Government Printing Office), 281.
73. Richard S. Bolan, "Planning and the New Federalism," *AIP Journal* (July

1973).
74. Subcommittee on Housing and Community Development, *Evolution of Role of the Federal Government*, 154.
75. Charles Orlebeke, "Carter Renews the Romance with National Urban Policy," *Planning*, (August 1978):2393.
76. Orlebeke, "Carter Renews the Romance," 2393.
77. Subcommittee on Housing and Community Development, "Evolution of the Role of the Federal Government, 155.
78. For details, see Subcommittee on Housing and Community Development, "Evolution of the Role of the Federal Government, 174; also Charles Orlebeke, "Carter Renews the Romance," 2393.
79. Orlebeke, "Carter Renews the Romance," 2393.
80. Subcommittee on Housing and Community Development, "Evolution of the Role of the Federal Government, 183.
81. Subcommittee on Housing and Community Development, "Evolution of the Role of the Federal Government, 202.
82. The original formula took into account the relative normalcy of a city's poverty population, per capita income, level of unemployment and change in total population. In 1976, percentage of pre-1949 housing was added as an optional measure, creating what is referred to as the dual formula, i.e., a city may choose the formula that will place it in the most favorable position with regard to dollar eligibility.
83. Subcommittee on Housing and Community Development, "Evolution of the Role of the Federal Government," [PAGE NO?]
84. Orlebeke, "Carter Renews the Romance," 2394.
85. Orlebeke, "Carter Renews the Romance," 2394.
86. Sundquist, *Power and Politics,* 154.
87. Clark and Hopkins, "A Relevant War Against Poverty," 252.
88. Seymour J. Mandelbaum, "Urban Past and Urban Policies," Department of City and Regional Planning, University of Pennsylvania, October 1979, 7.
89. Sundquist, *Making Federalism Work,* 278.
90. Haar, *Between the Idea and the Reality*, viii.

Chapter Three

The Intellectual Context

Urban improvement goals had resulted in many public programs throughout the thirties, forties, fifties and sixties.... Collectively, they were this country's urban growth policy, although we did not conceive them as such.

—K.C. Parsons and P.Clavel[1]

If an acceptable definition of "policy" is "...an organizing principle to guide action,"[2] the public programs that have been discussed are accurately described as this country's changing and fleeting national urban policies prior to 1977. Moreover, as Parsons and Clavel suggest, these policies were augmented by a series of publications by the federal government, called "Reports on National Growth and Development," that appeared every other year, starting in 1972.

Existing Policies and Prevailing Solutions

Biennial Reports on Urban Growth

Mandated by Title VII of the Housing and Urban Development Act of 1970, Reports on National Growth and Development were prepared by HUD for the President's transmission to Congress. These reports were designed to further Congress' declaration "...that the Federal Government must assume responsibility for development of a national urban growth policy related to seven enumerated objectives dealing with such matters as economic growth, strengthening institutions of general government, balanced use of physical and human resources,"[3] among others. The substance of these reports, however, again demonstrated that the central government continued to address urban problems and urban crises, rather than beginning to collect the growing body of federal experience into a coherent, if not comprehensive, national policy for urban communities:

> By dealing with "problems" and the "urban crisis," this country avoided formulating an integrated domestic policy. Problem-solving programs which lacked consistent central purpose were characteristic of national urban policies...[4]

The growth reports of 1972, 1974, and 1976 became increasingly adept at describing the complexity of the urban growth problem and the effects of various solutions. In fact, the 1974 report already had identified the "inadvertent impacts of Federal actions on growth," a theme that was to become central to the 1977 urban policy process. However, the subsequent 1976 report did not offer guidance for action in the traditional form of policy statements. The late Senator Hubert H. Humphrey, a long-time advocate of federal policy intervention in the cycle of city decline, was critical of this weakness in the 1976 growth report. He commented that the administration was not only neglecting its responsibility for coordinating national programs, but also was withdrawing from its commitment to provide programs for cities and depressed regions.[5]

In part, the failure of the biennial growth reports to be more directive and to provide policy guidance, can be traced to the philosophy of the Nixon and Ford administrations. Parsons and Clavel felt that such policy direction from the national level would have been inconsistent with the spirit of New Federalism, and a contradiction of the administration's intention to let local governments set their own priorities with as little interference from the federal government as possible. Further, if local governments were to decide how federal dollars should be spent, the federal government could not very well establish policies that required that federal money be spent by local governments in a specific way.

An equally important reason for the failure of the growth reports to enunciate policy, however, was the fact that responsibility for coordinating the achievement of consensus on values that such policies would address and for formulating the policies into generally acceptable language, rested with a single domestic agency, HUD. Graham insists that "...public forces who handed the administration the problem of growth policy in 1970...wanted an `identifiable unit' of the (White House) Domestic Council to prepare these reports and carry on the search for a NGP (National Growth Policy)."[6] Derthick makes a more generic point:

> When representatives of legally independent Federal agencies meet in a coordinating forum, they find it hard to reach agreement on issues of importance. Ordinarily they cannot settle disputes over jurisdiction or policy. They have neither the power nor an incentive to do so.... Coordi-

> nating forums may create good will, improve information, and reduce the appearance of conflict. They may also facilitate cooperation.... Beyond that, it is hard for any coordinating forum to do much good.[7]

Thus, the legislative mandate that implied that coordinating the development of growth policy should rest with HUD, probably also guaranteed that no substantive policies would be developed. It is this dilemma that generated amendments in 1977 to alter the tone and thrust of the subsequent reports.

Sections 702 and 703(a) of the National Urban Policy and New Communities Development Act, as amended in 1977, state in part that the newly mandated: "[N]ational urban policy...shall serve as a guide in making specific decisions at the national level which affect the pattern of urban development and redevelopment and shall provide a framework for development of interstate, State, and local urban policy."[8]

In these legislative sections, the scope of urban policy is described and its content is specified. The level of detail leaves no doubt that Congress was seeking a different and more commanding document.

That HUD was already in the analysis stages of the 1978 report when the amendments were passed offered strong support for HUD's arguments for continued designation as the urban policy development coordinator. Further, while the 1977 amendments did not mention that HUD would have the continued responsibility, this protocol was implied by the inclusion of the mandate in HUD's basic enabling legislation. Finally, HUD's Secretary Patricia Harris had made a point of HUD's role as the urban advocate in a number of her policy addresses, recalling that the agency was created to perform an advocacy function for urban areas paralleling the Department of Agriculture's traditional role vis-a-vis rural areas. These precedents probably were not lost on the President.

The Influence of Prevailing Urban Solutions

As is detailed in the following section, a number of thinkers were writing and speaking about ways to save the cities. However, three concepts were more significant than others in shaping the policy development process: triage, gentrification, and revitalization. An examination of their meanings and influence is instructive.

Triage. Triage was a concept advanced by several urbanists in different terms and with varying descriptions, but it was most closely identified with Downs, who coined the name.[9] Taking the word "triage" from the medical procedure that ranks patients according to the severity of their disease and gives priority to those likely to benefit the most from immediate attention, triage for urban areas proposed a similar priority system. Those cities, and portions of cities that were the most distressed, were viewed as the least likely to benefit from corrective intervention. Thus, these areas were to be left to their own devices while resources were directed to more healthy targets.

Thompson uses the phrase "checkerboard depopulation strategy" to characterize an orderly evacuation of core urban areas.[10] Evacuation would be accomplished by decreasing services for the areas and cutting off improvements.[11]

Sternlieb, while not necessarily advocating the abandonment of the city as a viable target for investments, still felt that big cities were not worth saving and that efforts to do so were largely symbolic:

> Would (I) give up on the central city? Yes...the bulk of our inputs into the central city are a form of what I would refer to as 'high-class ritual'—a form of symbolic reaction, of going through the motions.
>
> Much of our effort...is really trivial in terms of realistic throughput. In psychological terms—to show that somebody cares—it is very important. But in terms of putting real dollars into central cities, let me suggest that people put real bucks where you get the most bang for your buck—and the place where you get the most bang for your buck is not the central city.[12]

A rose by any other name is triage. The concept of triage became a rallying point for the staff developing the national urban policy. It energized the development process, and whether admitted or not, it became the bleak alternative against which all possible efforts of avoidance had to be directed. Triage was abhorrent as a viable concept for at least three reasons:

1) It flew in the face of the logic of the policy development process, i.e., if abandonment were inevitable, why was the administration making serious efforts to save the cities?
2) The political implications for the administration, if triage by default became a favored solution to distress, were grim in terms of Carter's commitments to the black, the poor, and other urban constituents.
3) Triage was not right. It condemned certain groups and classes of people to benign neglect. In addition to philosophical and personal objections that Secretary Harris and her staff had to

such a position, this was reminiscent of the acknowledged theme of the erstwhile Republican administration and, thus, additionally distasteful.

Gentrification. The term "gentrification" has its origins in the British experience of the return to the city by the gentry, an affluent, culturally refined, leisurely class of people, who had abandoned the industrialized urban areas at the turn of the century for the comparative exclusivity of the country. In American terms, gentrification has come to mean the affluent reclamation of housing and neighborhoods in the central city in response to fatigue with commuting, high energy prices, inconvenience, and other costs. Although the American gentry are largely white, they are more accurately described as middle-class people for whom some cities (or better, some precincts) hold the affordable attractions of a more diverse and economically attractive option:

> The truth—whatever cultural enlightment may be involved—is that the cost of a suburban split-level has only to soar so high, and the price of an innercity brownstone plummet so low, before people in Westchester start finding even certain neighborhoods in the Bronx colorful and cultivated places to live.... one of the northern cities' greatest present assets is their past misfortune. For thirty years the cost of innercity land, real estate, and labor has been declining, and the cost of those commodities in the suburbs rising, in relationship to each other. Whether the arsonists of the South Bronx have created a graveyard of urban civilization, or the biggest bonanza for the smart money developers yet depends on the eye of the beholder.[13]

Gentrification was not viewed as inherently bad by the developers of the national urban policy. Rather, it was seen as a sine qua non of any urban reinvestment strategy. It required, however, a system of control and direction in order to avoid the displacement of low-income and minority families, like that experienced during the predecessor urban renewal programs. Thus, a viable national urban policy had to accommodate and intensify gentrification trends, while constraining the negative impact on those unable to compete economically—specifically minorities and the poor—by retaining their stake in urban neighborhoods. Gentrification, therefore, offered a tool for urban revitalization as well as a challenge to its orderly and humane achievement.

Urban revitalization. Revitalization was the catch-all phrase for a variety of strategies to renew urban areas. Its origins are obscure, but logically derived from earlier images of the city as vital, and from feelings among urban advocates that a recapture of that vitality was possible, given sufficient determination. The federally sponsored urban programs, beginning with urban renewal in the mid-fifties, and continuing through to 1977 had been inspired to some extent by these images. Earlier analyses concerning dying cities,[14] saving cities,[15] cities in "twilight,"[16] and cities "emerging,"[17] all revolved around techniques to recapture urban vitality, however narrowly focused these techniques were.

A workable revitalization technique was the objective of the national urban policy development process. As will be elaborated later, a subliminal motivation was the belief that, once a set of coherent policies were written and pronounced, even if these were less than perfect and comprehensive, a commitment to revitalizing cities would be codified. The perfection of the revitalization tools then could be addressed with a singleness of purpose that was precluded by the prevailing debate about the advisability and practicality of saving or reclaiming contemporary urban areas.

In this context, an observation about human and philosophical motives—as opposed to local conditions and rational considerations—is appropriate. The reality cannot be ignored that a large portion of the motivation leading to the national urban policy grew out of a love of cities and a commitment to them on the part of the policy framers. While it is often difficult to explain this motivation through references to existing theories or strategies, it is true that those responsible for developing the urban policy believed that cities are important, that they contribute to the culture that is uniquely American, and that they provide a context for distinctly and characteristically American dynamics. The desire to preserve these urban characteristics, by rejecting triage, by controlling gentrification, and by revitalizing the urban environment, was a significant element of the national urban policy development process.

The Literature: Policy Proposals and Policy Issues

At least as early as 1969, the public and private sector were giving serious thought to what ought to comprise a national urban policy. On the one hand, there were valuative efforts to assess what we should have learned from what had gone before, as the nation undertook to improve upon these earlier experiences. On the other hand, there were those who felt that enough evaluation had taken place already and that some concrete proposals could be presented for drafting the long-overdue national urban policy.

Leading the evaluation-oriented group were contributions from Frederic Cleveland of the Brookings Institution,[18] looking at the problems that Congress presented in solving urban problems, and Robert Yin of the Rand Institute.[19] Yin assembled thirty-seven contributors to urban research who suggested ways in which the argument for greater resource availability versus a better policy approach might be reformulated. Graham,[20] Frieden and Kaplan,[21] and Harvey[22] all reviewed past experiences in an effort to divine how future action might be better and more equitably directed, and Muller[23] explored previous efforts to assess the artificial boundaries of the city that may have led to errors in understanding "the outer city."

The model builders of the national urban policy seem to have been led, at least chronologically, by the work of Moynihan,[24] based on his earlier working paper,[25] developed while he chaired President Nixon's Urban Affairs Council. At about the same time Harris and Lindsay[26] reported in the *State of the Cities* that racism and poverty still united to defy urban reform and offered recommendations for a viable urban policy. Sundquist[27] suggested that we should look abroad for models designed to decrease urban decline, while Jordan,[28] Caputo,[29] Long,[30] Downs,[31] and Wingo[32] all explored issues and alternatives for urban policy development.

Urban Growth Policy: A Point of Departure

The housing amendments of 1970, as discussed earlier, called for the President to report to Congress in every even-numbered year the progress being made in developing a policy to control unrestrained urban growth.[33] In part, this requirement was based on recommendations made by the Advisory Commission on Intergovernmental Relations (ACIR)[34] and by the National Commission on Urban Growth Policy, according to Canty.[35] Parsons and Clavel[36] and Humphrey[37] developed definitive criticisms of the series of presidential growth reports that were issued between 1972 and 1976, providing direction for how these reports might become more effective and useful policy statements. Meanwhile, the Urban Land Institute sponsored the independent growth studies of Scott, Brower and Miner,[38] and the Real Estate Research Corporation issued a three-volume study on urban sprawl,[39] reviewed critically by Altshuler.[40]

In a search for alternatives to the decline observed in spreading urban areas, control of city size was explored as a possible solution. Both Hoch[41] and Segal[42] addressed this issue in 1976, publishing just prior to the beginning of the urban policy development period.

Racism, Poverty, and Unemployment as Policy Issues

As was noted, the 1960s federal policy regarding cities emphasized the role played by race and poverty in the formulation of solutions to the urban crisis. This point was broadened at the turn of the 1970s to include unemployment as a corollary of race and poverty. Kain[43] and Feldstein[44] discussed the emerging dynamic of urban unemployment, reinforcing ongoing analysis of the demography of the black community by the National Urban League.[45]

Scheinder[46] explored the role of race in energy policy; Bryce,[47] the role of minorities and race in urban governance; and Brimmer and Terrell, the role of race in capitalism in the urban setting.[48] Green focused directly on race and poverty as the prime urban challenge,[49] and Porter explicated the concept of an urban Marshall Plan[50] as a model for urban policy. The National Urban League, following its annual practice of issuing a report on "The State of Black America," suggested a number of urban policy issues of importance to black America in its 1977 report, as noted above.

The Cities' Lobbies and Other City Experts

Chief among the organizations watching out for the cities' interests was, and is, the National League of Cities. In addition to issuing annual reports and producing working papers on various urban problems, the League prepared a special report in January 1976, that emphasized the growing concern for urban decline and fiscal crisis in urban governments.[51] The major recommendations of this report subsequently were adopted at the League's Annual Meeting later in 1976 and issued as a formal set of policy recommendations[52] to guide the President's urban policy effort.

Also during 1976, the major think tanks that conduct research on urban issues began developing sets of recommendations, as did a number of independent researchers. Notable among these were two study reports from ACIR, addressing the role of federalism in improving urban conditions.[53] The Urban Institute, which originated to answer the need for long-range urban research with reliable federal support, sponsored Gorham and Glazer's edited volume on the urban predicament.[54] The Brookings Institution's annual study report on the national budget, issued in early 1977,[55] contained a particularly influential contribution by Nathan and Dommel.[56] Also Bosworth and Dusenberry's[57] volume on the capital needs of cities was especially timely for the policy development effort.

The Joint Center for Political Studies,[58] which had sponsored the earlier Bryce study of urban governance, released a new book edited by

Bryce[59] that focused on the dynamics of growth and decline in smaller urban communities. Among the contributors to the Bryce volume was Bergh,[60] who, along with Vaughan and Vogel, had authored the Rand Corporation's study of the urban impacts of federal policies.[61] Bergh, Vaughan, and Vogel consistently stressed the need for the federal government to develop policies less inadvertently harmful to cities, and this became a prime theme of the final policy.

Issued after the national urban policy development process was underway in 1977, but still in time to influence the substance of the policy, were a study by the Council for Economic Development[62] and a report by the National Urban Policy Roundtable. The roundtable was conducted by the Academy for Contemporary Problems and sponsored by the Kettering Foundation,[63] which also had sponsored the Rand Corporation study.

The primary geographic focus of the Great Society's efforts of the 1960s reappeared as a primary focus of urban policy recommendations. Neighborhoods, as viable units of urban policy treatment, were discussed by Houstoun,[64] Lipsky and Mollenkopf,[65] and by Miller et al., in a National Institute for Advanced Studies report,[66] that echoed observations made earlier in the 1970s by Warren, Rose, and Bergunder.[67]

Guidance from Other Levels and Branches of Government

Hearings, policy documents, and reports by the U.S. Congress and by state governments were perhaps more influential than any other sources in the national urban policy development process. Because members of Congress ultimately must provide the legislative mandate and funds to support administration initiatives, attentiveness to congressional interest is often a wise posture for policy makers, in general. In the particular case of the national urban policy process, it has been noted that some members of Congress had established reputations in the area of urban research and policy development, particularly Congressman Henry Reuss of Wisconsin and Senator Daniel P. Moynihan of New York. The studies and reports for which they were responsible,[68] therefore, must be viewed as having been influential in the administration's determination to produce an unified national urban policy. The Reuss Committee's subsequent volume of analytical papers by urban experts in 1977[69] were substantively sound and useful in the policy process. Moynihan's work has been mentioned above as a paradigm for policy formulation.

The Reuss Committee also published the transcript of hearings on the implications of foreign experiences for American cities,[70] making a number of the same points that Sundquist made in the Brookings study of lessons from abroad.[71] The Committee's report on the impact of the federal budget on cities[72] offered recommendations that were directly incorporated into the policy.

Several state governments, primarily through their offices of community affairs, had undertaken urban policy development projects by early 1977. Massachusetts and California both published development strategies[73] and urban growth policies[74] that were well received and frequently cited by the national urban policy staff. Before the end of the 1977, the city of Baltimore also had prepared a set of recommendations to the federal government for the national urban policy,[75] and a HUD-sponsored conference of a coalition of Northeastern smaller communities in early 1977, produced a report on the special concerns of cities in the middle.[76] In this same context, the innovative demonstration undertaken by the state of Minnesota with tax-base sharing[77] received a close examination for possibilities of replication elsewhere as national policy.

Summary

All of the cited sources in the literature influenced the national urban policy development process, either because they offered encouragement that a policy could and ought to be written or through the guidance that they offered the staff concerning the substance of the policy. A few of the sources, however, were particularly influential—some negative and some positive.

The greatest negative influences were those against which the policy attempted to offer rebuttal and whose solutions were unattractive to the policy development staff and, thus, needed to be avoided at almost all costs. The most outstanding among these were Downs, Thompson, Sternlieb, and Jordan.[78] The former three propounded concepts for addressing the urban crisis that argued essentially that it was either not possible or not worthwhile to save cities. Jordan charged that the administration and the urban policy drafters were not doing worthwhile work, at least in so far as the black community's interests were concerned. None of these prophecies, of course, could be permitted to become self-fulfilling, in the view of any of the principals involved in the process.

In the category of positive influences are collected a small but prestigious group. Nathan and Dommel of Brookings, Moynihan, Reuss, Gorham and Glazer, the Advisory Commission on Intergovernmental Relations, and Vaughan were referred to frequently. In a number of instances they were contacted directly by the urban policy makers for their views. Incidentally, some of those whose overall influence has been characterized as negative were also contacted.

Notes

1. K.C. Parsons and P. Clavel. *National Growth Policy: An Institutional Perspective* (Ithaca, NY: Cornell University, Program in Urban and Regional Studies, 1977), 2.
2. Robert Morris, *Social Policy of the American Welfare State* (New York: Harper & Row, 1979), 1.
3. Subcommittee on Housing and Community Development of the Committee on Banking, Currency and Housing, House of Representatives, *Evolution of Role of the Federal Government in Housing and Community Development: A Chronology of Legislative and Selected Executive Actions, 1892-1974* (Washington, D.C.: U.S. Government Printing Office, October 1975), 167.
4. Parsons and Clavel, *National Growth Policy*, 2.
5. Hubert H. Humphrey, "Comments on the Draft of the President's 1976 Biennial Report on National Growth," mimeographed January 19, 1976, Washington, DC, passim.
6. Otis L. Graham, Jr., *Toward a Planned Society* (New York: Oxford University Press, 1976), 275.
7. Martha Derthick, "Hearings on New Federalism, Subcommittee of the Committee on Government Operations, House of Representatives (Washington, D.C.: U.S. Government Printing Office, 1974), 191–192.
8. See Appendix A for full language of Title VII, Sections 701–703.
9. Anthony Downs, *Opening Up the Suburbs* (Washington, DC: Real Estate Research Corporation 1976) and Anthony Downs, *Opening up the Suburbs: An Urban Strategy for America* (New Haven: Yale University Press, 1973).
10. Wilbur Thompson, transcript of remarks, Managing Mature Cities conference, National Urban Policy Roundtable, Academy for Contemporary Problems, sponsored by the Charles F. Kettering Foundation, Cincinnati, Ohio, June 1977, 9.
11. David Flick, "Let Some Areas Die to Save Others, City Told,"*Cincinnati Post*, June 10, 1977.
12. George S. Sternlieb, "Are Big Cities Worth Saving?" in *The City in the Seventies*, Robert K. Lin, ed. (New York, NY: Rand Institute, 1972) 266-267.
13. T. D. Allman, "The Urban Crisis Leaves Town—And Moves to the Suburbs," *Harpers Magazine* (December 1978): 5-6.
14. J. L. Johnson, *Los Angeles Times*, Friday, January 7, 1977, Part II, 7.
15. Sternlieb, "Are Big Cities Worth Saving?"
16. E. A. Gutkind, *Twilight of the Cities* (New York: The Free Press of Glencoe, 1962).
17. Scott Greer, *The Emerging City: Myth and Reality* (New York: The Free Press, 1962).
18. Frederic N. Cleaveland and Associates. *Congress and Urban Problems* (Washington, DC: The Brookings Institution, 1969).
19. Robert K. Yin, ed., *The City in the Seventies* (Itasca, IL: F.E. Peacock

Publishers, Inc. 1972).
20. Graham, *Toward a Planned Society.*
21. Bernard J. Frieden and Marshall Kaplan, *The Politics of Neglect* (Cambridge: The MIT Press, 1975).
22. David Harvey, *Social Justice and the City* (Baltimore: Johns Hopkins University Press, 1973).
23. Peter O. Muller, *The Outer City* (Philadelphia, PA: Association of American Geographers and Temple University, 1976). More recently, David Ruskin, *Cities Without Suburbs* (Baltimore: Johns Hopkins University Press, 1993) has quantified this research.
24. Daniel P. Moynihan, ed., *Toward A National Urban Policy* (New York: Basic Books, Inc., 1970).
25. Daniel P. Moynihan, "Toward a National Urban Policy," draft paper (became Introduction to Moynihan's 1970 book), July 1969.
26. Senator Fred R. Harris and Mayor John V. Lindsay, Co-chairmen, *The State of the Cities: Report of the Commission on the Cities in the '70's* (New York: Praeger Publishers, 1972).
27. James Sundquist, *Dispersing Population: What America Can Learn From Europe* (Washington, DC: The Brookings Institute, 1975).
28. National Urban League, Inc. *The State of Black America 1977* (Washington, DC: NUL, January 11, 1977).
29. David A. Caputo, *Urban America: The Policy Alternatives* (San Francisco: W.H. Freeman & Company, 1976).
30. Norton E. Long, "How to Help Cities Become Independent," unpublished paper, University of Missouri, St. Louis, Missouri, August 1977.
31. Anthony Downs, *Urban Problems and Prospects* (Real Estate Research Corporation) (Chicago: Markham Publishing Company, 1970).
32. Lowdon Wingo, "Issues in A National Urban Development Strategy for the United States" *Urban Studies* XIII (1976):3–27.
33. Mark J. Kasoff, "The Urban Impact of Federal Policies: A Preview of a New Rand Study," *Nation's Cities* (National League of Cities, November 1977).
34. Advisory Commission on Intergovernmental Relations, *Urban and Rural America: Policies for Future Growth* (Washington, DC: U.S. Government Printing Office, 1968.}
35. Donald Canty, ed., *The New City: National Commission on Urban Growth Policy* (New York: Frederick A. Praeger for Urban America, Inc., 1969).
36. Parsons and Clavel. *National Growth Policy.*
37. Hubert Humphrey, "Comments on the Draft of the President's 1976 Biennial Report on National Growth," mimeograph, Washington, DC, January 19, 1976.
38. Randall W. Scott, David J. Brower, and Dallas D. Miner, *Management & Control of Growth,* Vol. 1 (Washington, DC: The Urban Land Institute, 1975).
39. Real Estate Research Corporation, *The Costs of Sprawl* Vol. 1: Executive

Summary, Vol. 2: Detailed Cost Analysis; Vol. 3: Literature Review and Bibliography (Washington, DC: Government Printing Office, 1975).

40. Alan Altshuler, "Review of the Costs of Sprawl," *Journal of the American Institute of Planners* 43 (1977):207–209.
41. I. Hoch, "City Size: Effects, Trends, and Policies," *Science* 193 (1976): 856–863.
42. D. Segal, "Are There Returns to Scale in City Size?" *The Review of Economics and Statistics* 58 (1976):339–350.
43. John F. Kain, "Coping with Ghetto Unemployment," *AIP Journal* (March 1969).
44. M. S. Feldstein, "The Economics of the New Unemployment,"*The Public Interest* 33 (1973):3–42.
45. National Urban League, *Population Policy and the Black Community* B. William Austin, Research Department (Washington, DC: NUL, 1974).
46. Alvin J. Scheinider, "Blacks, Cities and the Energy Crisis," *Urban Affairs Quarterly* (September 1974).
47. Herrington J. Bryce, ed., *Urban Governance and Minorities* (New York: Praeger Publishers, 1976).
48. Andrew F. Brimmer and Henry S. Terrell, "The Economic Potential of Black Capitalism," presented paper, American Economics Association, New York, NY, December 29, 1969.
49. Robert L. Green, *The Urban Challenge: Poverty and Race* (Chicago: Follett Publishing Company, 1977).
50. Paul R. Porter, *The Recovery of American Cities* (New York: Two Continents Publishing Group, 1976).
51. National League of Cities, *State of the Cities: 1975—A New Urban Crisis?* (Washington, DC: NUL, January 1976).
52. National League of Cities, *National Municipal Policy* (Washington, DC: NUL, 1977). Adopted at the Annual Business Session, Congress of Cities, Denver, Colorado, December 1, 1976.
53. The Advisory Commission on Intergovernmental Relations, *American Federalism: Toward a More Effective Partnership* (Washington, DC: ACIR, August 1975).
54. William Gorham and Nathan Glazer, eds., *The Urban Predicament* (Washington, DC: The Urban Institute, 1976).
55. Joseph A. Pechman, ed., *Setting National Priorities: The 1978 Budget* (Washington, DC: The Brookings Institution, 1977).
56. R. P. Nathan and P. R. Dommel, "The Cities" in *Setting National Priorities: The 1978 Budget,* J. Pechman, ed., (Washington, DC: The Brookings Institution, 1977).
57. B. Bosworth and J. Dusenberry, *Capital Needs in the Seventies* (Washington, DC: The Brookings Institution, 1975).
58. The Joint Center for Political Studies is now known as the Joint Center for Political and Economic Studies.

59. Herrington J. Bryce, ed., *Small Cities in Transition: The Dynamics of Growth and Decline* (Cambridge: Ballinger Publishing Co., 1977).
60. Stephen Bergh, "The Urban Impact of Federal Policies: Their Direct and Indirect Effects on the Local Public Sector," in *Small Cities in Transition: The Dynamics of Growth and Decline*, Herrington J. Bryce, ed. (Massachusetts: Ballinger Publishing Company, 1977). Speakers: William B. Eddy, Stanley J. Hallet, Mark J. Kassoff, Lawrence Susskind, and Wilbur Thompson.
61. Rand Corporation, *The Urban Impacts of Federal Policies*, four volumes, prepared under a grant from the Charles F. Kettering Foundation, June 1977 (Santa Monica, CA: The Rand Corporation). Vol. I: Overview, Barbara Williams, project director. Vol. II: Economic Development, Roger J. Vaughn. Vol. III: Fiscal Conditions, Stephen Barro. Vol. IV: Population and Residential Location, Roger J. Vaughn and Mary E. Vogel.
62. Council for Economic Development, *An Approach to Federal Urban Policy: A Statement on National Policy by the Research and Policy Committee of CED* (New York: CED, December 1977).
63. Academy for Contemporary Problems and the Kettering Foundation, National Urban Policy Roundtable: Managing Mature Cities (Conference), June 9–10, 1977. Speakers: William B. Eddy, Stanley J. Hallett, Mark J. Kasoff, Lawrence Susskind, and Wilbur Thompson.
64. Lawrence Houston, "City Neighborhoods and Urban Policy," *Nation's Cities* (Washington, D.C.: National League of Cities, 1976.)
65. M. Lipsky and J. Mollenkopf, "Toward a National Urban Policy Based on Neighborhood Economic Opportunity and Vitality," report to *Action*, mimeographed, December 1977.
66. T.R. Miller, R.G. Bruce, Carol B. Shapiro, H.J. Tankin, *Strategies for Revitalizing Neighborhood Commercial Areas: The Role Application and Impact of Public and Private Resources,* final report (National Institute for Advanced Studies, November 1, 1977).
67. Roland L. Warren, Stephen M. Rose, and Ann F. Bergunder. *The Structure of Urban Reform: Community Decision Organizations in Stability and Change* (Lexington, MA: D.C. Heath and Company, 1974).
68. Hearings of the House Committee on Banking, Currency, and Housing from September 20, 1976 to October 1, 1976, "The Rebirth of the American City."
69. Hearings before the Subcommittee on the City of the Committee on Banking, Finance and Urban Affairs, "How Cities Can Grow Old Gracefully," House of Representatives, 95th Congress, First Session, December 1977.
70. Hearings before the Subcommittee on the City of the Committee on Banking, Finance and Urban Affairs, "Successes Aboard: What Foreign Cities Can Teach American Cities," House of Representatives, 95th Congress, First Session, April 4,5, and 6, 1977.
71. Sundquist, *Dispersing Population*, passim.
72. Hearings before the Subcommittee on the City, House Committee on

Banking, Finance and Urban Affairs, "Impact of the Federal Budget on Cities," July 1977.

73. Office of Planning and Research, *An Urban Development Strategy for California*, Advisory Committee Draft for Public Review and Comment, May 1977, Department of Housing and Urban Development, Washington, DC.
74. The Massachusetts Office of State Planning, *City and Town Centers: A Program for Growth,* The Massachusetts Growth Policy Report, September 1977.
75. William Donald Schaefer, *A New Federal Policy for Cities: The Baltimore Proposal* (Baltimore, MD: October 11, 1977).
76. Coalition of Northeast Interests, *Cities in the Middle: The Way Back to Prosperity, Trenton, New Jersey* (Washington, D.C.: HUD, February 1977).
77. A. Reschovsky and E. Knapp, "Tax Base Sharing: An Assessment of the Minnesota Experience," *Journal of the American Institute of Planners* 43 (1977):361-369.
78. V. E. Jordan, Jr., "Keynote Address to the 67th Annual Conference of the National Urban League," mimeographed, Washington, DC, National Urban League, July 25, 1977.

Chapter Four

The Presidential Mandate

The early stages of the decision-making process—identifying a disequilibrium, diagnosing the situation, and stating the problem—lead to the fourth step: selection of a particular course of action designed either to return...to a previous state of equilibrium or to bring...a new state of equilibrium. Skill in creating an operational solution to a stated problem is the test of all the preceding steps...and of the manager's decision-making ability.[1]

The Department of Housing and Urban Development (HUD) was preordained to lead the Carter administration's urban policy development process, and events occurring within HUD reinforced the inevitability of this leadership role. Several of HUD Secretary Patricia Harris' principal staff, notably Assistant Secretaries Robert C. Embry, Jr., Community Planning and Development (CPD), and Donna E. Shalala,[2] Policy Development and Research (PD&R), had asked Harris to prod President Carter about the crisis of the cities. As an indication of her own sensitivity to the problem, Harris concluded negotiations to hire Lynn Curtis as her urban affairs advisor shortly before March 1977. Curtis, a University of Pennsylvania Ph.D. in Urban Studies and Social Policy, at that time was on the staff of the Bureau of Social Sciences Research in Washington, DC.

While seeking a vehicle to advance the secretary's image as head of the urban advocacy agency within the new administration, Harris' immediate staff hit upon the idea of exploiting the urban convener power. Created for HUD's first secretary Robert C. Weaver by President Johnson, the Convener Executive Order 11297 was known to Harris' staff legal advisor,

Joseph Burstein, a veteran of previous Democratic administrations and a seasoned poverty warrior.

Undertaking the development of an urban policy began to emerge as an increasingly attractive strategy to Harris' staff as they sought to develop a distinctive theme for her stewardship of HUD. Thus, two of her chief executive assistants, Henry Hubschman and Andy Weisman, collaborated with Bruce Kirschenbaum, associate assistant to the President for intergovernmental relations, and Orin Kramer, White House Domestic Policy staff liaison to HUD, in sessions held in the White House, to draft the President's March 21, 1977 memorandum. (See Figure 4.1.) It was this memorandum that provided the mandate and direction and designated HUD as leader for the urban development process.

Addressed to the secretaries of Treasury; Commerce; Labor; Health, Education, and Welfare; Housing and Urban Development; and Transportation, with copies to heads of executive departments and agencies, the March memo directed the HUD secretary to convene a "working policy group on urban and regional development." The group was to have three responsibilities:

1) Conduct a comprehensive review of all federal programs that affect urban and regional areas;
2) Seek perspectives of state and local officials concerning the role of the federal government in urban and regional development; and
3) Submit appropriate administrative and legislative recommendations.

In addition to the specific charges to the working group, two statements in the memo set the tone for the group's structure and process. The first was the requirement that the process "be a joint project with full participation by each of the designated departments." The second was the commitment that two of the most senior White House staff members, Assistant to the President for Domestic Policy Stuart Eizenstat and Assistant to the President for Intergovernmental Relations and Secretary to the Cabinet Jack Watson were to be involved directly in the activities of the policy group. Calling the urban and regional policy effort "a high priority for my Administration," the President requested that he receive "a preliminary report on...progress and findings by early summer."

Thus, through a careful association of Harris' staff's agenda with priorities to which the President had committed himself during his campaign, HUD had created a vehicle for furthering its own image and simultaneously, had placed itself "in the driver's seat." The convener role assigned to HUD under the executive order included initial responsibility for chairing the policy group and ultimate responsibility for coordinating the entire urban policy process.

The latter responsibilities evolved into the organization and management role within the process, the role of secretariat for the subgroup task forces, and the role as principal author of the policy document itself. The following narrative describes the components of the policy working group structure, especially HUD's place in it.

HUD as Lead Agency

Taking its name from the function assigned to it by the President, the Urban and Regional Policy Group (URPG) got underway immediately in March 1977, at least at the staff level. Secretary Harris convened her principal staff exactly one week following receipt of the President's March 21 memorandum. Urban affairs advisor Lynn Curtis already had been informally designated by Harris to be executive director of URPG, with responsibility for "doing the writing and managing the substantive staff working on the urban policy."[3]

Curtis shared the URPG leadership with PD&R's Donna E. Shalala, who was to "handle the political role: diplomacy, representation of the Secretary, timing and convening the meetings, and mover of the URPG member agencies and their Assistant Secretaries."[4] As a presidential appointee who was confirmed by Congress, Shalala carried political clout and constituent support, which Curtis lacked. It was expected that she would be perceived by other assistant secretaries, who also had clout, constituents, and often their own agendas, as a peer with whom they could negotiate. Thus, Harris shrewdly divided URPG leadership along conceptual (Curtis) and political (Shalala) lines.

The duo's first assignment was to "prepare a first draft discussion paper and...lead the discussion, at the (March 29) staff meeting, of the paper and the approach to the policy group's task."[5] Curtis recalls that he had less than one week to prepare the draft paper to which PD&R staff contributed. PD&R's contributions were based, in part, on studies and research already underway for the fourth biennial growth report, newly required by Congress to be called the "Urban Policy Report." Shalala also had commissioned a number of analytical "growth" studies by outside expert consultants, some of which had been completed in draft.

The ten-page urban policy draft called for an examination of the "causal connections which link such problems as declining neighborhoods, deteriorating housing, inferior social services, urban employment and disinvestment."[6] As was to be echoed in subsequent drafts and in the final urban policy document a year later, an exploration was proposed of the "national and regional context" of urban problems and of the impact of federal policies on regional, metropolitan, and neighborhood conditions.

The paper suggested approaches, objectives, and specific agenda items that the policy should address, emphasizing that a coalition of state, local, public, and private forces would be needed to join with the national government in partnership. The paper disclaimed the validity of a "one best" solution to cities problems, citing the variety of conditions pertaining to location, size, and character of the urban area.

Two value premises were advanced in the Curtis PD&R draft:

> Urban policy and programs in the United States should *aim to achieve more than efficiency. Equity for all groups*, and particularly the less advantaged, should also be weighed in the balance in making choices.
>
> Where experience shows that private competitive forces alone do not produce results broadly deemed desirable, *public intervention* is both legitimate and necessary.

These premises supported seven important objectives. These objectives represented the secretary's posture, both at that time and throughout the policy development process. Some have argued that the final policy, not announced until one year later almost to the exact date, could and should have been refined essentially from these objectives, drafted early on.

Briefly summarized, these objectives were:

- Modernize existing cities and make them livable;
- Conserve existing suburbs and open them up so that people of every race and class can live close to where they work as a matter of right;
- Encourage pre-serviced, large-scale, full planning land development in outlying areas;
- Preserve the natural environment and better relate the built environment to it;
- Manage urban growth so that the quality of life can be improved; and

- Give as much attention to the redistribution of existing resources as to "trickle down" growth strategies;
- Address honestly the racial basis of much of the urban crisis.

Curtis reports that the draft was well received, given the short time devoted to its preparation. CPD Assistant Secretary, Robert C. Embry's[7] comments at the first meeting of the secretary's staff were that the policy should focus more on cities that were "troubled;" should identify more clearly exactly what the problems in the cities were, should detail a specific strategy to correct these problems, and should "prioritize—not take on everything." He also stressed that attention to regional concerns should occur primarily in terms of reversing the problems of the cities, not simply to develop the regions.[8]

The decision was made, based on in-house HUD meetings and discussions with White House staff, to form task forces to begin detailed work in specific areas. Simultaneously, the Curtis/PD&R draft was being revised for re-circulation within HUD and then throughout the other URPG member agencies. The refined draft was the subject of the first meeting of the cabinet members assigned by the President to the URPG.

The secretaries who attended the first URPG meeting on April 18, 1977, were: Patricia Harris, chair, for HUD; Secretary Juanita Kreps for Commerce; Secretary Ray Marshall for Labor; and Secretary Michael Blumenthal for Treasury, whom gossips reported to have arrived rather late by a side entrance and left early. Blumenthal was perceived by HUD staff to be less than enthusiastic about URPG and about HUD's leadership and to have had his own agenda, which emerged later. Joseph Califano, of Health, Education and Welfare (HEW), was represented by Undersecretary Hale Champion, and speculations about this substitution also will be discussed later.

Brock Adams, secretary for Transportation (DOT), was absent, but later evidence suggests that his absence did not necessarily reflect lack of interest. Both Eizenstat and Watson represented the White House. Table 4.1 gives a list of first URPG principals and their staff.

Secretary Harris viewed the first meeting as successful and as having endorsed the direction that her URPG staff was taking.[9] She indicated to Curtis that it was appropriate for secretaries' assigned deputies (usually a designated assistant secretary from each agency) to begin meeting to continue the work at the subcabinet level. Because the secretaries were overextended and tended not to have time to focus on the details required to develop a policy, Curtis supported convening such a group, to be chaired by Shalala.

The deputies' group met approximately ten times during the months of May, June, and July 1977. Those meetings have been described variously as "miserable," "disasters," and "fiascos." While Shalala's and Curtis' retrospective evaluations indicate that at least the deputies were given an opportunity to get to know each other better through the meetings, it is largely agreed that very little of substance was accomplished through this medium. A number of explanations have been given for the dynamics of the first URPG Deputies group and its reputation for being unproductive.

First, the HUD draft that was circulated to all URPG agencies was viewed as too conceptual, too academic, and too little oriented to the action needs of most of the deputies. Both Shalala, who chaired the deputies' group on behalf of the secretary, and Executive Director Curtis had come to HUD essentially from academic backgrounds.[10] This fact seems to have influenced some deputies' opinions about the draft.

Further, the research that served as the basis for the draft policy paper had been developed with a focus on causality and attempted to isolate value premises from which the policy itself logically would evolve. Thus, the subordinate role of "programs" tended to reinforce the perception that the academics in HUD were off on an intellectual exercise, of little or no relevance to the priorities of the other deputies. In an assessment memo prepared for Harris in July 1977. Curtis stated:

> [L]et's be clear about the problem. The perception that the URPG is 'too academic' is a smokescreen set up by, among others, Deputies who have not produced specific policy options, as requested by the White House. When HUD signaled that a number of policy options were being prepared internally for the URPG, there was a resentment by other agencies, which, nonetheless, did not have their own to initiate.[11]

Second, for reasons that require some inspection, the secretaries are rumored to have been unwilling to "be led by Pat Harris."[12] A paranoid interpretation of this rumor is that, as a black, as a woman, or both, she was resisted by the other secretaries who were white and, except for Juanita Kreps, male. As Harris said, "Just because I'm paranoid doesn't mean that they're not out to get me."

Another view is that the individual agency agendas were very much in the formulation stages at the beginning of the administration and each secretary wanted to devote attention to the functional responsibilities in his or her domain. As Shalala reflects: "They (secretaries) were all new in their jobs and were up to their ears in the responsibilities of their agencies."[13]

These constraints, along with the White House's "lack of commitment and...of basic values about the issues,"[14] and a reluctance to provide strong leadership, probably contributed equally to the resistance. Curtis recalls that the White House staff were attentive, generally supportive, and responsive but not leaders. Also, at the outset no White House staff were assigned to work actively on the policy; they only attended the meetings.

Moreover, Shalala described the agencies' deputies who were assigned the ongoing responsibility for working on the policy as "the wrong group of people. They hadn't read the literature. They were activists (not conceptualizers), and they wanted to get on with it,"[15] it being the programs of their individual organizations. Curtis added that "the early policy process was one of constantly refining fine points...and avoiding resolutions of larger issues. No one wanted to give up chips"[16] in the form of diminished program control in their individual areas. It is important, therefore, to review briefly the other principal agencies, their URPG representatives, and the issues consuming their attention at the beginning of the Carter administration.

URPG Participants

Department of Commerce

Led by Juanita Kreps, an economist on leave from a University of North Carolina professorship, Commerce was in the midst of at least two considerations that seemed to present conflicts to the URPG effort. The first was the President's reorganization study, a portion of which was underway by June 1977. One Office of Management and Budget (OMB) reorganization team was assigned to study "the government's community and economic development programs. The likelihood that the...team would ultimately recommend some consolidation of existing and new urban programs, particularly in the economic development area, initially heightened the tendency of the departments (Commerce and HUD) to fight for ascendancy in the development of urban policies."[17]

The second consideration was related to new HUD legislation, then under refinement in Congress. The Urban Development Action Grant (UDAG) proposal, a part of HUD's basic block grant reauthorization bill, provided for up to $400 million in new funds to support economic revitalization activities in distressed cities, in partnership with private-sector investments. Local economic development activities were the heart of

Commerce's Economic Development Administration (EDA). Commerce reportedly feared that a UDAG program under HUD's aegis would set the tone, both for recommendations by the reorganization team and for congressional constraints on refunding of EDA.

Added to these concerns were such interpersonal dynamics as Commerce Deputy Assistant Secretary Victor Hausner's possible discomfort with Embry, who had strong credentials because of his hands-on experience with successful economic development in Baltimore. ("He may be anxious that Bob Embry, who is now representing HUD...will overshadow him."[18]) Also, Juanita Kreps' Special Assistant Larry Houstoun was suspect because he had moved to Commerce from HUD under somewhat disagreeable circumstances involving his status within the HUD organization. Career HUD staff speculated that he exacerbated the tensions between the two departments.

Finally, from the beginning of the urban policy discussions, the predominant proposals to correct cities' ills were economic rather than social. With HUD in control of the policy's development, Commerce could not be entirely sanguine about the motives behind the proposals that would emerge. Turfing instincts anticipated pro-HUD recommendations:

> The HUD-Commerce competition was acute since both departments administer programs that assist economic development in urban areas, a major component of...urban policy.[19]

Department of the Treasury

As mentioned earlier, many were skeptical about Secretary Michael Blumenthal's commitment to URPG. Curtis reports that Blumenthal "sought to detach the Group from HUD control at the beginning."[20] Further, Treasury was at work on the administration's comprehensive tax reform package and an economic development initiative, under the direction of a departmental urban development task force, spurred primarily by the New York City fiscal crisis.[21] Both Roger Altman and Chester Johnson, respectively the assistant secretary and deputy representing Treasury on the deputies' group, were veterans of New York financial institutions—Altman, with a private investment banking firm and Johnson, with Morgan Guaranty Trust. While Treasury, unlike several other agencies, sent representatives to URPG meetings with some regularity, Curtis describes the participation as "critical and not always informed."[22] Staff were described as undermining the URPG progress and not assuming assigned task force leadership.

Department of Labor

Amid increasing Congressional charges that the Comprehensive Employment and Training Act (CETA) programs were being used to substitute for local taxes and that distressed cities were becoming hooked on CETA assistance, Labor Secretary Ray Marshall was preoccupied with concerns within his agency. Further, the deputy assigned to represent Labor on URPG, Assistant Secretary Ernest Green, was directly in charge of the CETA program. Unless CETA was reauthorized by September 1978, the program would end.

Thus, Green, who "almost never showed up and had made no written contributions,"[23] probably was a poor choice to represent Labor on the deputies' group. He was an urban activist, one of the pioneering black students who in 1955 integrated the schools in Little Rock, Arkansas. He was little inclined to respond to the early conceptual and non-activistic thrust of URPG discussions.

Marshall was perceived as receptive to some of the ideas being discussed by the URPG staff and had met with one staff consultant who was an old friend of his. However, Curtis speculated that the emerging fight over welfare reform (discussed below) might have acted as a constraint, especially since Marshall's reputation as a scholar and as an energetic thinker about urban problems suggested that his contributions to URPG efforts should have been substantial. He was thought to be friendly toward Harris.

Health, Education, and Welfare (HEW)

HEW Secretary Joseph Califano had, as early as 1977, developed a reputation for being a lone operator and for not following willingly most people's lead. He and Harris had become antagonists during the Kennedy-Johnson years and had had an adversarial relationship in both politics and the courtroom.

Trained as a lawyer, Califano, among all of the Cabinet members, had the most combined experience in the White House and in Washington lobbying circles, which probably contributed to his independence. Added to this background was his consuming obsession with welfare reform, which directly challenged HUD's programs.

In the week following Carter's inauguration, and in response to the President's campaign promise, Califano announced the formation of a consulting group to carry out "a great national debate on welfare reform."[24] Subsequent discussions led to a search for domestic programs that could yield money for the emerging welfare proposal. HUD began to appear to be a vulnerable primary money source:

> Harris' biggest battle (within the administration) is to prevent further erosion of HUD's housing subsidies. A couple of weeks ago she learned that top officials at the Office of Management & Budget and the Health, Education & Welfare Department were pushing a plan to fold $1 billion or more of HUD housing subsidies into a comprehensive cash payment to poor families.[25]

At an August 1977, hearing before the Senate Banking, Housing and Urban Affairs Committee:

> ... a bevy of witnesses assailed any efforts to change the subsidized housing program. They argued that housing subsidies play an important role in revitalizing urban areas...[26]

Thus, Califano's absence from the original secretaries' meeting of URPG, and the subsequent absences of Hale Champion from any of the URPG deputies' group meetings, largely were related to the bitter struggle between HUD and HEW over the developing welfare reform proposals. A special assistant to Califano, Sue Foster, did attend the meetings regularly. Although she developed respected written policy options, she lacked rank within the group, was over-committed, and could not be very effective because of the HUD-HEW imbroglio.

Department of Transportation (DOT)

DOT Secretary Brock Adams was viewed as a potential URPG supporter, primarily because he was perceived as comparatively uninfluential within the administration and could conceivably benefit from increased visibility. However, the deputy he assigned to the deputies' group, Assistant Secretary Chester Davenport, was viewed by HUD staff as openly hostile to the process. He rarely attended meetings and was seen as contentious when he was present. Davenport, a black lawyer and seasoned Washington lobbyist, has described the early URPG meetings as wasteful of time and prone to the pursuit of irrelevancies not designed to provide substantive help to troubled cities.

Davenport and others at DOT also were deeply engaged in the negotiation of a massive affirmative action program involving rail construction along the Northeast corridor. This probably seemed likely to respond best to the level of minority unemployment in the string of distressed Northeastern urban communities from Boston to Washington..

Also, the department contained one of the most powerful and heavily lobbied programs in the federal government, the Federal Highway Administration and its highway trust fund. HUD's early urban problem analyses asserted that interregional highways, and particularly ring-roads or beltways, contributed directly, although inadvertently, to urban decline. This allegation seemed to generate internal conflicts concerning DOT's policy posture. Thus, DOT was being both challenged as a villain of urban distress and courted as a savior with the potential to reverse urban decline through job creation and the infusion of funds into urban regions.

The White House

As mentioned earlier, the Offices of Intergovernmental Affairs and Domestic Affairs and Policy in the White House both assigned deputy-level staff to attend the URPG deputies' group. Both Watson and Eizenstat were present at the secretaries' first meeting, as was noted. Watson's deputies (Intergovernmental Relations) Bruce Kirschenbaum and Larry Bailey, usually attended the meetings and generally were viewed by HUD staff as supportive, although not as enthusiastic as Watson.

Eizenstat's deputy (Domestic Policy) Orin Kramer, however, rarely attended the meetings and usually did not contribute when he was there, Curtis reports. Junior staff member Marcie Kaptur attended and made valuable contributions, but like Foster from HEW, her lack of rank and Kramer's posture constrained her effectiveness. Unfortunately, it was precisely in the area of domestic policy that strong leadership for conceptualizing the policy was needed. Eizenstat had agreed to the conceptual approach, according to Curtis, but the lack of domestic policy staff's direction and visible reinforcement gave strength to some of the deputies' impatience with the academic thrust of the URPG effort.

Other URPG Participants

As issues began to be isolated for further examination, other federal representatives were included in the deputies' group. The Environmental Protection Agency (EPA) was invited and did send staff, although the principal deputy, Barbara Blum, attended only one meeting of the early group. The involvement of this agency was important because of the economic development considerations that required the resolution of conflicts between controlling pollution and slowing down the industrial disinvestment that was contributing to unemployment in cities.

OMB was included by fiat as a part of the Executive Office of the President and was represented by the ranking deputy administrator for policy, Dennis Green. A budget administrator from Detroit's municipal government with strong ties to national black civic and political networks, Green was perceived as highly critical of the group. He later reflected that he felt URPG's early efforts were courting disaster because they were leading inevitably to new budgetary requests, which he saw as impolitic. Carter had come into office stressing reduced federal spending, and OMB was deeply involved in program evaluations to accomplish that objective. Lofty concepts leading to new spending seemed to Green to be impractical.

The Office of the Vice President was included because Harris saw Mondale as a positive influence, given his liberal record on reversing social injustices. His deputy, James Dyke, a young black lawyer, was viewed as supportive. He did not, however, attend deputies' meetings regularly. Thus, the Vice President's influence on formulating the policy options and in encouraging agency cooperation was diminished accordingly.

The URPG-1 Task Forces

Meanwhile, the functional area task forces were decided upon and organized under the lead-agency concept. This meant that the domestic agency having the greatest expertise in a given area chaired, convened, and staffed the appropriate task force, with other agencies participating as members. The array of task forces organized by the end of July 1977 was as follows:

- Economic Development—Chaired by Commerce
  Representatives: HUD, DOT, Labor, Small Business Administration (SBA), EPA, HEW, CSA, and Treasury
- Public Finance—Chaired by Treasury
  Representatives: HUD, Commerce, HEW, and EPA
- Neighborhoods—Chaired by HUD
  Representatives: Commerce, SBA, HEW, Labor, DOT, CSA, Justice), and the White House Domestic Council (as surrogate for the upcoming Neighborhood Commission to be appointed by the President)
- Redlining—Cochaired by HUD and Comptroller of the Currency
  Representatives: The federal regulatory financial institutions (Federal National Mortgage Association, Federal Housing Ad-

ministration, Federal Home Loan Bank Board) and secondary market institutions

- States and Metropolitan Regions—Cochaired by HUD and Commerce.
  Representatives: Treasury, HEW, Labor, EPA, DOT, OMB, and the Advisory Commission on Intergovernmental Relations (ACIR). Regional and local officials as well as state and county interest groups were regular participants.

The track record of URPG-1's task forces was uneven and often discouraging. States and Regions, Redlining, and Neighborhoods Task Forces met, developed a structure, and began producing policy options, often with the participation of nongovernmental representatives. However, the Public Finance Task Force did not convene, nor did Treasury produce policy options for task force members' consideration. (As was noted above, however, Treasury had an in-house tax policy task force.) The Economic Development Task Force met, but its Commerce Department chair was accused of talking the members to death. Also, there appeared to be lack of coordination between the Commerce Task Force and deputies' group members.[27]

Curtis had three staff members, all highly trained policy professionals,[28] whom he used as task force coordinators. However, with no mandate to take the initiative, these staff were largely at the mercy of the lead agency's schedule. Since the coordinators were HUD staff people, they were even more constrained from having an impact where tensions existed between HUD and the lead agency, (e.g., Treasury and the Public Finance Task Force, and Commerce and the Economic Development Task Force).

SIC Transit URPG-1

On August 31, 1977, the *New York Times* carried the following headline on page one: "White House Orders Urban Policy Review; Revises Study Panel." Subheads were: "Urgent Response to Blacks," and "Cabinet-Level Group Gets Timetable to Act—Treasury Unit Drafts Complex Financing Plan."

The story behind that headline was much more evolutional than the *Times* implied and, furthermore, was one month old. The changes in URPG already had taken place officially on August 1, 1977. They were preceded by gradually building pressures, in the White House and within HUD, as well as from URPG members.

HUD Pressures

Within HUD, pressure for a change in URPG management had been building since the beginning. The characterization of that pressure varies depending on point of view. However, there is general agreement that the HUD program offices—Housing, and Community Planning and Development (CPD), in particular—felt that they, rather than Curtis and Shalala, should have responsibility for the preparation of an "action directive to produce change in cities."[29]

Shalala saw CPD's Embry as an adversary, perhaps not so much personally as in terms of power. Embry was very impatient with administrative detail, but very excited by the prospect of running the policy effort at HUD, she felt. "We were two ambitious people in the same generation, struggling to make their mark," she said.[30] The urban policy effort seemed an ideal opportunity.

Embry has stated that his impression of the first URPG was a group of people "sitting around, unstructured, with no firm assignments."[31] Because of his ten years' experience seeking solutions to the problems of Baltimore, Maryland—a classic case of a distressed city making a comeback—Embry had two concerns. First, since the President had "put his reputation on the line"[32] by undertaking the development of a national urban policy, this was an opportunity not to be lost—and Embry feared that it was being lost by default.

Second, he was concerned that HUD's performance, reflected by the lack of URPG productivity through July 1977, would confirm the President's opinion of HUD, expressed during Embry's preinaugural visit with Carter in Atlanta. Carter had characterized HUD as a disorganized agency, which was "all screwed up."[33] Embry's competition for the position of secretary of HUD after the 1976 election—and his near-win of the prize—was no secret to Washington cognoscenti. One can conclude, then, that Embry wanted HUD to look good to Carter since he identified with HUD so heavily.

Meanwhile, career staff from the CPD division, traditionally responsible for preparing the Biennial Growth Reports, sent Embry several position papers and drafts that generally challenged the wisdom of having two separate urban policy efforts going on in two different places within HUD—the secretary's office and CPD. Robert Duckworth, principal staff for the growth report and a trained urban planner, drafted a memo for Embry to Harris that urged coordination of the two efforts, at least in terms of the external image:

> It is important that there be a close relationship...between the (URPG) process and the 1978 urban growth report process.... If we are not synchronized within HUD, then cooperation efforts beyond the Department on urban policy run the risk of confusion.[34]

The memo pointed out work that already was underway on the growth report, and Duckworth recalled that he was very perplexed that the urban policy assignment had not been superimposed on the Growth Report process, so closely related were the two. Given the changes in the 1977 Block Grant legislation, which included re-naming the Biennial Report the "Urban Policy Report," duplication was avoidable. In fact, Duckworth had worked informally with the congressional committee responsible for drafting the amendment and feels that he had significant influence on the legislative shift to give the biennial report a more prescriptive urban policy name, image, and thrust.

While Embry has insisted that he really did not want the urban policy direction assigned to CPD, he felt that the Growth staff's concerns had some merit. Shalala also speculated that the secretary's immediate staff was dissatisfied with her and Curtis' leadership mostly because "they couldn't decide if they wanted to do the urban policy themselves." In fact, Shalala has said retrospectively:

> I was never given authority to run the urban policy (project effort). I had a representative role for the secretary only. Lynn Curtis was to be the staff person and Pat thought she preferred running (the policy effort) out of her office with Lynn as director.... I never had complete authority.

Curtis described the "tunnelling" within HUD as a type of turfing, which he later came to recognize as a legitimate action by those who were looking for a more action-oriented, programmatic policy effort.

URPG Members' Pressures

URPG members already have been characterized as critics of the academic thrust of the HUD staff's efforts. Additionally, as they began thinking about budget recommendations due for presidential review in December 1977, the urban policy obligation seems to have become increasingly burdensome. Cabinet members and subcabinet appointees are notorious for developing networks within the White House staff. Many have such ties when they are appointed, which often is why they are appointed. It is concluded, therefore, that dissatisfactions that other agencies felt about HUD, were communicated regularly to White House contacts.

There were, of course, blatant—and very human—inconsistencies. Jasinowski of Commerce, who in August 1977, characterized URPG to me as an overly academic exercise, is one case in point. He thought that the HUD staff, when they revised the working policy draft, took the liberty of ignoring practical recommendations from the deputies' meetings. Yet, he had written to Curtis the month before:

> The Group's work itself still suffers from the absence of an overall conceptual framework which would, among other advantages, enable it to establish task forces and measure their progress against some overall standards and priorities. We have tended thus far to treat the establishment of a Task Force as an implicit reflection of a priority setting process which does not in fact exist and we have not progressed on the larger purpose of determining what problems we want to address and in what sequence. This should be the subject of a carefully drafted plan for URPG's work.[35]

While Jasinowski wanted a conceptual framework, he balked at the process designed to arrive at one successfully within the context of the President's charge to URPG, to "be a joint project with full participation by each of the departments."[36] This cognitive dissonance was characteristic of many URPG participants, who understood the importance of exploring the values that an urban policy ought to reflect, while at the same time, wanting a program of immediate action for cities that would bring credit to their respective departments.

White House Pressures

Both Eizenstat and Watson were growing increasingly aware of the disquiet among those URPG deputies who were paying attention to the urban policy process. And, indeed, they received confirmatory reports from their White House staff. Moreover, they had settled into their governmental roles enough, it is suspected, to be ready for more active participation in the URPG process.

Additionally, late in June, the Kettering Foundation conference, mentioned earlier, called national attention to strategies for the survival of declining cities.[37] In July, the Reuss Subcommittee on the City, also mentioned earlier, released its report, urging "a new interagency urban and regional policy group, headed by...Harris, to assign a high priority to the development of a budget impact statement for cities."[38]

These events heightened the bureaucratic expectation that the administration ought to be coming out soon with its urban policy progress report, which the President had requested "by the end of the summer." The apparent lack of progress toward this end also probably helped to consolidate White House resolve to take a more active role.

During several conversations among Harris, Eizenstat, and Watson, it was decided that a reorganization of URPG's management would improve the group's performance. Harris made the decision to consolidate the staff leadership in a single policy person and to shift that leadership to Embry, relieving Shalala of her "deputy" assignment to URPG. Shalala agreed to the change with little resistance, reasoning that by graciously accepting Harris' decision, she could improve her bargaining position within HUD later on. Later, she reflected that she was outmaneuvered in what was largely a power play because she "was new and didn't know my way around government in Washington."[39] She was offered advocacy assistance in fighting to maintain her urban policy role by her White House network of old poverty warriors and friends. She declined this assistance.

Curtis, informed by Harris of the reorganization decision, was given the choice of negotiating a continuing URPG role with Embry, or resuming his more global role as the secretary's point-person on urban issues affecting HUD. When discussions with Embry revealed that Curtis would have to resign his appointment to the secretary's office and report directly to Embry in order to continue as URPG Executive Director, Curtis decided against the URPG role. He "decided that I wanted to stay in the secretary's office, doing the broader spectrum things that I had come (to HUD) to do, and that I did not want to lock my fate in with URPG."[40]

All of these events transpired during late July 1977. By August 1, Embry had accepted the assignment as Harris' URPG deputy. I reported to work on August 1, 1977, as deputy assistant secretary-designate, expecting to assume general planning responsibilities within CPD and to manage the department's discretionary grant programs. On that date I was informed by Embry that I also was to take over the staff leadership for URPG, to assist him in his new assignment.

Vernon Jordan's Pressure

It is appropriate to review the role of National Urban League president Vernon Jordan in the decisions to reorganize URPG. It was consistently reported, by the press and by other observers, that Jordan's criticism of the Carter administration's failure to produce an urban policy as promised caused the White House to force Harris to reorganize. This, in fact, may have been the case. A *New York Times* article stated:

> Stung by the recent criticism by black leaders...President Carter has ordered an urgent review of Federal urban policy.
>
> A Cabinet-level study group, which was formed early this spring to define the Administration's urban policy, but has been slow in doing so, has been reorganized and a timetable for new plans has been imposed...[41]

Jordan's speech was delivered on August 8, a week after the August 1 transition. By that time, decisions for reorganization already had been made. However, given Vernon Jordan's easy access to the White House and his behind-the-scenes style of persuasion, it is likely that he shared his misgivings with Jack Watson—an old Atlanta connection, well in advance of his public announcement on August 8.

Table 4.1
Principals and Staff of the Urban and Regional Policy Group

Convener of the URPG—Robert C. Embry, Jr., HUD Assistant Secretary, CPD
Executive Director—Yvonne S. Perry, HUD Deputy Assistant Secretary, CPD
Staff Director—John W. McLean
Staff Deputy Director—Robert P. Duckworth

Coordinators	Task Force	Lead Agency	White House Liaison
Wyndham Clarke	States & Metropolitan Regions	Commerce Houstoun	Kirschenbaum Johnston
Franklin James	Economic Development	Commerce Hausner	Spring Johnston
Claudia Pharis	Employment	Labor Packer Wyrch	Spring
Don Krumm	Transporta-tion	Transporta-tion Davenport Shefler	Johnston Schmoke
Janice Perlman	Neighbor-hoods	HUD Baroni McNeely	Kaptur
Judith May	Public Finance	Treasury Altman	Kramer Raines
Judith May	Redlining	HUD Shalala Heimann	Abramowitz Kramer

Figure 4.1
Presidential Memorandum
March 21, 1977

THE WHITE HOUSE

WASHINGTON

March 21, 1977

MEMORANDUM FOR

THE SECRETARY OF TREASURY
THE SECRETARY OF COMMERCE
THE SECRETARY OF LABOR
THE SECRETARY OF HEALTH, EDUCATION AND WELFARE
THE SECRETARY OF HOUSING AND URBAN DEVELOPMENT
THE SECRETARY OF TRANSPORTATION

During my campaign, I pledged an urban and regional policy based on mutual trust, mutual respect and mutual commitment between state and local governments on the one hand and the federal government on the other. Although we do not have as yet a national urban and regional policy, the first step toward achieving that goal must be coordination among federal departments and agencies.

I would like you to form a working policy group on urban and regional development. The purpose of the group will be to conduct a comprehensive review of all federal programs which impact on urban and regional areas; to seek perspectives of state and local officials concerning the role of the federal government in urban and regional development; and to submit appropriate administrative and legislative recommendations.

Under Executive Order 11297, Pat Harris has the responsibility to convene such a group and will do so shortly. I want to emphasize that development of an urban and regional policy should be a joint project with full participation by each of your departments, as well as from other federal agencies where appropriate. This is a high priority for my Administration, and I have asked Jack Watson and Stu Eizenstat to facilitate and support your collective efforts in every way possible.

I look forward to receiving a preliminary report on your progress and findings by early summer.

Jimmy Carter

cc: Heads of Executive Departments
and Agencies

Mr. Janis

Notes

1. Alvar Elbing, "Selection of Human Solutions," in *Behavioral Decisions in Organizations: A Framework for Decision Making* (Glenview, IL: Scott Foreman 1968), 132.
2. Embry was serving as assistant secretary for community planning and development (CPD); Shalala, as assistant secretary for policy development and research (PD&R). Both were Carter appointees who took office in early 1977.
3. Interview with Lynn Curtis, June 19, 1980.
4. Curtis interview, and affirmed in interview with Donna E. Shalala, June 21, 1980.
5. Memorandum from Harris to principal staff, March 29, 1977.
6. Lynn Curtis and PD&R Staff, "A New Approach to a National Urban Policy," unpublished mimeo, March 29, 1977.
7. Embry was soon to take over the URPG leadership from Curtis and Shalala.
8. Personal handwritten notes from the meeting on Embry's copy of discussion document.
9. Lynn Curtis to Principal Staff, "The Urban and Regional Policy Group," memorandum, April 25, 1977.
10. Holder of a Ph.D. in public policy, Shalala has had a distinguished teaching career, but also has impressive public service credentials, which include serving as a highly visible secretary of the Department of Health and Human Services during the Clinton administration, as well as serving as treasurer to the Municipal Assistance Corporation in New York City. Curtis' credentials have been cited in the text above. He had recently completed a book manuscript, *Future of the Inner Cities*. Both Shalala and Curtis had published widely.
11. Lynn Curtis to Secretary Harris, "The Politics and Procedures of URPG," unpublished document, July 1977.
12. Curtis interview.
13. Shalala interview.
14. Interview with Robert C. Embry, June 20, 1980.
15. Shalala interview.
16. Curtis interview.
17. Congressional Quarterly, "How Carter Urban Policy Was Developed," *Urban America: Policies and Problems* (Washington, DC: CQ, August 1978), 20.
18. Curtis, "The Politics and Procedures of URPG," 2.
19. CQ, "How Carter Urban Policy Was Developed," 20.
20. Curtis, "The Politics and Procedures of URPG,"1.
21. "Right now, most of the action (such as it is) is taking place deep inside the Treasury Department, of all places. A task force headed by Chester Johnson, formerly a vice president of Morgan Guaranty Trust Co., is working up a set of options to encourage economic development within the troubled cities." James M. Perry, "Mr. Carter's Cautious Urban Plan," *The Wall Street*

Journal, Tuesday, August 9, 1977, 14.

22. Curtis, "The Politics and Procedures of URPG,"1.
23. Curtis, "The Politics and Procedures of URPG," 3.
24. CQ, "How Carter Urban Policy Was Developed," 86.
25. "An Erosion of Aid to the Cities," *Business Week*, August 15, 1977, 36.
26. CQ, "How Carter Urban Policy Was Developed," 89.
27. Curtis reports: "Jasinowski (DOC Assistant Secretary) has faithfully submitted revisions to various papers, but the work is done by Deputy Assistant Secretary Victor Hausner and Special Assistant to the Secretary Larry Houstoun. Jasinowski was the one who criticized a paragraph at the last deputies' meeting–until I told him that he had submitted it." Curtis, "The Politics and Procedures of URPG." Of course, this type of ghost writing for policy-level officials is common in government. The point in this case was related, in part, to the extreme criticism that Curtis received from Commerce and a subtle tension and even antagonism that I perceived Jasinowski to have toward Curtis.
28. Judith May, Ph.D., Berkeley; Andrea Sullivan, Ph.D., University of Pennsylvania; and Gloria Cousar, MCP, Princeton University.
29. Curtis, "The Politics and Procedures of URPG."
30. Shalala interview.
31. Embry interview.
32. Embry interview.
33. Embry interview.
34. Robert Duckworth for Embry, memorandum, undated draft, circa June 1977.
35. Cited in Curtis' memorandum to Harris, circa July 1977, p. 3, Tab 2.
36. Carter's March 21, 1977 memorandum, Figure 4.1.
37. Academy for Contemporary Problems and the Kettering Foundation, National Urban Policy Roundtables: Managing Mature Cities, conference, June 9-10, 1977.
38. "Analysis Urged of Federal Impact on Cities," *Housing and Urban Affairs Daily*, Tuesday, July 19, 1977, 19. Refers to impact of the federal budget on cities.
39. Shalala interview.
40. Curtis interview.
41. *New York Times*, August 31, 1977, page 10.

Chapter Five

Reorganization: URPG-2

It's not personal and it's not that I don't respect you professionally. But I was (tenured in this office) before you got here, and I'll be here after you're gone, trying to make sense of decisions which you and your team have made while you're in power. I am unlikely to allow something to be instituted with which I don't agree, but which I will have to carry on afterward.

Nothing in the pre-employment conversations with Embry throughout June and July 1977 suggested that the national urban policy initiative would be included among my duties. I was hired as deputy assistant secretary to manage the planning, evaluation research, and environmental programs for Community Planning and Development (CPD), based on my experience as an urban planner with a work background in public and private city-oriented programs, including all of those dating from the 1959 evaluations of urban renewal. Additionally, the secretary's discretionary fund, which supported flexible programs such as technical assistance and innovative grants, was under my management. This was a particularly attractive responsibility in as much as some of the earlier dramatic efforts to help cities had been seeded with HUD grants from the secretary's fund.[1]

As was implied in the previous chapter, not much information was floating through the Washington grapevine, at least not much was reaching the ears of those outside of the federal bureaucracy, to suggest that serious work was underway in fulfilling Carter's campaign promise of an urban policy. In fact, unless one religiously read the *Congressional Record* or *Housing and Urban Affairs Daily* (bibles to bureaucrats—expensive, time-consuming pontifications to just about everyone else), little information was available at all about the URPG structure, about a growing focus within Congress on an urban policy, or about the progress of any then-current policy development efforts. That there was little visible activity simply encouraged public disinterest and cynicism.

A New Deputy Arrives

When I was invited by Bob Embry to become deputy assistant secretary for interprogram and areawide concerns, I was chairing the graduate and new undergraduate departments of city and regional planning at Howard University. I accepted Embry's offer after some initial hesitation based on reservations about how effective I, or any political appointee, could be inside an established bureaucracy, and fed by some measure of satisfaction with my independent and self-directed life as an academic.[2] My decision also was influenced by Embry's persistent recruitment and by his assurances that I would have primary influence in the areas of my greatest concern—planning policy and minority participation in CPD programs.

Not the least of the influences on my final decision, however, was a conversation with Secretary Patricia Roberts Harris. I had long admired her accomplishments. I had discussed with Dr. George Snowden (a respected consultant and sometime appointee in Democratic administrations, and then the director of the public administration program within Howard University's School of Business and Public Administration) what we might do from outside the government to assist Secretary Harris in her job. We both liked her style and wanted to be of help. Furthermore, she was a black and a woman in a very hot seat. But we had not arrived at any appealing plans by the time that Embry approached me.

Embry's recruitment process included a meeting with the secretary, scheduled for early July, which helped to strengthen my growing inclination to take the job. Had I known that the national urban policy would become my "baby," I would have been far less hesitant when Embry made his first overture in March 1977.

Assistant Secretary's Leadership

Embry, himself, also was a strong influence. He spoke of his commitment to minorities, and especially to blacks, and noted that he attended services at a different black church in Baltimore at least once each month to enrich his perspective on the black community. He said that people in my field respected my work, and that I was not seen as highly "political," although I was "difficult" on issues I supported. While my references described me as "strong willed" and sometimes "abrasive" in tough negotiations, Embry said that he needed these qualities in a deputy. He wanted someone who would not be intimidated by the forces that might seek to intervene in our efforts to improve conditions in cities and for minorities.

Embry had established an enviable record for himself in Baltimore by catalyzing the revitalization of the inner-city. I felt that I could learn from his experiences, while bringing a different dimension to his understanding of the dynamics of ghetto decline, based on my own work with neighborhood and community development organizations in cities.

He was direct, hard in his analysis, although naive in his liberalism—qualities that I found to be compatible with my perceptions of the way that the real world works. I agreed to begin as an on-call consultant in July 1977, and to assume my job as deputy, full-time, after August 1 of that year.

It is interesting to speculate, however, that had Lynn Curtis been willing to continue in his initial role as URPG Executive Director on Embry's terms, the outcome also might have been different. I would not have been as key to the process as I became and different decisions would have been made regarding the use of consultants and the structure of the URPG process, even though I might have had some limited influence on process.

URPG-2 under CPD Leadership

Throughout the first week following my URPG assignment, I reviewed documents, collected those materials that were written by the existing task forces, and absorbed the significance of the opportunity that Harris had delegated to Embry and, thereby, to me. The Curtis memorandum,[3] thorough and painfully candid, served as an organizing resource for assessing URPG's potential as an effective urban policy development mechanism. On August 7, following a weekend of nonstop reading and preparation of planning drafts, I submitted a memorandum to Embry recommending a series of transitional steps and decisions.

My memo presented management principles, organizational guidelines, a general approach to the use of consultants, and most important, a statement of tasks and tentative deadlines that constituted a preliminary work program. The recommendations in my August 7 memorandum took into account the past performance of URPG, suggested that we follow the new directions contained in Curtis' memo, and outlined my own general background in administration and management in the public sector. My commitment to the use of outside consultants, including women and minorities in the process, and my experience with coordination as an instrument for public action, all found expression in the document.

The memo was accepted and implemented without major adjustment.[4] Its basic elements were:

1) The deputies' group should not be disbanded, as had been informally proposed in July, but should continue to "assume leadership of Task Forces...assign agency staffing for each Task Force with clear directives...from (the responsible agency) Principal; monitor Task Force participation;" and serve as a forum for the discussion of task force progress.
2) New task forces should be created in the areas of fair housing/housing policy, urban employment and training, and transportation.[5]
3) The strategy...discussed concerning task force function should improve the performance of the task forces and make external agency leadership less problematic. For example, the assumption that policy option development will rest with coordinative staff and consultants—rather than waiting for initiation by task force membership—will shift major TF focus from development to review. ...Where TF members generate proposals, papers and ideas, these will become the agenda. Where this generation is delayed or of questionable quality, we will augment TF consultative support to keep the review and option-development function moving.[6]
4) Consultants were recommended for specific assignments, and a list of thirty-one names was submitted to begin a resource roster. Their assignments were to be: Direct an ongoing support to the task forces; periodic review of draft documents in the substantive areas; and preparation of various documents, summaries and *final drafts* that are indicated on the work program.[7]
5) Other details in the memo recognized the product deadlines imposed by anticipated events such as preparation of the 1979 budget, the State of the Union address, and the White House Conference on Balanced Growth scheduled for February 1978. A tentative deadline was proposed for completion of the national urban policy, March 1978, one year beyond the date of the President's initial mandate of March 22, 1977.

Finally, the closing paragraph of the memo outlined the protocols, reflecting my approach to the tasks that were proposed for guiding the policy planning process:

> Several operational imperatives guide the approach described in this memorandum. I intend to avoid duplication of effort and to facilitate coordination as fully as possible. This means working closely with the White House staff on the Growth Conference; continuing internal HUD relationships, such as with Donna Shalala and Lynn Curtis, as well as with (the Secretary's principal staff); and making every effort to influence the dynamics of the task forces positively. Much of the latter is a matter of timing and generation of substantive work for task force agendas.
>
> Also, I mentioned to you my concern that minorities and women have been excluded systematically from participation in policy exercised like this one because of the 'old boy' network and because one usually has to be known as an expert in order to be invited as an expert, to become 'known' as an expert. I want us to intervene in that circle, without the traditional constraints and pejorative screening which have institutionalized the exclusion of these groups.[8]

In the meetings with Secretary Harris, it was decided that primary activity in developing the policy would take place at the deputies' group level and within the task forces. Although a meeting of the secretaries was scheduled for early August, responses to the meeting notice indicated that attendance would be poor and the meeting probably should be cancelled. Harris agreed that she would not schedule another URPG secretaries-level meeting until there were substantive decisions to be considered. In view of the events scheduled in the planning work program, this would not be until draft materials were already for review and response.

Embry agreed that for purposes of continuity and name identification, the executive director's role should be retained. I had felt initially that this position was superfluous, since obviously as Embry's planning deputy assistant secretary, I was his chief aide for URPG. However, conversations with other URPG members emphasized their expectation that there would be a new executive director. It seemed advisable, therefore, to satisfy this expectation. In retrospect, it would have been disastrous not to.

Harris scheduled regular weekly briefings with Embry, me, and whomever we needed to include from the HUD staff from time to time. Usually, her personal staff also attended. The first of these meeting occurred on August 11, and they continued on schedule initially, with expected cancellations from time to time when the White House[9] preempted our time with the secretary.

Later, the agenda for these meetings expanded to include various troublesome CPD management or policy issues other than URPG. I attended most of these meetings. Also, almost immediately after the first meeting, HUD came under siege from OMB and HEW through the proposal to "cash out" HUD programs to fund the welfare initiative.[10] This and other survival issues had significant implications for HUD's strength and, therefore, for Harris' credibility in coordinating the interagency urban policy effort.

The Planning Work Program

Ordinarily, a planning work program is a management tool that serves as a reality check in the decision process, once agreement has been reached on its elements and tasks. The work plan, which appears as Figure 5.1, enjoyed a much more distinguished place within the national urban policy process for several reasons. First, in response to the amorphous grumbling by the assistant secretaries on the deputies' group about the URPG's lack of direction and purpose, the work program attempted to show that the new stewards in HUD knew what they were doing and how to do it.

Second, Embry and Harris were determined to see that a product did indeed emerge from the process. A schedule committed to paper seemed to be a good stick for prodding the reluctant. Finally, my own management style required the organization that a work program provided. Thus, in initial meetings with HUD staff, task force members, and leaders from other agencies, Embry and I focused attention on the work program, took it seriously—and so did they.

Some of the products' deadlines on the work plan were relatively arbitrary; others were not. For example, dates for initial budget submissions to OMB, for final drafting of the State of the Union message, and for the Balanced Growth Conference were public and bureaucratic expectations and fairly firmly set in concrete. By working within these constraints, I developed and assigned interim deadlines according to a reasonable estimate of minimal time requirements for product preparation and review. One of the deadlines that I assigned was the date for a respectable end to the urban policy development process—March of 1978.

Copies of Figure 5.1 were distributed to members of the deputies' group and to White House staff. No one questioned any of the dates. In fact, the work program was accepted as dictum, and the indicated deadlines began to be referred to in URPG meetings as realities. For example, Stu Eizenstat stated at one early meeting: "We have to complete the policy options by national goals categories by September 22," the work plan's target. Of course, as URPG became more deeply involved in the substance of the process, the specific deadlines slipped slightly. However, the planning work program remained throughout a symbolic measure of pace and expectation. And while it was HUD's instrument for coercion at the outset, toward the end its institutionalization by URPG and the White House transformed it into a potential instrument for ridicule: HUD had made a commitment, and HUD had better not fail in keeping that commitment.

Influence of the Players

Robert C. Embry, Jr.

The personal style of the primary managers of URPG-2 seemed to affect the responses of the URPG agencies, particularly at the deputies' group level. A very smart, Ivy League–educated lawyer, Embry's personal interaction style can best be described as passively/aggressively accommodating. He wanted to meet individually with the assistant secretaries as quickly as possible after the reorganization to show that he cared what they thought. He was willing to meet at any mutually convenient time, at a place of their choice, for as long as was necessary to give each of them an opportunity to air grievances and to make suggestions for improvement in the process.

Embry was not defensive about criticisms of HUD's lead agency role, adroitly conceding that he would have preferred for the policy development process to be taking place within the White House. Since the President had decided otherwise, however (and he might have added, with Pat Harris' skillful intervention), Embry encouraged the member agency representatives to call him and meet with him whenever they felt the need, and to expect to be included actively in decisions as these arose. He indicated that I was available whenever he was not.

Yvonne Scruggs Perry

This style coincided well with my own. I felt that open and easy dialogue would assist us in gaining credibility and in allaying fears that HUD was trying to keep the policy process close to the vest. Since I arranged each of the initial meetings, often directly with the URPG deputy, attended the meetings with Embry, and followed through on requests for information with each deputy and his or her staff, the agencies seemed to feel assured of a responsive URPG management team.

We believed that more could be accomplished by preparation before formal meetings than by expecting that participants automatically would come to meetings prepared to make decisions. Thus, the use of a feed-back system before and after URPG meetings generally kept Embry, me, and other staff in direct communication with each URPG deputy. The complaints to the White House staff appeared to be relatively few during the first months following the reorganization, permitting the HUD staff to carry out the steps of reorganization with little if any undercutting.

My flexibility and availability in interacting with URPG deputies grew out of a very difficult decision that I had made during my first week as full-time URPG executive director. This decision concerned the definition of my role and the precise activities in which I would engage directly and those which would be carried out by others under my supervision. The fundamental question was: Could I be more effective in gaining the involvement of other agencies in the URPG process, thus assuring that URPG did produce an urban policy, by devoting my time to administration, management, personal coordination of staff and participants, and to the review and revising of policy drafts produced by others? If the answer to this question was "Yes," this meant that *I would be unable actually to write the urban policy myself.* Instead, I would have to use experts on staff and hire outside expert consultants to do the writing.

I would then have to use late evenings, weekends, and any other available time to read policy drafts and recommend additions and changes. I also had the responsibility for administrative tasks required of me as deputy assistant secretary—apart from my URPG role. The old public administration aphorism—"The expert should be on tap and not on top"[11] came to life for me.

It had been stressful for me to concede to others the policy technician's role. Most professionals in the fields of city planning and urban problem solving at that time felt that they would want to write the first urban policy, if given the chance. I was no different. However, my administrative experience had convinced me that trying both to draft an urban policy and simultaneously to manage all of the different actors who were involved in the process would be suicidal.

CPD's Professional Urban Policy Staff

This admonition was borne out quickly when I began working with the HUD staff already assigned to the urban policy effort. The new chief of the CPD urban policy career staff, John McLean, was a former newspaper reporter who felt that he could write as well as anyone, and that the writing responsibility should become his. He saw the job as a "task," not as a process.

Aside from conceptual differences that I had with him on policy issues, it became apparent that this process was too slow and excluded other more junior staff from contributing according to their skills. Also, time was too short for me to win a tug of war with McLean over who would produce policy drafts.

Additionally, the deputy chief, Robert Duckworth, had been responsible for developing the Fourth Biennial Growth Report, re-named the Urban Policy Report in the 1977 HUD re-authorization legislation. (Mention of Duckworth's role in formulating the language of this legislation appears in Chapter 4.) I needed his skills with the nongovernmental sector and with career staff in other agencies with whom he already had been working, to assist me in my ongoing management of URPG.

If McLean wrote, Duckworth would have to manage the rest of the staff and the task force coordinators and, consequently, would not be available for the transactive tasks. If I wrote, the entire operation would get out of control because no one would be "minding the store" on a daily basis, that is, seeing that all of the necessary pieces were being produced on time.

Adding to these complexities was Embry's administrative style. He encouraged all career staff, especially office directors and division chiefs, to approach him directly whenever they chose rather than through his deputies. The opportunity for a classic bureaucratic end-run, indeed, was exploited, more often by some than by others. Unless roles were precisely defined, therefore, in terms that were unassailable, I would constantly be reacting to career staff's forays in support of, or in objection to, some issue or another emerging from the policy development process. I needed to be in the position of recommending resolutions to such issues, not as a personal advocate of any single one. Being the avowed administrator gave me the immunity that I needed to exercise control in that rather inhospitable environment.

Finally, turfing within HUD, and between HUD and other agencies, was so lethal that the distractions of contemplation and creativity required to write the policy, would have provided ample opportunity for an internal or external predator to snatch control of the policy process from CPD, or alternatively, from HUD. While neither Embry nor I held the intractable position that CPD was best qualified to develop the policy in terms of resident staff expertise, we both felt strongly that we were better able to negotiate among program assistant secretaries and their deputies in other domestic agencies. We seemed to represent the best balance between practical, hands-on experience and a conceptual approach to resolving urban problems successfully. In an imperfect world, we felt that the cities had the best chance with CPD as their advocate.

Donna Shalala's Research Staff

Donna Shalala and her principal PD&R (Office of Policy Development and Research) staff gave their commitment to continue their development of working papers that already had been commissioned—either for the original URPG or for the renamed growth report. We established a series of briefings, to be attended by Embry, our top urban policy staff, and me, that would expose us to the thrusts of the papers under development.

Although both Embry and Shalala took pains to allay appearances of tension following the shift of URPG leadership from PD&R to CPD, nuances of competition continued throughout the effort. Usually the perpetrators were neither Embry nor Shalala, but staff people fighting old battles between the two offices that transcended both the tenure and the interests of the Carter administration appointees. Such behavior is a fact of life in bureaucracies, as Heclo points out:

> When bureaucrats fight among themselves, often over the integrity of organizational boundaries and missions, only rarely is it the pitched contest of the open battlefield. Left to their own devices, bureaucrats battle about stability and change in much the same way gardens encroach on each other, through a slow, twisting struggle where only the most rigorously enduring species will see the light of day.[12]

PD&R by definition had a vested interest in any policy development that was going on within HUD, regardless of how anyone else viewed CPD's advantages. That career staff members in PD&R were less than enthusiastic about the location of the policy effort outside their office is understandable.

A Stable of Consultants

The final group of actors involved in the policy development process were the consultants. This was a diverse group, some of whom came and went on a regular basis, conforming to the normal pattern of consultants. Others came, settled in, and did not leave even after the national urban policy was written, announced, and from all appearances from the White House, long since forgotten. Still another group was called on to produce a single particular product, or to advise on a limited specific issue. This was the largest group, drawn primarily from the list submitted in my August 7 memorandum.[13]

Thomas Reiner, professor of regional science at the University of Pennsylvania, and R. Joyce Whitley, former director of planning for the National Model Cities Office and vice president of her own firm in Cleveland, were key among the first group of consultants. They were related to the process throughout, without being permanent attachments to the URPG staff. They were my principal advisors, and as friends of long standing and recognized experts in the planning field, I valued their perceptions both about the substance of the policy drafts and about the process by which they were produced.

Both prepared extensive reviews of the policy documents as they began to emerge, and often I would submit their comments into the URPG review process unaltered. Frequently, however, I incorporated their views into memoranda that I wrote for broader circulation as guidance to the other consultants and the policy staff.

Anthony Downs and Richard Nathan of the Brookings Institution and Richard F. America, a free-lance consultant on economic development in inner-cities, were also consulted regularly for their views. They, along with Timothy Jenkins, president of the MATCH Institution; Conrad Weiler of Temple University; the late Andrew Bennett, then a economic development consultant; Hans Speigel of Hunter College; Donald Warren from the University of Michigan; and Bernard Anderson, the Wharton School of the University of Pennsylvania, among many others, developed position papers and substantive working documents for the policy through a process of intense interaction with URPG staff.

Two consultants were placed under contract initially and later became full-time appointees. Marshall Kaplan met with, and subsequently in July 1977, wrote to Jay Janis, HUD's undersecretary, who was his former colleague from the Kennedy-Johnson administrations. I knew Kaplan also from the Great Society years and felt that his energy and experience were a good fit with the tight schedule required by the URPG work plan. He had stated in his letter to Janis, after URPG, that I was well underway:

> My conversations with people in other agencies indicate that "everyone is looking for an urban handle." I would think, again, HUD could take the lead in putting together a useful interagency strategy which, at a minimum, would link together various planning programs and hopefully, ultimately, address such key problems as the trade-off between environment and housing; social services and community development, etc.... I would like...to spend some time with persons whom you designate to develop a working paper on interagency thrusts in light of previous experiences.

Since Kaplan had written about urban issues,[14] I negotiated a three-month contract with him to take lead responsibility for drafting the policy,[15] based on working papers produced by consultants, URPG staff, task forces, PD&R, and others in the private and institutional sector who were developing policy statements. This arrangement proved effective for the initial period.

Kaplan, who described himself as an insomniac, could work eighteen to twenty hours a day for weeks at a time. While definitely *not* an insomniac, I nonetheless felt that such an intense daily schedule was going to be required in order to meet the deadlines. I was willing to make this investment and needed an aide, along with several other masochistic members of my urban policy staff, who would be willing to do likewise. My assessment was correct. Without our total commitment and nonstop pace, the urban policy would not have been produced.

The second long-term consultant was Franklin James. Initially borrowed from the Urban Institute in Washington, DC, because of his expertise in economic development analysis and conceptualization, James held a Ph.D. and had published widely.[16] He remained a consultant until the HUD personnel office was able to arrange an official appointment for him. His appointment fulfilled Secretary Harris' expressed desire to attract top-flight professionals and academics into the career ranks, especially people who shared her values for saving cities and for helping those who lived there and were in need.

Planning Protocols: The Place Is the Thing!

During three days in mid-August, the protocols that would guide the policy planning process throughout were established. They were to be a healthy balance of cost and benefit, but in the views of Harold Wolman and Astrid Merget, they served to confuse White House staff and URPG members alike as to who in fact was in charge of the process.[17]

After a Monday meeting with Eizenstat that followed a long Saturday afternoon White House[18] meeting with Bert Carp, one of Eizenstat's bright, able, and hyper-kinetic principal aides, several protocols for URPG conduct were established. These included designations of where meetings would be held, who would attend, and how much money was available for serious urban policy development.

The secretary's group would be scratched, and the assistant secretaries would meet every week. Eizenstat himself would be there. He identified assistant secretaries and further agreed to ask them personally to serve on the deputies' group and to chair the task forces in their related functional areas.

With regard to resources, Eizenstat stated, since there had been:

> [A]pproximately a $10 billion margin in the FY'81 budget, $3 billion of which has been consumed in the proposed welfare initiative, there will be roughly $7 billion available with which to launch urban programs. This does not include revenue sharing, countercyclical or other major administrative initiatives that have been around.[19]

Carp's arithmetic further indicated that programs developed "must cost less than $5 billion in FY'81."We can have as many meetings in the White House as necessary," Eizenstat stated. This reinforced Carp's view, that: "The White House staff should show that HUD (is) strongly supported as the lead agency."

This meeting arrangement offered another control over the content and accountability of the URPG process: *only people specifically invited to meetings were cleared by the Secret Service to attend when these meetings were held in the White House.* Thus, one disruptive characteristic of earlier URPG meetings was eliminated, which was the musical chairs quality of participation reflected in last-minute substitutions of lower-level staff for top-level people. These staff usually were not in positions of authority or decision-making and often lacked the continuity needed to participate in the dialogue.

Meetings with Carp and Eizenstat were productive and useful. Both were substantively knowledgeable and were experienced Washington hands. Eizenstat had served as an aide to former Vice President Hubert Humphrey in his national campaign in 1968 and had worked on the White House staff during the Johnson years. Carp had worked on "The Hill" as well as within Great Society programs.

Bert Carp served as my liaison initially, facilitating access to the White House or agency people whom we needed to fold into the process. Probably the second most important decision—the first was about the available funds—and perhaps the one with the most lasting influence on the outcome and fate of the national urban policy was made in these three days. After consultation by Eizenstat with President Carter, it was decided that health, education, welfare, environment, and energy, all of which were critically important to the urban policy formulation, but were then being developed "on a separate fast track," should not be integrated into the URPG process. *Thus, these issues were to remain permanently inde-*

pendent of URPG and were excluded from the final national urban policy document.

Reorganized Task Forces

Discussion of task force reorganization should take place from two perspectives. The first concerns the structure and protocols that accompanied the reorganization, since these appear to have influenced the task forces' productivity to a large extent. The second perspective concerns the series of most critical substantive considerations taken by the task forces after URPG was reorganized. These priorities necessarily reflect my own biases. They reflect, also, the perspective of an effort directed from within HUD, which saw itself as the advocate of urban areas.

Task Force Structure and Protocols

Each task force was assigned a HUD staff coordinator, who served as the secretariat for each group. Embry's and my individual meetings with deputies produced "lead agency" commitments for chairing new task forces or for continuing with those already in existence. Also, where an assistant secretary would not be able to devote full attention to his or her task force, a specific policy-level staff person (usually a deputy assistant secretary, per our request for a high-level appointee) was formally identified. Additionally, following a productive meeting with Stuart Eizenstat in mid-August, White House staff members from his and Jack Watson's staff were assigned as liaison members to each task force. They attended the meetings, facilitated various task force efforts, and served as monitors and White House links with the process.

During August and September, in meetings with Embry, Eizenstat, his staff, and me, specific deadlines were established for task force products within the context of the work program time schedule. Where, in spite of HUD's coordinators' efforts, task forces were slow in organizing or producing materials for review, the White House sought to encourage more effective lead-agency management.

Task force reports were standard agenda items for deputies' group meetings. Eizenstat had agreed to co-chair these meetings with Embry. He usually honored this commitment, although occasionally the President detained him. Thus, the prospect of having the White House become aware that one or another agency was or was not producing seemed to serve as an additional incentive for cooperation. Table 4.1 in the previous chapter reflects the URPG administrative and task force structure as it had evolved by September and essentially remained throughout the process.[20]

In addition to the HUD staff directors and the three coordinators who were career staff from within HUD, non-career, full-time consultants were hired as coordinators because they were experts in the task force area to which they were assigned. Several coordinators had written widely in their fields. Janice Perlman was a Ph.D. and faculty member from the University of California at Berkeley, and Judith May was a Ph.D. on loan to Lynn Curtis from NASPAA (National Association of Schools of Public Affairs and Administration) and Rutgers University.[21] Franklin James, the economic development coordinator, has been mentioned above. Aside from being bright and energetic, the coordinators from HUD's career staff had program experience and had worked on urban issues for CPD or PD&R prior to the formation of URPG.

White House Task Force Participation

The staffing of the task forces and the request for White House liaison for each were not guileless acts. Since any federal agency could choose to participate on any task force, and in several instances representatives of the public interest sectors also held permanent task force membership, at least three task force malfunctions always were possible. Philosophical differences among members could bring deliberations to a screeching halt, creating interminable delays in the development of recommendations and proposals. For this problem, the White House liaison staff were to serve as enforcers and expediters for the lead agency chairperson.

Also, turfing conflicts continued, as Heclo has observed,[22] and were a constant threat to cooperation and consensus. Again, White House staff were expected to reflect the "party line" from the President—albeit, several times removed—and to help the coordinators soothe ruffled feathers through one-on-one contacts with antagonists between meetings.

The most serious threat to the success of the task force structure, however, was the inclination of such a diverse, interdepartmental, and public/private membership to reinvent the wheel at every meeting and to talk sub-issues into the ground. Lynn Curtis had been right in his analysis. This dynamic avoided the requirement of producing substantive recommendations.

White House liaison members helped to neutralize this threat by representing a visible link, through their presence, between the White House (i.e., the President) and the task forces. They also offered dissenters and disgruntled task force members a channel for stating their positions "for the President's benefit,"so to speak. However the battle over any given issue might be resolved, the White House would always know what the losers' positions had been.

Unfortunately, White House staff served as obstructors as well as facilitators of the task forces' process. The youthful junior staff members (the mean age of all White House staff immediately after the transition was calculated to be 32 year) lacked their own budgeted programs to administer. Therefore, they sought opportunities to "make a difference," which usually had been their inspiration for entry into public service in the first place. Their collective inexperience in administration propelled them into kinetic activity, setting up parallel task groups and duplicating planning efforts already underway within the executive agencies working on URPG.

The conflicting effects of the White House behavior had also been the basis for concern to others. Harold Wolman and Astrid Merget, professional students of administration and among PD&R's observers of the policy process, commented:

> White House participation could be merely passive and facilitative (which would seem to capture the spirit of 'Cabinet Government'...) or it could be active and directive (what we have termed the White House Lead-Interagency Task Force model). In fact, during the first 18 months of the Carter administration, it was both, sometimes within the framework of the same set of policy deliberations...

However, what most junior staff lacked in experience and maturity, they often made up for with jawboning and by no little measure of posturing, with career staff as well as with the non-career coordinators. Both the Neighborhoods Task Force and the Economic Development Task Force fell victim to these bad habits. In both instances, a parallel bureaucracy for urban policy began to surface in the White House as the policy development process matured. There seemed to be little understanding of the impediments set up by such White House centrality in the daily technology of policy formulation. Heclo points out the weakness of this governance style:

> Since the end of the Eisenhower administration, enough experience has accumulated to suggest that whenever an activist president tries to run ...government operations directly from the White House he also runs into considerable trouble...

> Rather than helping the President, these arrangements increasingly sucked problems into the White House, complicated major choices with irrelevant details, confused signals going out in the President's name, and made the White House itself into a slow-moving bureaucracy.[23]

These costs to the President, of course, did not become obvious until much later. The difficulties presented to the URPG task force staff, however, were apparent after the first two months of reorganized operation. Inherent in the definition of the HUD coordinators' role was a mechanistic response to task force dynamics. The coordinators sought to keep the process more or less on track through a number of actions: by working with the lead-agency chairperson in developing the agenda; by recording and circulating minutes that magnified progress and accomplishments (or the lack thereof); and by providing substantive materials for task force discussions if necessary. In some instances, none of these safeguards worked.

Task Force Performance

As might be expected, dynamics within each task force varied, according to the membership and the relevance of that membership to the specific mission of the lead-agency. In this sense, task force performance can be reviewed by cluster groups within which there were similarities. It is difficult, however, to make general statements about task force performance, or to make a blanket assertion that one task force's recommendations were more or less fully reflected in the final urban policy document than were another's. The process for developing drafts was complex and idiosyncratic. While task force deliberations did influence these drafts, the extent, form, direction, and strength of that influence varied according to the issue involved and who cared most about it.

Task forces on States and Metropolitan Regions, Neighborhoods, and Redlining form one cluster for examination. Their commonality was based on their broad membership, which included substantial representation from both the public and private sectors, and on the specificity of their agenda, which had fairly clearly defined issues.

A second cluster grouping consisted of the Employment and Transportation Task Forces. Both of these were primarily intra-departmental, having a preponderance of members from the Labor and Transportation departments, respectively. Both task forces also had White House staff. However, when a particular initiative required the direct involvement of other domestic agencies in order to be implemented, representatives from those agencies joined the task forces for the duration of discussions on that initiative. Many of the employment and transportation recommendations in the final urban policy document were primarily crafted by the Departments of Labor or Transportation.

Economic Development and Public Finance Task Forces were a breed apart, serving as battle grounds for larger national and interdepartmental issues. Economic development was the theme of struggles between HUD and Commerce for hegemony over programs and, therefore, dollars appropriated by Congress for urban revitalization. On the issue of the locus of the proposed urban development bank, Treasury joined the fray. Public finance was the avenue for efforts to influence the nascent tax policy proposals that were being developed unilaterally in the Treasury Department.

States and Metropolitan Regions Task Force. This task force was created because URPG-1 decided that states must play a key role in helping local units of government solve their problems. As stated in a draft progress report to the President:

> By setting the conditions of local government participation in area-wide planning and decision-making, defining the powers of metropolitan organizations, and determining the distribution of state aid within metropolitan areas, state laws and practices can affect the ability of local jurisdictions to pursue metropolitan areawide solutions to urban problems.[24]

The first task force meeting was not held until after the URPG reorganization, but once convened, the group met regularly and frequently until final recommendations were submitted for the policy. Co-chaired by Commerce and HUD, task force membership included representatives from HUD, several divisions within the Economic Development Administration (EDA), Transportation, OMB, the Environmental Protection Agency (EPA), HEW, Labor, Treasury, and top staff from the appropriate interest groups.[25] The Advisory Commission on Intergovernmental Relations (ACIR) was a strong participant and the substance of early discussions was supplied by the various definitive ACIR studies on state and regional behavior and characteristics.

Taking direction from two public positions expressed by President Carter,[26] the task force resolved to address the following issues:

> The extent to which federal programs benefitting local governments and metropolitan agencies can address common national objectives...on a metropolitan basis through joint federal incentives.

> The extent to which state initiatives in behalf of declining neighborhoods, central cities, and suburbs can be advanced through cooperative federal policies providing incentives for special efforts.
>
> The extent to which the federal government can induce greater cooperation among local and state governments in resolution of metropolitan problems.[27]

Initial meetings were devoted to general discussions with a focus on a specific proposal developed by Embry and his staff and submitted by HUD. This regional strategy proposal[28] sought to target funds from existing federal programs to metropolitan regions engaged in pro-city activities. As this proposal was refined, the group's emphasis shifted to tackling broader gauge issues, involving the responsibilities and strengths of state governments and the need for innovative funding and new arrangements at the sub-state levels. For this exercise, the task force scheduled a series of hearings and consultations with individual interest groups.

This mode continued until December 1977, when a group of governors arranged to meet with the President because of their concern that states were not being seriously integrated into policy recommendations, in spite of the President's earlier promises. This meeting escalated direct White House involvement in the matter of fashioning a state role, and Jack Watson personally began monitoring the activities. He hired a state specialist from New Jersey to work on the final recommendations, revised the final draft report himself, and often met with a smaller core group of task force members—usually the HUD coordinator, co-chairpersons from HUD and Commerce, and his staff liaisons and specialists.

The final task force report was a thorough reflection of the groups' work, and included comments from participants with regard to their position on the recommendations. Four specific proposals were advanced:

1) A federal-state urban partnership, including the preparation and funding of "state urban development strategies;
2) A federal policy for metropolitan development, which was to foster cooperation among metropolitan municipalities and counties in the preparation of unified plans to combat distress;
3) An intergovernmental commission on urban revitalization, composed of distinguished representatives of federal, state, and local governments to explore in depth the options available under federal policy to assist distressed communities; and,

4) Federal funding of state urban development or investment strategies, which would provide incentives for state governments to reorder their own funding and investment decisions to more favorably affect cities and older suburbs.

The Task Force on States and Metropolitan Regions had some success in accomplishing its mission and addressing the issues before it. The "energy that it dissipated assuming the dressing of decision through interagency coordination,"[29] was seen by coordinator Wyndham Clarke as an impediment to the process as it unfolded. Also, the tension that developed because of the joint HUD/Commerce leadership Clarke felt contributed to a lack of clarity "about who was doing what to whom." This dilemma was exacerbated by the power struggle between the two agencies.

However, another point of view is that both of these criticisms were a product of the inherent complexity of the URPG process of coordination and normal conditions of interagency efforts. Also, although the tensions made life difficult for the coordinator, they were creative enough to generate reasonably satisfactory task force performance and to contribute significantly to the final urban policy document.

Neighborhoods Task Force. It seemed that every task force chairperson and coordinator combed Presidential comments to isolate a specific statement by Carter to provide a raison d'etre for the group. In the case of the Neighborhoods Task Force, the search yielded a relatively obscure speech at Brooklyn College in September 1976, in which the President described neighborhoods as "the living fiber that holds our society together." Carter stated that neighborhoods must be "at the very top of our national policy.... If we are to save our cities, we must revitalize our neighborhoods first."

Based on this mandate and on the nationally recognized commitment of HUD's Assistant Secretary for Neighborhoods[30] Geno Baroni, who "led a nationwide fight to save and revitalize urban ethnic neighborhoods,"[31] the task force got underway in early April 1977. A number of meetings took place prior to the reorganization, and much staff time was devoted initially to establishing broad participation on the task force and to organizing immediate and conceptual issues. Consequently, by August, the task force had prepared a lengthy conceptual paper, conducted a White House workshop on neighborhood reinvestment and made preparations for plugging into the work of the Neighborhoods Commission, then in the process of being formed through Presidential appointments.

Task force membership included representatives from every federal domestic agency except Treasury: HUD, Commerce, Labor, Transportation, HEW, Small Business Administration (SBA), Justice, Interior, and Community Service Administration, as well as White House staff who formerly had worked with Baroni at the National Center for Urban Ethnic Affairs. Both Curtis' staff coordinator and the task force coordinator whom I hired in August were highly trained specialists in neighborhood and community programs.[32] While the task force meetings were open at all times to citizens who wished to participate, and large numbers frequently did attend, these were not regularly the same people. Nonetheless, at any meeting, nonpublic-sector attendees usually outnumbered public-sector members.

Task force issues emerged in the following forms:

1) A neighborhood's policy must apply with equal weight to white and nonwhite neighborhoods;
2) What exactly are "neighborhoods"? How do they differ from "communities," "slums," or "ghettos"?
3) Should a "neighborhood policy"apply to both deteriorating "transition" neighborhoods and hard-core impoverished ghettos?
4) What are the overlaps and difference when "neighborhood policy" is compared to "economic development policy" or "community development policy?"[33]

These questions, through refinement, were considered within the context of the task force's desire to develop a two-pronged strategy:

> On the one hand, we must develop policies and actions that deal with the macro issues of jobs and employment, income transfers, welfare, fiscal redistribution, etc. On the other hand, we must have a special or turf-based strategy that deals with people's everyday problems in the communities in which they live.[34]

The agenda and mission of the Neighborhoods Task Force presented far fewer problems for the URPG process than did the internecine warfare between factions of professionals within the neighborhoods movement. Unfortunately, these factions divided along agency lines as well, with one faction that worked from the White House influencing the Neighborhoods Commission and a portion of the opposing faction located within HUD. While Baroni himself also was at HUD, many of his closest supporters were on the White House staff. Janice Perlman, HUD's task force coordinator, was identified with the "other" group, and when she sought to advance concepts or to organize a meeting of neighborhood representatives at the White House, White House staff objected.

The neighborhoods specialist on the domestic policy staff had prepared a lengthy discussion draft[35] for Eizenstat that included the names of neighborhood people with whom the White House had been in contact. Called their "outreach efforts," the White House procedure coincided with the task force agenda in some instances and diverged in others. In all instances it duplicated URPG staff and consultant activities in the neighborhood area. This observation is of no little import: well-respected experts Hans Spiegel and Donald Warren, mentioned earlier, served as on-call consultants to the Neighborhoods Task Force and were guiding and monitoring the agenda. Perlman herself had a solid reputation and deep experience in the field. The staff person engineering the White House position was not of comparable rank or experience. Yet, she intervened to cancel the original neighborhoods meeting and directed the design of the participant list and the agenda for a rescheduled meeting a month later.

Perlman pointed out the substantive problem of this sequence of events in a lengthy, analytical memo following the cancellation:

> The original list was created through a careful process of names submitted by the White House, the URPG staff, and Assistant Secretary Baroni and was balanced to reflect not just geographic and ethnic diversity but an array of styles, philosophies, and approaches.
>
> The present reduced list has two women, three blacks, and four Latinos and has a fair geographic spread but has no diversity at all in terms of type or approach. It reflects only those...that have a "development orientation" which means that it excludes some of the most innovative, dynamic, and successful groups around the country which have worked on urban policy issues...[36]

The Neighborhoods Task Force had more impact on the policies finally recommended by virtue of its existence and general activity rather than because of substantive agreed-upon recommendations finally presented. The concept of neighborhood is a complicated one. Thus, underlying the task force's deliberations was the dilemma of whether or not any policies formulated for a subsystem within a city can, or should, differ from overall policies for cities. At the core of this dilemma is the reality that neighborhoods are not self-sufficient economic or social units and that the interaction effect between them and their environment is great, even in the case of neighborhoods with strong name identification and traditions.

Sensitive to this reality, the task force's preliminary draft for the urban policy reflected the following worldview:

> We view the world of government as a facilitator and catalyst of citizen and neighborhood capacity. The recognition of neighborhoods, we believe, must be a new consciousness. We must direct policy toward the positive role of neighborhoods in the life of the individual and family rather than the more restrictive concern with neighborhood pathology.[37]

Redlining Task Force. The Redlining Task Force succumbed to the intractibility of its banking industry representatives and was unable to reach consensus on final recommendations after a year of URPG activity. This occurred in spite of numerous meetings, strong joint leadership by HUD and the comptroller of the currency, and top quality work by the coordinator. In fact, at one time this task force boasted fourteen HUD staff regularly assigned to provide support by the secretary's office, and various other divisions of the department, in addition to the full-time URPG coordinator, Dr. Judith May. Half of these assigned staff were top-level political appointees, the other half, equally senior career staff.

In one sense, the highly organized, specialized nature of the task force membership and its abundant staff may have contributed, in part, to its constipated performance. The URPG staff director noted at the end of September:

> [T]he URPG Redlining Task Force is taking a much more detailed and formal approach to developing its recommendations than are the other Task Forces. The group has a very structured work program ... Ironically, the Redlining Task Force may be doing the most but being heard from the least, at the upper levels of URPG decision-making. By its nature, it has no budget recommendations...it has not been represented at the deputies' table...(and) no written recommendations will be) available for deputies or other decision points before October 20.[38]

The agenda that this task force developed when it was reorganized included the following items:

- Determining community credit needs;
- Developing neighborhood-tailored marketing techniques;
- Developing application processes and information collection procedures necessary for marketing and monitoring;
- Developing nondiscriminatory uniform and objective appraisal and underwriting standards;

- Developing uniform methods for informing consumers about loan decisions; and,
- Presenting alternative risk-reducing techniques.[39]

The major work on formulating this agenda was done by the URPG coordinator, in collaboration with PD&R staff experts loaned to the task force. The membership of thirty-four participants alone gave the group a difficult dynamic. More than half of that membership came from the Federal National Mortgage Association, Government National Mortgage Association, Federal Reserve Board, Federal Home Loan Bank Board, Federal Deposit Insurance Corporation, and Treasury Department.

In the opposite corner, so to speak, were ACTION, the Civil Rights Division of the Department of Justice, the Office of Minority Business Enterprise in the Department of Commerce, the White House Domestic Policy staff representatives, and the Offices of Fair Housing and Equal Opportunity, PD&R, and URPG within HUD.

In gross liberal and conservative terms, these two collectivities represented polar extremes. Between these two factions, representatives of inner-cities stepped from time to time, attending the meetings of the task force and making the point that redlining had racial as well as economic implications. The members of the task force, however, continued to disagree on a definition of redlining.

Work on single-family redlining proceeded during the policy drafting period, along with discussions of multi-family redlining. However, as the urban policy final draft neared completion in 1978, it was agreed that the task force was not ready to submit options for inclusion in the President's announced policy.

Employment Task Force. After several abortive attempts to develop recommendations with full interagency participation, the reorganized Employment Task Force retreated to functioning mainly within the Department of Labor. Its membership was augmented regularly by a White House domestic policy staff expert and a deputy assistant secretary from Treasury. Its meetings also were attended by an unappreciated URPG coordinator. Labor constantly was suspicious of her motives and regularly complained that she was interfering with its productivity. In fact, the coordinator challenged Labor's slavish commitment to designing urban policy initiatives that reinforced existing Department of Labor policy and programs, rather than more critically assessing whether CETA, for example, offered the best avenue for attacking the unemployment of inner-city minorities and youth.

From the beginning of URPG activities following reorganization, DOL, represented by Arnold Packer, Assistant Secretary for Policy, Evaluation, and Research, had sought to augment public service jobs and to focus "attention...(on) the total array of Labor Department programs, currently underway or planned..."[40] Packer expected to expand the budget of the economic stimulus package for FY'79 and to piggyback on the jobs portion of the welfare reform proposal, both of which he described as "integral parts of DOL's present and future employment program."

Neither of these approaches met with much enthusiasm. OMB and the White House were concerned about the substantial increase in budget authority for the next two fiscal years that Labor's proposal required. Task force staff felt that Labor's approach was self-serving. Further, according to specific criticisms from the expert consultant to the task force, the Wharton School's Bernard Anderson:

> [F]iscal and monetary stimulus alone will be inadequate to deal with the deep set employment problems of many urban areas, especially the hardship cities of the Northeast and the Midwest. To be specific, no amount of economic growth will be sufficient to stir the economic backwaters of inner city ghetto areas suffering from decades of neglect. Bold and imaginative policies are required to accomplish that task and the federal government must assume the major responsibility for leadership in getting the job done.[41]

Claudia Pharis, task force coordinator, prepared an employment initiative, "Reaching the Hardcore Unemployed," based on recommendations from Anderson and Andrew Bennett, a consultant experienced in union behavior, and gleaned from a broad-based "Labor Forum," which she organized and held in November 1977. Not only did Packer register strong objections to the idea of an employment proposal coming from somewhere other than the Labor Department, but DOL staff also complained to both Embry and me that the forum should not be held. Claudia Pharis' efforts to gain a fair hearing for the URPG proposal resulted in DOL also lodging objections with the White House, to which Pharis responded:

> I do not know why (DOL) was so opposed to this proposal ever seeing the light of day, but in the spirit of openness which has characterized the workings of the URPG to date, it strikes me as inappropriate to withhold perfectly viable options from consideration.[42]

It also struck others as a perplexing stance since it was understood that the management of any employment initiative necessarily would rest in the Department of Labor. None of the reasons suggested to explain Labor's recalcitrance, including neurotic hysteria on the part of a couple of the actors, made any sense. Ultimately, both the Secretary of Labor and White House liaison agreed that someone other than Packer might be a more collegial representative of Labor on URPG.

Thus, Labor's Assistant Secretary Ernest Green, the civil rights activist and former Little Rock Seven hero, who had served on the URPG-I task force, was reassigned to URPG. He participated fully this time around and a number of employment initiatives ultimately were presented in the final policy document. These included programs to link EDA- and HUD-funded projects with Labor programs, but also expanded and targeted CETA funding more sharply.

Transportation Task Force. The fact that most of the Transportation Task Force's activity really was a reflection of Department of Transportation's internal policy planning is not a pejorative observation. For reasons that were not very clear, the task force never quite took off. On the other hand, DOT's efforts to support URPG's work and mission, while sometimes testy, were well above average.

Contrary to Curtis' assessment that during URPG-1 a lack of cooperative spirit characterized Assistant Secretary Chester Davenport's participation, following reorganization of URPG-2, Davenport immediately created a mechanism within DOT to assure a constructive departmental response. In a definitive memorandum to DOT's secretary and deputy secretary, Davenport outlined three principal objectives of URPG to which he felt DOT could respond without delay: new urban programs; improved coordination; and urban policy initiatives.

Affirmative Action and Set-asides

Davenport indicated that officials at HUD and the White House had suggested specific ways in which DOT could link into neighborhood, business and economic development programs. His conversations with Eizenstat and top staff at OMB had indicated that there could be between $3 billion and $7 billion available for such new initiatives."[43] Further, the Young Amendment, then under consideration in Congress, provided for business and economic development in the area of transit stations. Davenport already had undertaken "to assure that this department complies with the mandates of the URPG. I have set up a working group representing the various modes and assistant secretaries within this department who are concerned with the urban revitalization process."[44]

The interaction between Davenport and his staff, and the URPG Coordinator and staff, was open and frequent. Numerous informal exchanges reflect mutual probing to expand the range of DOT's commitment, and the department submitted three specific formal initiatives and policy recommendations into the URPG process—once in late September and twice in October—in an effort to accommodate suggested program expansions.

In addition to upgrading track and station facilities along the Northeast Corridor,[45] DOT designed direct transportation construction grants for minority enterprises, sought to target employment to distressed communities, designed a transfer of funds from the interstate highway system to urban use, and targeted rapid rail benefits to distressed cities as a first order of priority. To facilitate implementation of the various initiatives, DOT designed changes in certain Federal Highway Administration decision mechanisms governing the use of funds, along with changes in matching formula requirements to better accommodate the disadvantageous negotiating position of distressed cities.

By the end of October, specific ranges of increases in jobs and program value had been projected for the Northeast Corridor Improvement Program:

> To enhance the employment effects of this program, this Administration has established a goal of directing 15 percent of the aggregate dollar value of the program to minority-owned businesses (in distressed cities along the corridor).... The Department has estimated the projects will result in about 20,000 jobs during the period from 1977–1980.[46]

Often during the final policy drafting period it seemed that, in spite of the department's responsiveness, and its working as a single-agency task force most of the time, DOT was being pushed to go even farther, and frequently beyond the limits that were being required of other agencies. HUD continued to press for a policy of relief for cities plagued by ring-roads and beltways that siphoned retail shopping, commercial and industrial resources into the suburbs, and strangled the cities economy as effectively as if they, in fact, were nooses around the cities' necks.

These discussions were not very productive. The beltways causing the most current damage, like the one castigated by the mayor of Richmond, Virginia, were well into the construction phases. Thus, they were past the point where capital investment, financing, and building plans realistically could be changed. Besides, in cases such as Richmond, the damage to downtown shopping areas already had been done. Atlanta, too, had a deserted minority neighborhood as a prime exhibit, through which access roads had been partially constructed to link into a ring-road, and to which Mayor Jackson attributed several of his city's serious social and economic problems. The ultimate response to this and several similar dilemmas was the urban impact analysis, which was later proposed as a policy.[47]

Public Finance. A well-balanced group with at least one representative from each major federal domestic agency, the Public Finance Task Force was chaired by Treasury and closely monitored by almost everyone else. Judith May, who also served as coordinator for the Redlining Task Force, had less developmental work to do in Public Finance than in Redlining, but more analytical assessments of a substantial number of initiatives being proposed in the public finance area. Fiscally conservative Treasury often was seen as "the fox guarding the chicken coop" with regard to pro-city proposals.

With the exception of the tax policy being prepared for Presidential announcement, Treasury appeared to fold much of its urban-oriented work into the task force, or at least into the deliberations of the URPG deputies' group. In addition to "analyzing the varied fiscal activities of state and local governments," the task force proposed to "develop policies that improve the impact of federal programs on the fiscal condition of these governments."[48] In response to the task force's general call for agenda items from domestic agencies, the following reflects the range of submissions for task force consideration:

1) Metropolitan fiscal disparities
   Tax increment sharing
   Statewide tax base equalization
   Annexation
2) Municipal credit problems
   Short-term borrowing
   Reducing supply of tax-exempt bonds
   Taxable bond option
   Urban Development Bank
   Municipal bond guarantees
   Pension fund reform
3) Adequacy of federal assistance
   Adequacy of formula grants
   Keeping pace with inflation

Federal assumption of welfare costs

4) Adequacy of state assistance
   State assumption of education costs
   State housing finance agencies
   State economic development corporations
5) Maintaining tax base
   Altering tax code to increase incentives for investment in rehabilitation rather than new construction
   Discouraging fiscal and snob zoning
6) Equity issues
   School tax equalization
   Property tax circuit breakers
   Real estate assessment practices
7) Municipal economic development strategies
   Leveraging private investment
   Community development corporations
   Infrastructure
   Housing development and rehabilitation
   Manpower strategies
   Federal program coordination

The task force devoted considerable time to conducting an analysis of the fiscal impact of proposals submitted by domestic agencies to URPG on state and local governments. This analysis posed several questions, including:

- To what extent is the problem to be met by the proposed program perceived to be an excessive fiscal burden at the state and local government level?
- The general means by which the program will be financed, the size of the program in fiscal years 1979 and 1980, and the projected federal budgeting cost over the first five years after its enactment; and
- The projected responses of state and local governments to the proposed programs, e.g., are they likely to substitute federal assistance for state and local funds or will the program design attempt to maintain present effort or stimulate more state and local funding?[49]

As Treasury was conducting its assessments of fiscal impact and pro-urban forces were becoming increasingly nervous about what appeared to be a very restrictive fiscal posture in OMB and Treasury, particularly with regard to urban needs, HUD was undertaking an assessment of the urban impact of the tax reform proposals. Of the eight changes proposed by Treasury in the tax reform package, two were judged to negatively affect urban areas, one had negligible effect, and the remaining three were felt to be beneficial.

Briefly summarized below, along with anticipated urban impact, the tax reform proposals were:

- Limitation on the deduction of mortgage interest: Negligible probable urban impact
- Liberalization of treatment of gain realized on sale of owner-occupied homes: Beneficial probable urban impact
- Shift from deduction to a credit and reduction in the tax rates: Beneficial probable urban impact
- Creation of a taxable bond option (localities could issue securities with federal interest subsidies): Beneficial probable urban impact
- Elimination of deductions for some state and local taxes: Mixed to negative probable impact
- Limitation on depreciation deductions: Mixed to negative probable impact
- Termination of exemptions on industrial development bonds: Negative probable urban impact
- Revision in the investment tax credit: Negative probable urban impact

Perhaps the most important task performed under the aegis of the Public Finance Task Force was, in fact, Treasury's evaluation of the countercyclical review-sharing program[50] and the recommendations that were forwarded to URPG. With assistance from the Urban Institute, Treasury's staff argued that a continued but modified program was justified because "the benefits afforded by this program to those units of government with the greatest fiscal need support a recommendation for continuance."[51] A more sharply targeted program was designed and included in the urban policy document, reflecting a successful offensive by EDA, HUD, Labor, and Treasury, working through URPG, to salvage an initiative felt to be important to cities.

Economic Development Task Force. There was, of course, a linear relationship between many of the fiscal and economic development proposals. Almost every tax proposal—credit, incentive, exemption, equalization or base-sharing—had implications for economic development. And the most glamorous urban policy initiative of all—at least, according to the daily press—was both a fiscal *and* an economic development proposal: The Urban Development Bank.

But while it may have appeared otherwise to outsiders, the Economic Development Task Force was devoting much of its time to discussing a range of issues, not the least of which was the difference between community development and economic development. This distinction lay at the core of the controversy, discussed earlier, between HUD and Commerce. If community development were accepted as the more generic term, then HUD's argument would be supported, that:

> increases in economic development assistance to cities should be channelled through (1) Community Development Block Grants, in order to meet particularly the need for land assemblage, and (2) Urban Development Action Grants in order to provide a level of immediate economic assistance to distressed cities.[52]

If, however, economic development were decided to be the more generic term, Commerce's Economic Development Administration (EDA) would be supported in its efforts to increase EDA funding, especially for use in urban areas, a relatively new geographic focus for the department. EDA also had improved its competitive advantage vis-a-vis HUD, as well as somewhat improving its targeting with regard to cities. A change in the language in its reauthorization legislation in 1976 permitted EDA to designate any depressed neighborhood or area as a "redevelopment" area. Thus, funds could be granted to urban or nonurban areas with little delay, an improvement over most of HUD's grant-giving mechanisms.

As Embry pointed out in a memorandum to Stu Eizenstat:

> One of the major thrusts of the Urban Policy we are working on will be "economic development." The principal Federal programs of economic development are those administered by HUD and Commerce. As you are acutely aware, there has been some rivalry between these two Departments as to which will take the lead in this area. I, for one, find this rivalry healthy. It keeps both Departments on their toes and encourages an increase in responsiveness to cities and a decrease in bureaucratic delays. In addition, it has a corrective influence in requiring HUD, a city and poverty oriented agency, to concern itself with the needs of busi-

ness, and Commerce, an operation oriented toward businessmen and rural areas, to become more tuned to cities.[53]

Actually, there were two real issues between HUD and Commerce, and these underlay the ongoing definitional thrusts and parries and verbal hyperbole. The first issue revolved around the Urban Development Action Grant Program, (UDAG), its sexy appeal to Congress, and the threat, therefore, of fund transfers from the previously facile EDA program to the newer UDAG. Since upwards of $400 million was at stake, the game was played without humor and with sudden-death moves. HUD prepared an analytical paper showing that anything EDA could do—public works, economic development, private enterprize efforts—HUD could do better—water, sewer and public facilities; urban renewal; contracts with commercial and industrial and housing developers and builders. EDA charged, on the other hand, that because of HUD's housing programs for the poor, the business sector did not trust HUD to have its best interest at heart. This was especially true with regard to creating the conditions necessary to encourage the alliance with the private sector needed for effective economic development.

The second real issue dividing HUD and Commerce was mentioned earlier. This dealt with the President's reorganization plans and how such definitional questions, about economic versus community development, would affect rumored options for the creation of an Economic and Community Development Department. One signal of the way in which the wind might be blowing in that regard, therefore, would be the organizational placement of the Urban Development Bank.

On the issue of definition as well as on the location of the Urban Development Bank, HUD felt beleaguered. OMB had prepared a position paper that favored Commerce as the primary sponsor of economic development activity. HUD charged that the paper was full of "sufficient numbers of misleading and inaccurate statements."[54] In addition, the secretary's staff suspected that Orin Kramer, White House domestic policy staff assigned to HUD's programs, was quietly undermining HUD in the White House and encouraging OMB and Commerce to lobby against HUD with the Reorganization Task Force.

While the basis for this suspicion probably was somewhat uncertain, Kramer's general behavior did little to inspire confidence among HUD's top staff. Indeed, his behavior in some Economic Development Task Force meetings was openly hostile to HUD staff and reflected a distorted view of how HUD's programs worked.

Other items on the task force agenda included developing new incentives and supplements to existing programs; obtaining the authority to encourage the private sector to expand or locate in distressed cities; and adjusting programs to be more targeted to distressed cities. Both HUD and Commerce submitted initiatives to the task force to revise, redirect, and target more narrowly, and link their existing programs and policies with other programs.

Finally, the agenda included proposals for a dozen studies, including research to generate data about economic development on a regional basis, as well as studies and assessments to make regional coordination of programs more effective. Commerce proposed to develop research papers in some of these areas, and did prepare some of these papers. It is suspected that the URPG member who complained that the Economic Development Task Force meetings were burdensome and that members got "talked to death" had in mind meetings where these more abstract concepts were discussed.

Summary

On August 23, at the first full URPG meeting following reorganization, commitments were made by URPG deputies to the deadlines in the planning work program. Eizenstat chaired this meeting, with Embry providing the details for the substantive discussion, thus enabling Eizenstat to establish the pattern for his continuing URPG role.

An analysis of urban problems was due from URPG/HUD staff by September 1, with comments from other agencies due by September 15. Budget proposals were to go to OMB by September 15, and task force products were due by October 1. A fully developed options paper that would present products then under preparation was needed for the President by November 15. These products included, among others, proposals on tax credits, property tax relief, municipal bond financing, and an urban extension service, designed and submitted to URPG by Jack Watson. It was pointed out to the deputies that the President's State of the Union Speech was in January and the urban policy document and the message to Congress had to be completed by March 15, 1978. The offensive was underway, and everyone had his or her marching orders.

In all visible respects, URPG's design and structure was quite consistent with Carter's intentions, if Wildavsky's conjecture about the President's administrative style is correct:

> Our hypothesis is that Carter's basic beliefs are about procedures for making policy—procedures about which he speaks with passion, deter-

> mination, and consistency. He is concerned less with particular goals than with the need for goals, less with the content of policies than with their ideal form—simplicity, uniformity, predictability, hierarchy, and comprehensiveness.[55]

The intent of the process-oriented structure, however, was not to please the President. Rather, the intent was to create a context of order within which "power exchange" activities of the bureaucracy could occur purposefully rather than haphazardly. The structure of the deputies' group, with its precise protocols and high-level leadership, might be classified by some as an "exchange interstitial" form.[56] The informal design of the task force system, with its generally open membership and public/private composition, provided "coordinative interstitial" opportunities for transactions between the public interest and citizens sectors and the policy planning mechanisms. These structures, however, labeled, were obvious and uncomplicated enough in their mission to encourage, rather than suppress, external transaction and internal interaction.

I have referred previously to the "interactive and transactive" nature of the urban policy development process. By "interactive," I mean the give and take, combat and compromise, horse trading and negotiating, that went on constantly within the deputies' group. In the final analysis, this dynamic interaction accounted for sufficient consensus to permit the departments to sign off on the policy document and President Carter to announce it on his Cabinet departments' recommendation. This process of *creative contention* characterized most encounters between the lead agency and the other actors.

Heclo emphasizes the ability of the bureaucracy to obstruct exercises such as URPG, that, unless neutralized, pose a diffuse but inexorable obstacle:

> ...bureaucrats are able to generate their own power through an ability to give or withhold compliance, advice, and information. Their circuits are firmly based in loyalties to particular programs, functional specialties, and institutions rather than to any particular leader of the day.[57]

Indeed, infinitely more than any particular urban policy issue was always at stake in these interactions. Budget decisions, decisions on priorities within the reorganization plan, program control decisions, staffing levels—all of these informed each ostensible encounter about urban policy. To ignore this reality was to misunderstand an entire dynamic of bureaucratic survival and to voluntarily relinquish any hope of achieving some level of consensus on the substance of the urban policy itself.

Moreover, the entirely fundamental reality of career service exerted an often subliminal and always powerful influence on the behavior of the agency staff people. Given the fluid nature of management priorities and values in a system with rotating ideological leadership—this time, the Democrats, next time, the Republicans—career staff are adroit in avoiding loose ends and incomplete circles for which they may have to design closure at a later date. As I was told early in my tenure as a top political appointee by one of the office directors who reported to me:

> It's not personal and it's not that I don't respect you professionally. But I was (tenured in this office) before you got here, and I'll be here after you're gone, trying to make sense of decisions which you and your team have made while you're in power. I am unlikely to allow something to be instituted with which I don't agree, but which I will have to carry on afterward.

The transactive quality of the urban policy process refers to the constant, desirable, and frequently overwhelming dialogues with those from the private sector that characterized Embry's days, my days, and the lives of all of the top URPG staff members. These contacts included one-on-one meetings with many experts, including some like Richard Nathan of the Brookings Institution, who called the urban policy process "a work in search of a mission," and, in fact, "question(ed) the viability of urban policy," as a concept that anyone seriously ought to try to capture.

Members of the Congressional Black Caucus with whom Embry and I met were more specific in their criticisms. Congressmen Conyers and Augustus "Gus" Hawkins, cited "the internal conflicts between long-term needs (of distressed cities) and the comprehensive character of a policy that also must look at farm and energy elements." They wondered what superman was going to "pull together such a comprehensive policy."

Private citizens, in "Equity Forums" assembling in San Francisco, Chicago, and Washington, introduced their personal perceptions of the priorities that an urban policy should address. Not unlike their predecessor from the Northeast's "Cities in the Middle," who met in New Jersey earlier in 1977, Equity Forum participants called for "job creation and economic development; reduction of fiscal and service disparities, physical revitalization, and local capacity building.[58]

Between August 23 and November 15, I held more than 200 meetings and private conferences with individuals and groups from the private sector in an effort to gain the broadest possible exposure to ideas, priorities, and concerns among those outside the public agencies. For the same reasons, Bob Embry held an almost equal number of meetings; so did the urban policy director and his deputy. We made conscious efforts not to "double-team" or duplicate each other. In all, well in excess of one thousand individual and group meetings were convened by the most senior URPG staff members to seek in-put, feed-back, and consensus.

Clarence Mitchell, elder statesman of the civil rights movement; directors of the National Urban League, the National League of Cities, National Association of Counties, Conference of Mayors, National Governor's Association, NAACP, and the Joint Center for Political Studies; state legislators; mayors and local legislators from Atlanta, East Orange, Connecticut, California—the list of our appointments and conferences was endless and was substantiated on the schedules that were printed for Embry and me daily. In addition, there were highly structured White House meetings that the President sometimes attended. There also were the regular URPG deputies' and task force meetings, both of which were attended by public- and private-sector participants. The opportunities for transaction were infinite, and we exploited them all.

Phyllis Lamphere, President of the National League of Cities, was critical of the intensity of the URPG schedule and of the short turnaround deadlines. Moreover, she feared that the URPG approach would not, in fact:

> [L]ead to a policy but to a series of programs.... There has to be a reason for this programmatic, mechanistic approach, and I wonder whether it is wrapped up on the same sort of thinking that makes schedules and deadlines so important to this administration .[59]

At the time, I dismissed the NLC's assessment as being cavalier and of the type normally made by those who did not have the ultimate responsibility but could afford to be the ultimate critics. Later, I came to think that it was a good thing that we had developed such a tight schedule; otherwise, we would not have been finished with writing the national urban policy before we lost the President's attention. On the other hand, there are those who seriously question that we ever had his attention. I certainly now wonder, in retrospect, what difference it made that a written national urban policy was completed.

HUD was given the responsibility of being the lead agency for URPG. But because of problems and dissatisfactions within the deputies' group, the fact that URPG was created so early in the new administration and because of various pressures and turf wars, URPG was viewed as being ineffective in constructing proposals that were less academic and more practical. When Shalala was relieved of the leadership position and Embry was asked to assume the URPG responsibility, the effort gained new momentum. The project was now housed within CPD, and the White House assumed a more pro-active and responsible position in facilitating and concluding the policy development process.

Table 5.1
Work Plan
August 1977 Through March 15, 1978

Key: ▬ = ongoing effort, ■■■■ = revision, adjustments, O = product, X = intermediate drafts

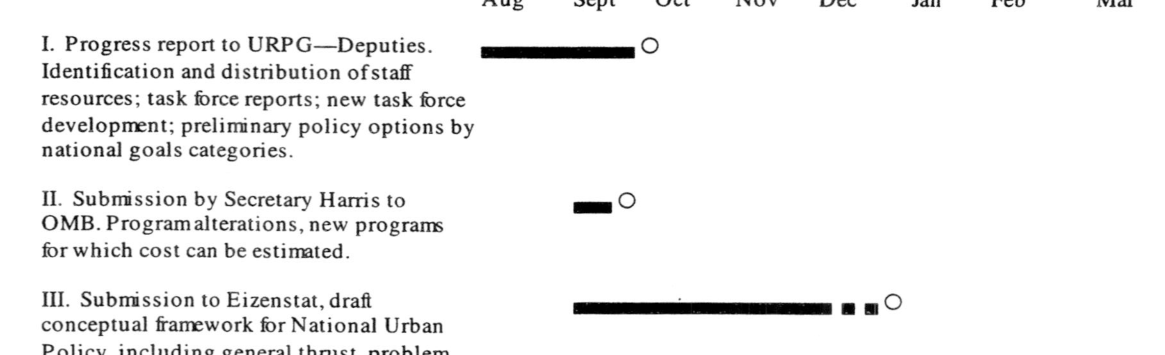

	Aug	Sept	Oct	Nov	Dec	Jan	Feb	Mar
I. Progress report to URPG—Deputies. Identification and distribution of staff resources; task force reports; new task force development; preliminary policy options by national goals categories.								
II. Submission by Secretary Harris to OMB. Program alterations, new programs for which cost can be estimated.								
III. Submission to Eizenstat, draft conceptual framework for National Urban Policy, including general thrust, problem statement, and tentative range of options. URPG Review—deputies								

Table 5.1
Work Plan
August 1977 Through March 15, 1978

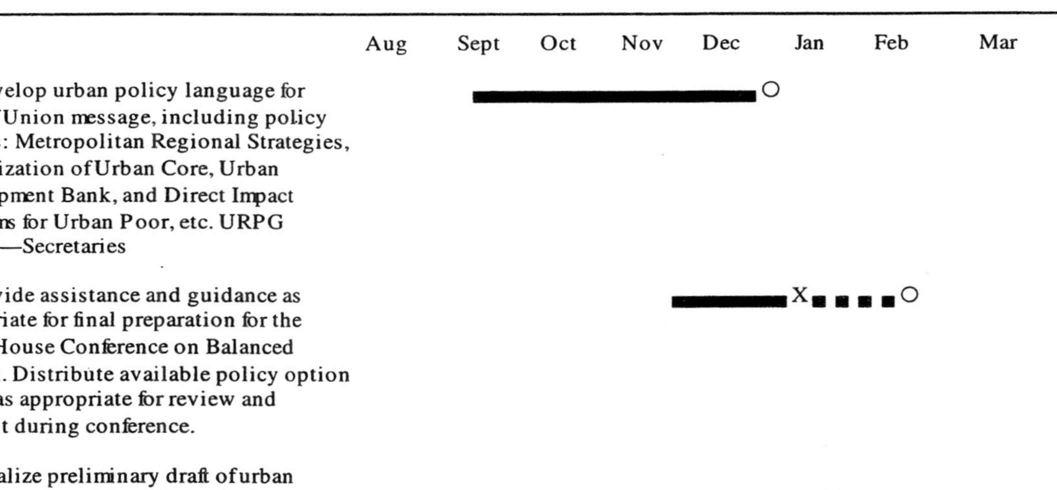

	Aug	Sept	Oct	Nov	Dec	Jan	Feb	Mar
IV. Develop urban policy language for State of Union message, including policy options: Metropolitan Regional Strategies, Revitalization of Urban Core, Urban Development Bank, and Direct Impact Programs for Urban Poor, etc. URPG Review—Secretaries								
V. Provide assistance and guidance as appropriate for final preparation for the White House Conference on Balanced Growth. Distribute available policy option papers as appropriate for review and comment during conference.								
VI. Finalize preliminary draft of urban policy statement. Tentatively decide on specific recommendations in programmatic terms. URPG Review—deputies								

Table 5.1
Work Plan
August 1977 Through March 15, 1978

	Aug	Sept	Oct	Nov	Dec	Jan	Feb	Mar
VII. Review recommendations from Balanced Growth Conference. Review National Urban Policy report recommendations as appropriate. URPG Review—deputies							■■■	X
VIII. Consultation with URPG and revision of National Urban Policy Report to accommodate language and other procedural concerns; finalize time tables for policy implementation and priorities. URPG—secretaries								■■■ O
IX. Delivery by Secretary Harris and URPG of final National Urban Policy Statement, 1978 to President Carter								O

Table 5.2
Work Plan Deadlines
August 1977 through March 15, 1978

URPG Task	Deadline	Product
Presentation of preliminary policy options along with new programs for which costs could be estimated	Sept. 22, 1977	See Appendix A: TOWARD A NATIONAL URBAN POLICY: CITIES AND PEOPLE IN DISTRESS #1
Presentation of new budget initiatives to OMB	Oct. 1, 1977	See Appendix B: Letter from Dennis Greene to URPG Deputies requesting Budget Review Procedures for URPG and other urban Initiatives
Submission of draft NUP to White House	Nov. 15, 1977	See Appendix C: URPG Draft #2
Development of language for President's State of Union Message	Dec. 15, 1977	See Appendix D: Memo for President from Harris and Eizenstat
Finalize preliminary draft of Urban Policy Statement with specific recommendations	Jan. 28, 1978	See Appendix E: Summary of Policies, 3rd Draft
Review Balanced Growth Conf. recommendations against NUP statement recommendations	Feb. 15, 1978	See Append F: Embry memo
Delivery by URPG of final National Urban Policy Statement, 1978, to President Carter	Mar. 15, 1978	In process

Notes

1. Most notable of these programs was Model Cities, which in 1967 began its planning phase with a $25 million earmark from the Secretary's Discretionary Fund (SDF). In 1977, the SDF supported the following programs by congressional mandate: New Communities; Native American Community Development (CD); CD in Guam, the Virgin Islands, and Puerto Rico; Disaster Relief; Areawide Organizations (Housing Deconcentration); Innovative Grants; and Technical Assistance Grants. The SDF appropriation level was $98.3 million in 1977.
2. The constraints of public office and the indiscriminate exposure of an administration appointment also dampened my enthusiasm, since as a very private person, I valued the order and seclusion of private life and the discretion that I was able to exercise over my social and professional calendar. Finally, the foreclosure of private consultation, which the deputy's job necessarily required, would affect my earning power for the duration of the appointment. My final decision to accept was influenced by the opportunity that I saw for affecting HUD policies, governing funding to urban planning organizations—a diminishing priority under the previous Republican administration—and governing work-study assistance, provided through HUD's 701 Metropolitan Planning Program to minority graduate students enrolled in planning and public administration degree programs.
3. Lynn Curtis to Secretary Harris, "The Politics and Procedures of URPG," unpublished document, July 1977, passim.
4. Yvonne Scruggs Perry to Robert C. Embry, Jr., "Transitional Considerations Involving URPG," unpublished document, August 7, 1977, passim.
5. Task forces on energy and environment as well as on federal grants policy were proposed, but never organized. The former will be discussed more fully later. The latter simply became an increasingly less independent function and the idea was incorporated in all task force agendas.
6. Perry, "Transitional Considerations Involving URPG," 2.
7. Perry, "Transitional Considerations Involving URPG," 4. The list included: Anthony Downs, Brookings; Herrington J. Bryce, Academy for Contemporary Problems (formerly, Research Director, Joint Center for Political Studies); Graham S. Finney, Philadelphia consultant; the late R. Joyce Whitley, city planner and Cleveland businesswoman; Thomas A. Reiner, University of Pennsylvania; Brian Berry, Harvard University; Morton J. Schussheim, Library of Congress, LRS; Norman Glickman, University of Pennsylvania.; John Kain, Harvard; William G. Grigsby, University of Pennsylvania; Ann Louise Strong, University of Pennsylvania; George Sternlieb, Rutgers University; Robert Green, Michigan State University; Reginald W. Griffith, Howard University; Thomas Muller, Urban Institute; Phillip Clay, MIT; Bennett Harrison, MIT; James L. Sundquist, Brookings; Grace Milgram, Library of Congress LRS; Lowdon Wingo and Roland Warren, Brandeis University; Donald Warren, University of Michigan;

Marshall Kaplan, Dallas/San Francisco consultant; David R.Godshalk, University of North Carolina; Norman and Susan Fainstein, Columbia and Rutgers Universities; Roger Starr, Columbia and Pratt Universities; Herbert Gans, University of Chicago; Carol D. and Ortiz Walton, University of California at Berkeley; and Antionnette McAllister, American Society of Planning Officials/consultant. This list is composed of more than 25 percent blacks and more than 20 percent women.

8. Perry, "Transitional Considerations Involving URPG," 5.
9. The "White House" means the President or any of his six or eight principal assistants, irreverently referred to as the "Georgia mafia" in informal circles or sometimes in the press.
10. "An Erosion of Aid to the Cities," *Business Week*, August 15, 1977, 36.
11. Guy Benveniste, "The Prince and the Pundit" in *The Politics of Expertise*, (Berkeley, CA: The Glendessary Press, 1972), 1–21, and also Herbert A. Simon, Donald W. Smithburg, and Victor A.Thompson, *Public Administration* (New York: Alfred A. Knopf, 1956), passim.
12. Hugh Heclo, *A Government of Strangers: Executive Politics in Washington* (Washington, DC: The Brookings Institution, 1977), 144.
13. Others on the consultant roster included: Charles Washington, George Washington University; Jerome Zeigler, NYU; George Paterson, Urban Institute; David Dayton, Technical Development Corporation; and Herbert Franklin, from a private Washington law firm.
14. For example, Marshall Kaplan and Bernard Frieden, *The Politics of Neglect: Urban Aid from Model Cities to Revenue Sharing* (Cambridge, Mass.: MIT Press, 1977); and Marshall Kaplan, *Urban Planning in the 1960s: A Design for Irrelevancy* (Cambridge: MIT Press, 1973).
15. His contract later was extended. Following President Carter's announcement of the final national urban policy in 1978, Kaplan was named a deputy assistant secretary in CPD, an appointment that he had coveted. During the first months of Carter's administration, Kaplan was rumored to be lobbying energetically but unsuccessfully to become assistant secretary (or deputy) of HUD's policy development and research, the position to which Shalala, in fact, was appointed by Carter.
16. See, for example, Franklin James, "Private Reinvestment in Older Housing and Older Neighborhoods: Recent Trends and Forces," mimeo, Urban Institute, June 1977.
17. Harold Wolman, an economist affiliated with the White House Conference on Balanced National Growth and Economic Development, and Astrid Merget, deputy to Donna Shalala and specialist in governmental administration.
18. Both the actual White House on Pennsylvania Avenue and the Old Executive Office Building (EOB), usually entered from 17th Street, are loosely referred to as the White House. This is partially because offices that normally would be in the real White House, were there enough room, often spill over into

available space in the elegantly marbled and vaulted-ceiling rooms of the next door neighbor, the Old EOB. Another likely reason that the occupants of the Old EOB refer to it loosely as the "White House," is because that is a more prestigious designation. One can, in fact, enter either the White House or the Old EOB from the main driveway, accessible from the Pennsylvania Avenue White House Gate, located roughly on a line up the center of that driveway. However, those who have been tempted to move freely from one building to the other by means of the driveway—especially those who do not work regularly in either building—can verify that the practice is frowned upon by the Secret Service and therefore, risky.

19. Personal notes taken during August 1977 meetings.
20. In November, Robert Duckworth replaced John McLean as Staff Director. This change occurred in part because of a new assignment for McLean, who was a career staff member; in part, because of tensions mentioned earlier between McLean, and some of the staff and consultants concerning who was responsible for actually writing the urban policy drafts.
21. I recruited Perlman during my first week as URPG Executive Director. She had done empirical research on grassroots and neighborhood organizations and had published her findings. I invited May, also of NASPAA, to join the new urban policy staff because of her research on fiscal and administrative problems of local governments. She also had produced several monographs in her area.
22. Heclo, *A Government of Strangers*, 144.
23. Heclo, *A Government of Strangers*, 13.
24. Draft Progress Report, Urban and Regional Policy Group, July/August 1977, 2.
25. The major interest groups were the National Association of Regional Councils (NARC), the National Governor's Association (NGA), the National Council of State Legislatures (NCSL), and the Council of State Community Affairs Agencies (COSCAA).
26. Carter speech to the Conference of Mayors, Milwaukee, Wisconsin, July 29, 1976: "I pledge to you an urban policy based on a new coalition—recognizing that the President, Governors, and Mayors represent the same urban constituents."
27. Lawrence O. Houstoun, Jr., "Organization of the URPG Task Force on States and Metropolitan Regions," unpubl. document, July 28, 1977, attachment, 2.
28. Robert C. Embry, Jr., speech to annual Conference, National Association of Regional Councils, San Antonio, TX, May 3, 1977.
29. Interview with Wyndham Clarke, July 1980.
30. The division within HUD is officially named Neighborhoods, Voluntary Associations and Consumer Protection.
31. Charles A. Krause, "Geno Baroni to Get HUD Housing Post," *The Washington Post*, March 2, 1977.
32. Andrea Sullivan, Ph.D. from University of Pennsylvania in sociology,

formerly of the Urban League and Janis Perlman, Ph.D., assistant professor at University of California at Berkeley and author of "Grassrooting the System."

33. URPG Staff, Neighborhoods Task Force Outline, unpublished document, July 1977, 5.
34. J. Perlman, "Enhancing Neighborhoods Capacity; A Preliminary Assessment," memorandum, URPG, September 1977, 2.
35. Marcy Kaptur, memorandum to Stu Eizenstat and Bert Carp, "Urban Policy Process: Draft I for Discussion."
36. Janice E. Perlman, memorandum to Yvonne S. Perry, "White House Neighborhood Meeting of URPG Policy Process," December 16, 1977, 1.
37. Janice Perlman, memorandum, "The Neighborhood Component of a National Urban Policy," September 1977, 1.
38. John W. McLean, memorandum to Robert C. Embry, Jr., and Yvonne S. Perry, "Timetable of Redlining Task Force," September 30, 1977, 1.
39. Task force archives, Red Lining Task Force, August 19, 1977.
40. Arnold Packer, memorandum to URPG, "Department of Labor Proposed Program—Urban and Regional Policy," September 1977.
41. Memorandum to Yvonne S. Perry, "Employment Policy for Urban Areas," October 17, 1977, 1.
42. Memorandum to Yvonne S. Perry and Bob C. Embry, October 5, 1977.
43. Chester Davenport, assistant secretary for policy, plans, and international affairs, memorandum to secretary and deputy secretary, "Priority-Status Report of the Urban and Regional Policy Group," August 31, 1977.
44. Davenport, memorandum, "Priority-Status Report,"2.
45. The Northeast Corridor referred to the high-speed main line of Amtrak which runs from Boston, MA, to Washington, DC, through the states of Rhode Island, Connecticut, New York, New Jersey, Pennsylvania, Delaware, and Maryland.
46. Chester Davenport, memorandum for Yvonne S. Perry, "DOT's Northeast Corridor Improvement Program" October 20, 1977, 1.
47. For a full discussion of this process, its genesis and application, see Norman J. Glickman, ed., *The Urban Impact of Federal Policies* (Baltimore: Johns Hopkins University Press, 1980). See also Mark J.Kasoff, "The Urban Impact of Federal Policies: A Preview of a New Rand Study," *Nation's Cities* (November 1977). Mentioned earlier as a significant consultant and advisor to the process, especially in association with PD&R staff, Glickman developed a series of "impact statements" that were proposed by the URPG directors, and especially Harris, Embry, and me, as a process for protecting cities. It ultimately was decided that every proposed public policy should be subjected to a litmus test, the Urban Impact Assessment, to see whether the policy might hurt cities if it were implemented and if so, how badly. Obviously, numerous objections were lodged against the notion of such a test, not the least of which was the confounding reality that one person's

passion is another person's poison, that is, if it helped cities, did that then mean that it would harm the suburbs? rural areas? the counties? Whose quality of life was preeminent?

48. Roger C. Altman, assistant secretary for domestic finance, memorandum for Public Finance Task Force, "Interim Work Requirements for Members of the Public Finance Task Force," August 22, 1977, 1.
49. Public Finance Task Force, memorandum to Urban and Regional Policy Group, "Review of Fiscal Impact of Federal Urban Policy Proposals on State and Local Governments," September 23, 1977, 2.
50. This program, also more formally called Anti-Recession Fiscal Assistance, is described in Title II of the Public Works Employment Act of 1976, as follows: "Efforts by the Federal Government to stimulate the economic recovery will be substantially enhanced by a program of emergency federal government assistance to State and local governments to help prevent those governments from taking budget-related actions which undermine the federal government's efforts to stimulate the economic recovery. "The aid was in the form of CETA, Public Works and Revenue Sharing Funds," triggered by an excessive level of unemployment.
51. Roger C. Altman, memorandum to URPG, "Evaluation of Counter-Cyclical Revenue Sharing: Recommendation for Modification of the Program," September 15, 1977, 1.
52. Robert C. Embry, draft memorandum to Office of Management and Budget, April 1978.
53. Dated March 1, 1978, no subject.
54. Ibid., p.1.
55. Aaron Wildavsky, "Jimmy Carter's Theory of Governing," *The Wilson Quarterly* 1 (2, Winter 1977).
56. See Frederick L. Bates and Lloyd Bacon, "The Community as a Social System," *Social Forces* 50 (March 1972). Bates and Bacon describe a mechanism for linking elemental groups in complex organizations, where both exchange and coordination take place through the medium of an "interstitial" group or device. In the exchange interstitial group one position is occupied by the same actor in a large number of cases (i.e., the President or his surrogate). Actors occupying the other position change according to the client or issue involved. The function of the coordination interstitial group is to manage relationships among two or more distinct groups or organizations with differing and potentially conflicting interests. In this type of interstitial group, each position is occupied by a person representing the interests of a different group or organization.
57. Heclo, *A Government of Strangers*, 7.
58. Timothy L. Jenkins, *Final Report: National Urban Policy Statement Equity Forum Feedback* (Washington, DC: The Match Institution, March 15, 1978), Part II, 22. Also see "Coalition of Northeast Interests, *Cities in the Middle: The Way Back to Prosperity, Trenton, New Jersey* (Washington, D.C.: HUD,

February 1977).

59. Editorial, "R.S.V.P.," *Nation's Cities.* 15 (10, October, 1977). Also, Lamphere was a member of the City Council from Seattle, Washington—hardly a novitiate in local government. The National League of Cities, moreover, had produced a comprehensive, 125-page document, *National Municipal Policy*, which was in print before the onset of URPG-2., having been adopted by NLC membership at its National Congress of Cities business session, in Denver, Colorado, on December 1, 1976.

Chapter Six

Producing a Draft

The genius of the United States is not best or most in its executives or legislatures, nor in its ambassadors or authors or colleges or churches or parlors, nor even in its newspapers or inventors...but always most in the common people.[1]

Walt Whitman

A number of forces acted on the policy writing process within the Urban and Regional Policy Group (URPG), which essentially occurred within HUD's offices. Continuous interaction with the task forces and their interagency and private-sector membership necessarily focused staff's attention on the issues of highest priority to these participants. Task force recommendations, where these were being formulated, and the deliberations reported through the coordinators were intended to provide the substance for the policy document.[2] Thus, task force influences were planned and legitimate. White House meetings and consultations with persons representing many different groups, including unions and public interest, civil rights, and women's organizations as well as with various groups of elected officials from all levels of government, generated numerous position papers and other forms of written recommendations for the policy as well.[3] Consultants under contract also were beginning to complete special assignments and parallel studies for URPG. One of these was a set of recommendations from Joyce Whitley for a black community needs study. Her review of existing and emerging papers from within the federal agencies, including HUD, strongly suggested such a study. Whitley stated:

> I think there is a need for the Department to examine and evaluate the impact of federal policies and administrative regulations on low/mod-

> erate income black communities more rigorously than I think has been undertaken to date.
> ...The thrust of such a study should not be to document the failure or success of given efforts to achieve measurable benefits ... or to assess federal program impact in gross terms... Rather the study should be designed to answer various specific questions such as: ...
>
> ...To what extent have community groups participating in the planning of their community improvement programs been able to achieve any of their community improvement goals and objectives; and to what extent do their priorities parallel federal priorities?[4]

All of these varied recommendations and products had to be taken into account. If they were not ultimately included in the policy draft, then there had to be evidence that they at least had been considered. Otherwise, this aspect of the transactive process would have been violated.

During the period of serious drafting and redrafting of the policy document, several senior-level policy makers within HUD also contributed their views through guidance memoranda circulated to the URPG staff. Among these were two internal papers drafted by Embry, a quasi-internal memorandum of "Off the Top of my Head Reactions to URPG Papers" from Shalala, and a discussion memorandum from me, all addressed below.

Finally, the local and national press, reflecting an increased interest in the emerging urban policy, stepped up its coverage of the policy development process. News stories and articles began to appear regularly, reporting on policy recommendations that were accidentally or, at times, intentionally leaked to them. Reporters commented on the wisdom of some of the approaches being followed, and at times, their interpretation was informed by "off the record" and "deep background" conversations that they had with staff or with consultant Marshall Kaplan. Usually their source was Kaplan, in as much as their biases constrained several of them from taking me seriously and, therefore, from seeking my views, even through I was executive director of the entire process.

Some published accounts were more accurate than others. Frequently, the errors lay in the unique perspective of the journalist who enjoyed a reputation of sorts as an urban expert in his own right, thus adding either authenticity or skepticism to the report.[5] Collectively, however, the press coverage developed into a formidable force to be countered or accommodated as the policy drafts emerged.

Assembling the Content and Setting the Tone

Most of the task forces' contributions were not in the form of policies. They submitted new programs, or refinements and adjustments to existing programs, so that a particular policy emphasis was reflected. This condition led to URPG staff's concern with cognitive dissonance in the process and to my concern with definitions:

> One of the problems which we are having in our effort to develop a National Urban Policy is the differentiation between policy and program.
>
> It plagues us less internally than in our relationships with other agencies. However, it also may be a constraint on our internal efforts to consolidate a number of disparate notions about what will make cities better places to live.... A policy is a normative statement. It should evoke an expected end state.... It suggests a desirable plateau of effort...toward which resources should be directed in the interest of stated goals.[6]

Bob Embry also felt the dilemma of the policy-versus-program tension. A particularly direct expression of his views included the suggestion that the policy draft cite the oath of the Athenian City State in its text,[7] and take a principled stand:

> Please make sure that the urban policy statement leads off with a position on the poor and black of our cities, and how the first aim of an urban policy should be to transform this group into a stable community with dependable and adequate income, social equality and racial mobility.[8]

The ultimate priority consensus about what the policy should be, supported by URPG staff leadership, grew out of the numerous meetings held with city proponents, regular citizens, and interest groups. These views were summarized as follows:

- Poor and minorities must be helped in a more targeted fashion. Benefits must be direct, not trickle down. The assistance must be economic first and foremost. Minorities must be aided as employees as well as employers.
- Imbalances faced by cities must be corrected. A national effort must be made to attract and hold jobs in cities, particularly those jobs accessible to the poor;

- Federal efforts in city areas must be rationalized and pro-urban strategies encouraged for all federal agencies;
- For the working population, disincentives to city living must be removed.
- There should be an increased emphasis on neighborhoods;
- There should be permanent and focused public employment for all those who cannot find jobs;
- Fiscal viability of city government must be restored;
- Those who want to find jobs in areas of higher employment must be helped to migrate; and
- The partnership role of state governments must be articulated and efforts made to encourage needed state urban initiatives.[9]

A joint URPG staff paper asserted that "this is a nation of cities. They are important to our society and should not be allowed to deteriorate. They form the core of our cultural and economic strength."[10]

After reading the task force papers, Donna Shalala reflected an approach with a different emphasis. She suggested ideas that "while one could not describe them as bold and visionary there are elements that point toward a policy":

> If I were President and had limited resources I would spend them on very specific, measurable activities. More important, I would recognize how complex previous plans have been and do some simple straightforward programs.
>
> The most central is the structural unemployment. ... Second...a whole series of visible physical changes. Third, we should do something about children. ... Fourth, the regional strategies might be too planning oriented—tax base sharing is more specific...Fifth, if we want to do straight fiscal relief we might just increase revenue sharing with a formula change. Finally, economic development—urban—the capital formation proposals [are] understated because they are high risk in the worst-off cities.[11]

Thus, the three major drafts of the urban policy prepared by URPG, including the final policy document announced by President Carter in March 1978, represented a struggle of reconciliation and compromise. Each draft was subjected to the scrutiny of various specialists and was shepherded through the review process by a group, many of whom themselves were not in agreement on how the policy finally should look and what it should be for whom. A document surviving such ambiguity and conflict was destined to be less than any single participant wanted.

Transactions with the Public

Mentioned earlier was the intense schedule of meetings and conferences with representatives of all types of public interest groups to get their views on what the policy should include and to gain their support for the emerging urban policy document. It is difficult to convey the importance attached to this series of meetings that occurred at the end of 1977 and early in 1978.

In the main, the meetings were held in the White House or next door in the Old Executive Office Building's Indian Treaty Room. One exception to this pattern was a series of equity forums. Organized by a wholly minority-owned consulting firm, the Match Institution,[12] these forums were purposely scheduled for locations other than Washington, DC. This was to provide an opportunity for participation in the urban policy development process by ordinary people, especially minorities and the poor, whose views, even if they lived in Washington, were not characteristically sought.

The White House meetings were dramatic, coveted, and effective. They served to emphasize that the urban policy process indeed was being President-driven—otherwise, why would he permit us all to meet in the White House? Whenever elected officials were present in the group, the President made an appearance, unless he was out of town. After I observed that Carter would always honor those occasions with a visit, one of the criteria for scheduling the meeting was the availability of the President to drop by if he felt so inclined so he rarely missed a meeting. He often did not appear when nonelected officials were meeting, although it seemed that this pattern was driven more by relative priorities, than by any particular desire to avoid meeting with private citizens.

When the President attended the meetings, which usually were held in the Roosevelt Room of the White House, he always made it a point to walk around the conference table and shake each hand. He also would make a few comments about the importance of having an "inclusive and fair" urban policy that was coherent and unbiased and did not add much to the budget deficit. In fact, after most of the interest group meetings had been held and the press had commented on the impressions of various interest group leaders as to whether or not the policy would be useful, a nervous Carter sent one of his familiar handwritten notes to Harris, Eizenstat, and Jim McIntyre of OMB: "[B]e sure that the urban policy principles are defined clearly. I do not want the interest groups writing the (urban policy) report."[13]

The best characterization of the dynamics of the interest group meetings in the White House was made by Secretary Harris, in a briefing memorandum that she wrote to presidential "enforcer" Hamilton Jordan:

> Consistent with the President's and my commitment to an open administration, the public has been directly and consistently involved in the development of the National Urban Policy since March 1977. The contacts have been with interest groups and representatives of virtually every sector of the population.[14]

A summary of the outreach and interface followed, including:

Corporate forums: Conducted in Washington, DC; Santa Barbara, California; and New York City, with participation by corporate presidents, board members, and corporate leadership of more than 300 businesses of all sizes (including Fortune 500) for day-long policy review and comment sessions.

Citizens forums: More than 2,000 private citizens met in ten cities across the country to review and comment on the national urban policy. The cities were Boston, New York, Philadelphia, Atlanta, Chicago, Dallas, Kansas City, Denver, San Francisco, and Seattle.

Labor forums: Leadership of organized labor met in all-day sessions in the White House with Stu Eizenstat and Secretary Harris to present their views and recommendations on the second draft of the national urban policy statement.

White House conferences: Secretary Harris and Stuart Eizenstat convened nine separate White House meetings with groups and organizational representatives. These groups were the National Governors' Association; the National Conference of Mayors; the National League of Cities; the National Association of State Legislatures; more than a dozen civil rights organizations;[15] the National Association of Counties; the National Neighborhood Association Members; the National Black Caucus of Local Elected Officials; and twenty leaders of labor organizations (primarily AFL-CIO and affiliates).

Equity forums: Described above, these involved 200 leaders "of sectors normally referred to as minorities," convened in Chicago, San Francisco, and Washington, DC. Attendees included women, the disabled, the elderly, ethnic and racial minorities, and the poor.

Academic Forums: Described more fully below, these consisted of more than fifty leading experts on urban policy from the academic community. These experts reviewed the initial drafts of the national urban policy document.

Drafting the Urban Policy

The first full draft of the urban policy document, dated October 29, 1977, was a "working staff draft" called the *National Urban Policy Statement: Toward Cities and People in Distress.* That draft was followed by a substantially revised draft issued a few weeks later, in mid-November, entitled, *Cities and People in Distress: National Urban Policy Discussion Draft.* Voluminous comments were received in writing about both documents, which were informally circulated, passed out, shared, and otherwise offered as trial balloons.

The difference between the two drafts was partially in substance, but largely in the color and tone of the language. The preface of the October draft opened with these paragraphs:

> America is an urban nation. Its greatness, its vitality, its sense of direction has depended and will continue to depend, to a large degree, on the health of its cities and the quality of life available to their residents.
>
> .....Although available, reams of statistics are not necessary to confirm the frequent statements of harried city officials concerning the "urban crisis." Neither are extended studies required to lend credence to the poignant declarations of many urban blacks and poor that something is basically wrong with their urban America.

The November draft focused more directly on the concerns of race and poverty. It also reflected efforts to accommodate strong opposition to the perceived URPG bias in the first draft, in favor of large Northeastern cities. The first two paragraphs of the second draft's preface read:

> America's cities, old and new, small and large, have provided opportunity and hope for generations of immigrants from foreign countries and their descendants, and for migrant Americans—white, black and

> Hispanic—all of whom sought to better their lives and their children's futures. But the hopes of today's city residents, and the ability of cities to fulfill them, face formidable obstacles.
>
> Far too many city residents, particularly black and other minority residents, are without jobs and live in poverty. They lack adequate housing, good services and the other amenities of American life as it is known to most.

While both drafts included fairly detailed discussions of the problems of urban distress—fiscal disparities, population and jobs exodus, inconsistency in federal urban policies and programs and the inadvertent effects on urban areas of non-urban federal programs—one dramatic difference existed between the two. The first draft offered dollar estimates associated with the recommendations. The second draft did not mention money at all.

The first draft introduced the concept of "policy clusters," which were derived from the seven major policy directions intended to guide the administration's urban actions and initiatives. These were:

- Provide immediate jobs, income, and services for the poor, blacks, and other minorities;
- Take steps toward long-term urban economic viability
- Reduce fiscal, social, and economic disparities
- Increase local capacity
- Develop and revitalize neighborhoods
- Revitalize cities' physical environments
- Improve the urban impact of federal activities

Within the lengthy discussion of each cluster were program recommendations and options by which the policy goal might be achieved. It was in this context that dollar estimates of the level of required spending were suggested for carrying out the programs. While there were several predictable points of disagreement expressed by the White House staff when they reviewed the first working staff draft, none of their comments compared with the consternation, mainly of Stu Eizenstat, that the draft contained dollar target levels.

The Working Press

The White House was afraid that the policy draft might raise expectations of new money for cities just at a time when federal agencies were being required to zero-base (and reduce) their budget requests to OMB.

Press coverage of the document further aggravated these fears. Newspaper headlines after reporters obtained copies of the working draft were not temperate:

> Carter Gets $7B Blueprint for the Cities[16]
> Carter's Task Force on Cities Urges $7.7 Billion Job Program for Poor[17]
>
> U.S. Report Urges Larger Commitment to Cities and Poor[18]
>
> Plan Favors Cities, Poor[19]

Interpretation of the 110-page document by the national press tended to ignore the policy issues and policy recommendations and to focus on the program options. Characteristic of much of the reporting was the *New York Times* article by Robert Reinhold:

> While the report deals with a broad array of "options," it lays its heaviest stress on creating jobs for the poor and promoting the economic development of center-city areas.
>
> ...Confirming earlier reports, the recommendations contain few suggestions for new social programs, despite intense lobbying on the part of black leaders and some mayors.[20]

The *Philadelphia Inquirer* echoed this sentiment, adding:

> The central question is how much money the administration is ultimately willing to spend on the nation's cities.
>
> The paper does not contain an overall dollar figure for its recommendations, which go beyond direct job programs. However, scattered throughout the report are a variety of suggestions which, added together, come to more than $12.5 billion.
>
> An administration official who asked not to be identified said he strongly doubted that Carter was willing to commit that much money.[21]

Most of the dollar figures quoted in the press either were wrong or, at best, only half true. It puzzled the URPG staff, in fact, that anyone could arrive at any intelligible total based on the estimates scattered throughout the draft. Even in the case of the so-called jobs programs, what was to one reader a jobs initiative conceivably to another reader was an economic development initiative. I suspect that, by exploiting various "deep background" sources, the reporters learned what I had been told by the President's staff much earlier in the process: that, regardless of the shape or direction of the final recommendations, OMB and the budget would allocate no more than $5 billion to $7 billion in new spending for the urban policy proposals. The press then pushed the policy recommendations to fit into this leaked dollar ceiling.

Academic Critics and Private-Sector Comments

Additional influence came from the academic community. Based on the belief among top URPG staff that useful concepts and perhaps newer approaches to the problem of urban distress could be contributed by experts from colleges and universities from across the country, an academic panel was assembled in Washington in November 1977.[22] The panel then submitted a series of individually or collaboratively prepared position papers, assessing the policy process and the direction that the drafting was taking.

There is something to be said for having a constituency on which to rely for friendly criticism. All of the academics were well known to me, my principal staff director Bob Duckworth, or my chief consultant Marshall Kaplan, from our own academic lives. They valued our transient efforts as public servants and, therefore, took seriously the task set before them of critiquing the evolving national urban policy drafts.

They were asked to provide comments that would make the policy document more viable and more likely to gain acceptance in the larger community. Their comments were dispassionate, yet leavened by a sensitivity to the consensual nature of the URPG undertaking. Their views, while by no means unified, reflected a reasonably narrow range of differences. They offered creditable guidance to the URPG staff, largely fine-tuning such concepts as the centralizing effects of technology; the need for a policy framework to better identify trends in certain conditions; and "qualitatively and quantitatively how the policy package would alter types of programs, levels of funding, infusion of funds into various types of municipalities...,"[23] among other concerns. However, their views often thrust against the direction of the interdepartmental task forces' priorities, further intensifying the search for consensus in the policy-drafting exercise.

They found the "draft Urban Policy Statement a sound and constructive proposal for redirecting federal actions that affect the cities. It is a marked improvement over earlier, more limited attempts to cope with urban problems."[24] They expressed concern over whether the administration was prepared to give necessary support to the proposals in the draft and to act on the high priority for urban issues that the report recommended.

The panel's comments concentrated on several themes: reviewing the commitment, the city in context, suggestions on programs, and miscellaneous. Indicating that "URPG's process, unlike similar Johnson and Kennedy processes, secured understanding and commitment at the expense of absolute coherence,"[25] they recommended that the document emphasize needed changes rather than weaknesses in existing programs. They supported the economic and cultural importance of cities, while arguing for coalition-building by relating the problems of cities to those of metropolitan areas and regions. One of their strongest arguments was to:

> ...urge a reaffirmation of the national commitment to eliminate the racial, economic and social disparities through a strong Presidential statement, an aggressive Federal effort, and the delivery of adequate resources.[26]

The panel supported the general multipolicy approach of the urban policy draft, favoring that over a "centerpiece" approach, such as the press had emphasized with its focus on the Urban Development Bank. A sharpening of the language concerning the role of the private sector also was encouraged.

General Public- and Private-Sector Responses

For its part, the general public and the private sectors responded mainly through institutions and interest groups. The U.S. League of Savings Associations and the National Urban Coalition—two organizations actually at polar positions on an ideological continuum—urged that a climate be created in cities to entice the middle class to return.[27] This view was consistent with Embry's concern, expressed to me in a memorandum:

> One issue which we do not come to grips with is whether we should encourage the middle class to move into the city, if so why, and how do we minimize the negative impact on the poor. This is the central issue today and we should face it.[28]

Other private-sector comments dealt with expanding the base of involvement in the ongoing URPG structure. The American Institute of Planners, the official professional organization of urban planners, and the National Housing Conference, "the oldest national organization concerned solely with provision of decent housing and good communities for all Americans," were the most specific and substantive in this regard. Both stressed the importance of expanding the scope of the policy document through "the development of a broad-based coalition of interested organizations to develop a consensus of support for (the Administration's) upcoming National Urban Policy."[29]

These, as well as other organizations mentioned earlier, convened committees of the boards of directors and of their general membership to review the policy drafts and submit comments to the administration or directly to URPG. While the specific editorial, philosophical, and programmatic recommendations are too varied and numerous to list, the predominant response was consistent with that expressed by the Charles F. Kettering Foundation:

> All of us who have waited for an American leadership response to the plight of cities take heart in the work of the Urban and Regional Policy Group to date and the prospect of the Nation's first intentionally developed national urban policy. It is even more encouraging to note the evidence that the Group both understands and proposes to deal with the negative consequences of existing piecemeal federal policies that have at least contributed to current urban problems. We are most impressed with the depth of this effort and eager to help in any way we can.[30]

No one felt, however, that the draft policy document even approached perfection. Anthony Downs, writing from his perspective within the Brookings Institution, felt that the document ignored the context of national trends and developments that created the problems of distressed cities, partly because it focused too narrowly on conditions within those cities. Further, Downs cited the draft policy for "ignoring basic tensions or inconsistencies among key social objectives related to urban problems, such as the trade-off between high-level housing production and high demand for housing in older neighborhoods."[31]

The main weaknesses of the document were intimated by the proposed titles of the first two drafts: "Cities and People in Distress." A *New York Times* editorial summarized the dilemma:

> The two problems, of cities and of people, obviously overlap. Everything is related to everything else. But the answers to one problem may, and sometimes must, diverge from the answers to the other.
>
> ...A responsible society cannot choose between the problems of cities and the problems of people. Both must be urgently addressed. But

> surely it cannot be wise to try to address both problems with the same machinery. Creating jobs in cities may help cities and, to some extent, their poor residents, but to stop there limits what might be done for those people. Yet that is what the emerging Administration policy tries to do; the lumping together of aims is indicated even by its title, "Toward Cities and People in Distress." And that seems to us a serious flaw in an otherwise praiseworthy enterprise.[32]

The *Times* was not alone in its view. Providing a critique for the American Institute of Planners, George Sternlieb wrote:

> The fable of Balaam's ass—the animal tethered midway between two piles of foodstuffs which starves to death since it cannot make up is mind which of them it should address first—has its equivalent in the political realities. Thus the issue of regeneration of city as place versus the care and feeding of its unfortunates creates only immobility. Illustrative of the phenomenon is the verbal support given to the back-to-the-city movement, but at the same time a pious warning that the attempt to attract middle-class households should not be done at the expense of the poor.[33]

The Issue of Distressed Cities

The issue of cities versus people sounded the clarion for both liberal and conservative arguments about what the policy statement ought to address. Contrary to the views expressed by both Sternlieb and the *Times*, as well as to the focus of the drafts on the neediest urban populations in the neediest urban places, was the argument that this narrow urban policy focus on the dynamics of distress was misdirected. While some critics felt that it was proper for a national urban policy statement to give highest priority to the problems of inner-city areas, they suggested that this focus should not have been construed as the entire national urban policy.

This public argument mirrored a dilemma that had been central to the internal policy debate within HUD and in the URPG deputies' group. Early in the process, the Department of the Treasury had created an analytic construct for assessing the "Fiscal Impact of the Economic Stimulus Package (ESP) of 48 Large Urban Governments."[34] This index—of distress or hardship—attempted to measure the interaction of a number of variables—per capita income, level of unemployment, level of federal payments as countercyclical relief and other population trends—to rank and array localities in relationship to each other. From this analysis, forty-eight cities were identified, and from this group, fifteen cities emerged as the most distressed communities in America.

The internal arguments were concerned with the political implications of including this list, or portions of this list, in the problem analysis section of the urban policy draft. There was a concern within the White House domestic policy staff and with Harris, Embry, and our regular HUD program managers as well, that the designation of a city as "most distressed" would mandate funding and resource allocation decisions that always favored these cities. This, in turn, would dampen support among all other constituencies for an urban policy that eliminated them from serious consideration for relief since they were "less" distressed than the cities on Treasury's list.[35]

Ultimately, while the policy document did specifically cite the twenty-five largest cities in rank order according to population, it labelled them "cities with both high unemployment rates and declining population." Although many of these cities, did, in fact, appear on every known list of cities with distressed factors, this exact language was not used in the policy report. Nonetheless, these indexes were always a part of our analytic context and were intentionally and unintentionally reflected in the name initially given the policy drafts: "Cities and People in Distress."[36] But the camouflage really fooled no one. Charging that the policy drafts omitted the vast majority of urban residents from its purview and left out many significant urban problem areas, the argument continued:

> Just to equate policies focused upon "cities in distress" with a "national urban policy" is...factually and politically unwise.... There are 123 "distressed cities" in the United States with a combined population of about 32.8 million. That equals 22 percent of the total of 148.3 million persons living in 266 metropolitan areas in 1970. Hence, a "national urban policy" that focuses entirely upon "distressed cities" leaves out 78 percent of the nation's metropolitan-area population—including over half the residents of all cities over 100,000 (as of 1970).[37]

Response from the Federal Establishment

The same arguments advanced by the private sector were echoed within federal bureaucratic agencies, augmented by a continued preoccupation with the urban policy drafts' implications for existing or proposed agency programs. Also, federal agencies whose responsibility areas had not been accommodated by any specific task force, introduced additional considerations from their particular perspectives. One such agency was HEW.

The HEW comments noted the absence from the drafts of any indication of how current HEW initiatives fit into the "policy directions" presented. "Specifically...welfare reform, hospital cost containment, and national health insurance should be briefly discussed. Further, current agency programs concentrated in urban areas should be acknowledged."[38] HEW also called for a more rigorous definition of terms, for less "journalism" and more scholarship by using hard data references to support assertions about urban demographic characteristics.

The Commerce Department's comments were both more extensive and had a greater negative impact than those of any other cabinet agency. Not only were these comments widely circulated and reported in the press, but they also were viewed as a continuation of the intense turfing battle that had been going on between HUD and Commerce. Thus, Commerce was perceived as even more critical than might have been intended. Moreover, Commerce's document was so lengthy that it undoubtedly required extensive internal review before it was issued to Secretary Harris in early December. Unfortunately, this timing coincided—intentionally or accidentally—with a White House budget review of great import for the URPG process, which appeared to give the Commerce paper added influence.

While complimenting HUD for "orchestrating the first national urban policy statement, a remarkable achievement in itself," with tact and dedication, Commerce complained that the draft contained no basis for setting priorities and lacked a rationale for providing special aid for distressed cities and their residents. Commerce found the most serious deficiency of the draft concerned the relative roles of the federal and state governments in addressing urban distress. The emphasis on a role for states was called inadequate and gave the impression that states were not a part of the problem facing cities, Commerce charged.

> In consequence, the draft report mistakenly implies that the federal government is the primary cause of urban problems (and, through the use of "we" throughout the text, that this Administration is at fault).

This led to the *Washington Post* headline that URPG views the federal government as both "cause" and "cure." Nothing could be more mistaken, politically or substantively.[39]

Having obtained a copy of the Commerce document from "a source close to urban groups," the *Washington Post* headlined on December 14, that "Carter Aides Untangle Urban Policy." The news article quoted Commerce's criticisms broadly, fitting that department's demurrers into the context of a reported meeting between the President and OMB.

In this meeting, the President was angry when presented with budget recommendations by OMB to fund various URPG-designed urban initiatives. However, these recommendations were not accompanied by any of the proposed urban policies, and indeed Carter had not seen any of the URPG's drafts to date. Further, OMB met with the President without Secretary Harris or any of the URPG staff present. Stuart Eizenstat, the most knowledgeable of any of the President's principal deputies and the President's point person on urban policy, also was absent. In a reflective chronology that Secretary Harris sent to Hamilton Jordan, Carter's closest adviser, the OMB scenario was described:

> In early December, the OMB had a meeting with the President to discuss budgetary and programmatic issues concerning URPG. Although neither I nor any member of the URPG staff participated in drafting options for the President or attended this meeting, it was widely reported in the press that the President indicated his displeasure with the options presented to him. Apparently, the President was distressed by the fact that he was asked by the OMB to make budgetary and programmatic decisions without first having been provided with a policy framework. It also was reported that the President indicated his belief that programs he was being asked to approve constituted little more than a "laundry list" of programs. The President at that time had not been presented with an options paper on urban policy. Nevertheless, the press interpreted the President's remarks at the meeting as a rejection, in part, of the URPG.[40]

None of the URPG principals believed that OMB had met with President Carter innocently and simply as one step in a sequence of fiscal year '79 budget preparations. Rather, it was suspected that this meeting was part of an offensive by OMB against HUD that had been foreshadowed by OMB's support of Commerce in the community development/economic development dispute.

Also feeding URPG staff's scepticism were the rumors that OMB had supported HEW Secretary Califano in his attempts to structure welfare reform on the ashes of billions of dollars worth of HUD's "cashed out" housing programs. These suspicions were substantiated by a lengthy OMB working paper that later came to light. OMB's paper was addressed to Eizenstat and Harris and stated in part:

> During the budget discussions of urban programs with the President, he indicated the need for the development of a clear conceptual underpinning which would support our urban policies. Your memorandum to the

> President ... began the process of clarifying key concepts and policies. The attached paper was developed by OMB staff to continue this process and to provide a possible approach to the development of a fuller conceptual framework.[41]

Aside from the deviousness of the OMB strategy, the temerity of any single agency to suggest that a unilaterally developed policy statement should supersede the policy derived from the efforts of thousands of public and private contributors, was insulting to URPG leadership. Yet, the influence of OMB on decisions about new urban initiatives' spending, and about a maintenance of effort in existing urban programs, was undeniable. A truce had to be negotiated, a task that OMB policy director Dennis Green and I undertook immediately.

The State of the Union Address and the Decision Memorandum

Task number four in the work plan[42] for URPG had specified December 10, 1977, as the product deadline for "Urban Policy language for the State of the Union Message, including policy options: Metropolitan regional strategies, revitalization of urban core, Urban Development Bank, and direct impact programs for urban poor, etc." URPG staff, therefore, simultaneously worked on the urban policy draft, incorporating suggested changes and ameliorating criticisms, while developing language for the State of the Union address.

The statutory date for the President's State of the Union speech is January 20 of each year. Therefore, URPG—more precisely Harris and Eizenstat—undertook to reverse the damage done to the URPG process by the Commerce/OMB offensive and to convince the President to take a strong pro-urban position in his speech. On January 9, they sent the President a decision memorandum that provided a summary of urban problems and recommended general principles and objectives for the administration's urban policy.

The memo's intent was two-fold. First, it offered an opportunity for the President to focus, for the first time substantively, on the issues and contentions about the "the urban problem" and optional solutions. Second, by demonstrating that URPG was more than the conduit for a "laundry list of programs," as Carter reportedly had called URPG's effort, we hoped that the memo might encourage Carter to offer directions that could be converted into a "crowbar" for leveraging recalcitrant departments. Already, the private sector was informally encouraging the President to forcefully support the urban policy in his speech, and URPG reinforced this effort.[43] The memo, therefore, did the following:

- Reviewed characteristics of the urban problem;
- Discussed the scope of the problem;
- Described underlying causes;
- Outlined a strategy for the policy statement's structure and the president's announcement;
- Listed the seven principles and five objectives that had emerged from the draft policies.

The President was given three multiple-choice decision options: Approve principles and objectives as a basis for the analysis of programs and new initiatives, disapprove of the principles, or meet with Secretary Harris to discuss his concerns. Carter chose the first of these and conveyed his choice to Harris and Eizenstat in a handwritten note on January 25. (See Figure 6.1.) The President sent another note several days later when he finally realized that the OMB policy paper had received public attention and was causing negative comments among the interest groups who had worked with URPG on the drafts. The second note implied that Harris, Eizenstat, and McIntyre were quarreling among themselves. They were directed to "get together and...resolve differences." Otherwise, they were to report to him. (See Figure 6.2).

None of the efforts succeeded in getting the President to take a definitive urban policy position in his State of the Union address. After URPG failed to solidify its position and to legitimize the urban policy through the medium of the State of the Union address, all URPG staff attention was concentrated on completing draft revisions and scheduling the formal announcement of the national urban policy. Although the final policy statement went through the normal rewriting and editing phases, the final document was completed, for all intents and purposes, by February.

Meanwhile, much of the assault from within the bureaucracy continued. Domestic agencies were diverted somewhat by the budget-making process, in which favored programs and existing funding commitments were at stake. But some of the public increasingly became cynical.

Writing in February 1978 in the *Washington Star*, Carl Rowan was less than optimistic. He characterized much of the difficulty of URPG as reflecting a bias against Secretary Harris, as a woman and as a black. Further, he intimated that Carter's views were being influenced by OMB and by HEW's Califano, who was exploiting the opportune tension between Harris and Commerce's Secretary Kreps over community and economic development to gain advantages for a commitment to people rather than to cities:

The notion of grabbing housing money so as not to have to ask for more money for welfare reform seems to have originated in the Office of Management and Budget (OMB). ...Califano and his advisers apparently decided ... that the "cash out" slogan wouldn't sell. So they importuned the president to "aid needy people, not needy cities."

But the politics of a "new urban policy" may weigh heavier with Jimmy Carter than the economic and social realities. Already he seems to have bought the argument that we must appease the suburbs rather than the heavily black cities if he is to get any program through Congress.

... If Jimmy Carter wants an urban policy that will change America for the better, he is going to have to take political risks, alienate a lot of racists, take sides in jungle warfare within his cabinet—and even spend some money.[44]

Figure 6.1
Presidential Memorandum

THE WHITE HOUSE
WASHINGTON

1-25-78

To Pat Harris
Stu Eizenstat

Proceed on urban policy as indicated on memo, but

a) include all cities

b) analyze existing programs first

c) encompass federal state, local gov'ts, + private & neighborhood groups + volunteers.

I would like to place a major emphasis on c) & try to do it in an inspirational & exciting way if possible.

My whole family will help.

Jimmy

January 25, 1978

Figure 6.2
Presidential Memorandum

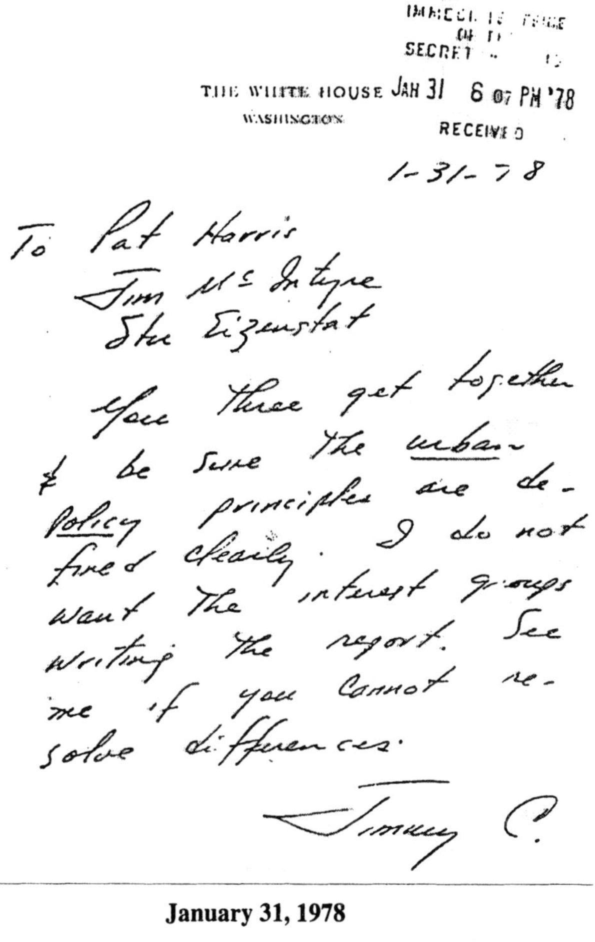

IMMED[illegible] OF[illegible]
SECRET[illegible]

THE WHITE HOUSE JAN 31 6 07 PM '78
WASHINGTON RECEIVED

1-31-78

To Pat Harris
Jim McIntyre
Stu Eizenstat

You three get together & be sure the urban policy principles are defined clearly. I do not want the interest groups writing the report. See me if you cannot resolve differences.

Jimmy C.

January 31, 1978

Notes

1. Walt Whitman, *Leaves of Grass.*
2. URPG Staff, "Outline of November Draft—Urban Policy Report," October 6, 1977, 1, states: "Theme: Cities and People in Distress."
3. Among the more than one hundred contributors were: Timothy Jenkins, Chairman, The Match Institution, "National Urban Policy Statement," February 28, 1978; Dr. John M. DeGrove, "The Impact of Federal Grants-in-Aid on the South and its Cities," The Southern Growth Policies Board, September 1977; Gage B. A. Haskins, "The Impact of International Trade and Investment: Policy on Employment in the United States," November 1977; Seymour J. Mandelbaum, "Urban Pasts and Urban Policies," University of Pennsylvania, January 1978; The National Urban Coalition, "National Urban Policy Paper," March 1978; Dr. Conrad Weiler, "Urban Reinvestment and the Displacement of Low and Moderate Income People: The Emergence of an Issue," Temple University, November 1977; Morton J. Schussheim, "The Housing Outlook," Congressional Reference Service, Library of Congress, September 1977 (with a note to Yvonne Perry, which read: "Where's that urban policy?"); Anthony Downs, "Creating a National Urban Policy," Brookings Institution, paper transmitted Fall 1977; Herrington J. Bryce, "Priorities in the Allocation of Federal Funds to Aid the Cities," Joint Center for Political Studies, September 1976, transmitted for URPG consideration September 1977; Benjamin Chinitz, "Urban Economic Development: The Federal Role," SUNY Binghamton, New York, October 1977; Robert L. Lineberry, "Public Services and Economic Development," Northwestern University, September 1977; and T.D. Allman, "America is an Urban Nation," report outline, Office of Urban Research, University of California at Berkeley, September 1977. These contributions were *in addition* to the ongoing submissions by the official consultants to the URPG Executive Director's office and to the scholarly works referred to and discussed in Chapter Three, above.
4. Memorandum to Yvonne Perry, August 26, 1977, 1, 4, 5.
5. I recall no women reporters regularly covering the urban policy process, although Meg Greenfield commented occasionally. Neal Pierce, John Herbers, Robert Reinhold, and David Broder were the principal chroniclers of URPG's proposals.
6. Yvonne S. Perry, internal memorandum to URPG Staff, November 1977, 2.
7. Athenian City State Oath:
   "We will ever strive for the ideals and sacred things of the city, both alone and with many: we will increasingly seek to quicken the sense of public duty; we will revere and obey the city's laws; we will transmit this city, not only not less, but greater, better, and more beautiful than it was transmitted to us."
8. Robert C. Embry, Jr., memorandum to Yvonne Perry, September 1977.
9. Embry, memorandum to Perry.

10. Embry, Perry, and several staff, "Some Assumptions Underlying a National Urban Policy," draft collaborative paper, September 15, 1977.
11. Memorandum to Embry, "Off The Top of My Head Reactions to URPG Papers," October 26, 1977.
12. Timothy Jenkins, an African American attorney, was the president and founder of the Match Institute and had the distinction of being an active Republican who was a welcome participant among the team of URPG consultants and URPG leadership, in the Democratic Carter Administration.
13. Personal Memo, dated January 31, 1978, and signed "Jimmy C."
14. Memorandum, "Chronology of National Urban Policy Development," with 10 appendices, March 2, 1978.
15. The attendance list of the civil rights group was a veritable Who's Who of activist leadership: Clarence Mitchell (Chair), Marvin Caplan, and Arnold Aronson for the Leadership Conference on Civil Rights; William Taylor, Center for National Policy Review; M. Carl Holman, President, Walter N. Rothschild, Jr., Sarah S. Austin, for the National Urban Coalition; Mario Anglada, Aspira of America, Inc.; Dr. Bernard Watson, Temple University Vice-President; Eddie N. Williams, Joint Center for Political Studies; Councilman Jerry Moore of Washington, DC; Leon Finney, TWO, Chicago; Samuel Jackson, Esq. Washington, DC; Vernon Jordan, Ron Brown, Maudine Cooper, Robert Hill, William Hasking, and Tom Gale, National Urban League; Rev Joseph E. Lowery, NAACP; and Berkeley Burrell, National Business League.
16. *New York Daily News*, November 9, 1977.
17. *Philadelphia Inquirer*, November 9, 1977.
18. *New York Times*, November 5, 1977.
19. *Atlanta Constitution*, November 7, 1977.
20. *New York Times*, November 5, 1977.
21. *Philadelphia Inquirer*, November 9, 1977.
22. Members of the Academic Panel were the late William L.C. Wheaton, then Professor of City Planning, University of California at Berkeley; Robert L. Green, Dean of the College of Urban Development, Michigan State University; William Grigsby, Chairperson of City and Regional Planning, University of Pennsylvania; Herrington J. Bryce, Vice President, Academy for Contemporary Problems, Washington, DC, and Columbus, Ohio; Bernard Frieden, Professor of Urban Studies and Planning, Massachusetts Institute of Technology; Harvey S. Perloff, Dean, School of Architecture and Urban Planning, University of California at Los Angeles; Edward E. McClure, Associate Dean for Planning, School of Architecture, University of Texas at Austin; Arthur Naparstek, Director, Washington Public Administration Center of the University of Southern California. Also, Robert C. Wood, President, University of Massachusetts; Paul N. Ylvisaker, Dean, Graduate School of Education, Harvard University; James L. Sundquist, Director,

Governmental Studies, Brookings Institution; Thomas A. Reiner, Professor, Department of Regional Science, University of Pennsylvania; R. Joyce Whitley, Whitley/Whitley Architects and Planners, Shaker Heights, Ohio; and Paul Davidoff, Executive Director, Suburban Action Institute in New York City.

23. William Grigsby, University of Pennsylvania, Department of City and Regional Planning, letter to "Yvonne and Marshall (Kaplan), November 29, 1977, 1.
24. Summary of academic panel's deliberations was prepared by Bernard Frieden, "Report of Review Panel on Draft URPG Policy Statement," memorandum to Robert C. Embry, December 6, 1977.
25. Frieden, "Report of Review Panel," 2.
26. Frieden, "Report of Review Panel," 1.
27. Donald Krumm (a Task Force Coordinator), "Interest Group Proposals for National Urban Policy," memorandum to all URPG staff, December 1, 1977, 8.
28. Memorandum to Yvonne Perry, dated November 7, 1977, 1.
29. Carl A. S. Coan, Legislative Counsel, National Housing Council, Inc., to Orin Kramer, White House Domestic Council, letter, January 6, 1978.
30. Robert G. Chollar, Chairman of the Board and President, Charles F. Kettering Foundation, to the Honorable Patricia Roberts Harris, letter, November 28, 1977.
31. Anthony Downs, memorandum to Robert Embry, December 4, 1977, 2.
32. Editorial page, November 21, 1977
33. "Sailing Directions for Urban America: Beating, Reaching and Running," *Journal of the American Institute of Planners* 44 (3, July 1978):355.
34. U.S. Department of the Treasury, Office of State and Local Finance, January 23, 1978. This was the sanitized final report from Treasury's study. URPG staff had access to a series of working papers and memoranda in which the actual rankings and evidence of the analysis were presented.
35. The cities on the Department of Treasury's list of fifteen cities were, in rank order of severity of distress: New York City; Newark; Los Angeles; Buffalo, New York; Cleveland; Long Beach and Oakland, California; Chicago; Detroit; Boston; Toledo; Minneapolis; Seattle; and St. Louis and Kansas City, Missouri. New York and Newark were numbers 1 and 2 on three of the six "distress" lists.
36. For a full discussion of a refined much expanded analysis, see R. P. Nathan and P. R. Dommel, "The Cities" in *Setting National Priorities: The 1978 Budget,* J. Pechman, ed., (Washington, DC: The Brookings Institution, 1977), 283–316.
37. Downs, memorandum, 3.
38. Hale Champion, Deputy Secretary, HEW, to Embry, memorandum, November 17, 1977.
39. Sidney Harman, Under Secretary of Commerce, "Comments and

Recommendations On 'Cities and People in Distress''," memorandum, December 2, 1977, 2.

40. Patricia Roberts Harris to Hamilton Jordan, Assistant to the President, "Chronology of National Urban Policy Development," memorandum, March 8, 1978, 4.
41. James T. McIntyre, Jr., to Patricia Roberts Harris and Stu Eizenstat, "Concepts to Guide Our Urban Policy," memorandum, received January 10, 1978, 1.
42. See Figure 5.1.
43. Carl A.S. Coan, National Housing Conference, wrote to Orin Kramer Associate Director of the White House Domestic Council: "...we urge that the President's State of the Union message to Congress indicate his intention to deal with the Nation's urban problems in a separate message in March. ...We also recommend that the President indicate in the State of the Union message, as well as in his Fiscal Year 1979 Budget Message that he intends to submit a supplemental budget request in March in conjunction with his urban policy proposals...." Others also urging State of the Union mention include Dr. Robert C. Weaver, first Secretary of HUD, then Professor Emeritus at Hunter College, New York; and the National Housing Conference. (See Archival papers, 1976–1977.)
44. *Washington Star*, Wednesday, February 8, 1978, editorial page. Rowan also challenged Carter to take seriously his pledge that White House staff would not be "permitted to push his cabinet officers around," a pledge made three days after his inauguration:

> There will never be an instance while I am President when the members of the White House staff dominate or act in a superior position to the members of our Cabinet.

Chapter Seven

Selling the National Urban Policy to the President and to the Public

We will ever strive for the ideals and sacred things of the city, both alone and with many: We will increasingly seek to quicken the sense of public duty; We will revere and obey the city's laws; We will transmit this city, not only not less, but greater, better, and more beautiful than it was transmitted to us.

Code of the Athenian City State

As the national urban policy announcement day approached, different types of battles raged within the federal bureaucracy. There were contests between agencies and departments for hegemony over the dollars that such a policy might generate, or defensively, over maintenance or acquisition of program-operating authority. Within the URPG policy staff, the strife was about which language would prevail in describing and rationalizing the federal government's commitment to cities.

The former battle—between the federal departments and some of their constituents—was the ground upon which consensus was finally forged, between January and early March, and was articulated on March 27, 1978, when the President made his announcement. Consensus emerged from the analysis of base programs, from the acceptance of the concept of urban impacts and the refinement of its subtheme of "targeting," and from resolution of the role of the states in solving urban problems and, thus, of their position and prominence in the final urban policy statement.

Clearly, damage was caused by OMB's "poorly timed and ill-advised decision to present proposed new programs to the President, independent of their policy context."[1] However, in response to Harris' and Eizenstat's January 9 policy decision memorandum, the President directed URPG to:

> Proceed on the urban policy as indicated on memo, but
> a) include all cities,
> b) analyze existing programs first
> c) encompass federal, state local govts, + private & neighborhood groups +volunteers.
>
> I would like to place a major emphasis on (c) & try to do it in an inspirational & exciting way if possible.
> My whole family will help.[2]

These instructions broadened the focus and the scope of the urban policy process within URPG and began forcing the policy itself into a more familiar, traditional mold. In effect, URPG was instructed to move away from sharp targeting ("include all cities"), to work within a more bounded reality ("analyze existing programs first"), and to reach consensus with *all* stakeholders ("place major emphasis on (c) & try to do it in an inspirational and exciting way").

HUD also took seriously the President's offer of help from his family. When Mrs. Carter paid an orchestrated "surprise" visit to HUD, Secretary Harris took full advantage of the opportunity to plug the national urban policy.

Addressing Black Concerns

Additionally, the priorities that the President identified in late January had to be reconciled with the mandate that he issued in mid-February, directing Harris and Eizenstat to:

> Be sure to get written suggestions re urban policy from black leaders and other groups so as to derive good ideas and to minimize the inevitable criticisms later on.[3] (See Figure 7.1.)

In fact, black leaders already had provide ample evidence of their priorities, in the White House meetings with the President,[4] as well as through their written submissions into the URPG process. Typical of most of these comments and documents was the testimony during that period by the Joint Center for Political Studies before Congress. Entitled "Priorities in the Allocation of Federal Funds to Aid the Cities," the Joint Center's testimony noted that targeting resources and remedies to central cities and federal compensation to cities, through policies and oversight, for the disproportionate control of suburban and regional bodies, offered the best solutions to the problems of distressed urban areas and their black populations. Evidence from extensive research showed that:

> We cannot escape the link between the quality of our cities and the state of the black population.... Policies which fail to address the conditions of blacks will also fail to address the condition of many of our cities.
>
> Federal spending programs must take into account the limitations imposed upon city governments (by an)...intricate web of intergovernmental connections. (T)his web places a constraint on the initiatives of cities to help themselves...and in the hands of regional bodies with different racial compositions and pressures.[5]

Later in his decision process, the President was to reject a regional approach to urban remedies. He already had softened the concept of targeting considerably. These choices were trade-offs with influential suburban and "sun-belt" areas, which wanted both to benefit from and not to be penalized by the national urban policy.

Analysis of Existing Programs or "Base Evaluation"

URPG immediately undertook the evaluation of existing programs as the President had instructed. An early March memorandum reported the outcome of this analysis and identified three purposes for the exercise. The evaluation summarized the growth and existing level of federal aid available to states and cities, reviewed the performance of key urban aid programs, and recommended ways to increase program effectiveness in light of "statutory objectives and emerging Administration urban policies."

The study was made possible by the submission to URPG staff of program assessments by each major department. The evaluation report traced the historical growth of the federal inventory according to dollar volume and overall impact. It also presented a summary analysis of key urban aid programs, by selected policy area. Finally, it recommended improvements to assure that the program would meet statutory mandates and urban policy objectives. URPG selected approximately forty programs from those submitted by the agencies for intense analysis. These programs provided almost 80 percent of all funds going to cities and were thought to have strategic impact on the localities. At the conclusion of the analysis, a summary document, "Outline of Action Required to Implement Base Recommendations"(Appendix B) was prepared and transmitted to Stu Eizenstat. The actions recommended were largely administrative, with some joint administrative/legislative initiatives and a few purely legislative initiatives.

The base evaluation served two purposes. It responded to the direct order from the President that such information be assembled, although the

President was not clear about how it would be used. Secondly, the outcomes of the evaluation found their way into the final national urban policy. The very first of the ten policies fed directly off the base study and the President's directive:

> The Federal Government will administer existing and new programs in a coordinated, efficient and fair manner. Before approval, all key federal activities will be evaluated to make sure they are as consistent as possible with the Administration's urban policy.

The final version of Policy No. 8 also reflected the awareness of overlapping federal programs that the base study had revealed. This policy referred to the federal government's efforts "to strengthen the long term fiscal condition of older central cities and suburbs *and reform the current chaotic system of intergovernmental aids.*" (Emphasis added.)

The Base Evaluation outcomes also appeared throughout the policy's implementation strategies. For example, in Policy No. 3, concerning local planning: "Consolidate all Federal planning assistance aids to provide flexible tailored aid." And the outcomes frequently triggered changes or adjustments that would be needed in order to achieve a given policy objective. The application of base analysis outcomes was important. On one hand, the base evaluation was circulated widely throughout the government and in the White House. Thus, departments with vested interests in the status quo had greater difficulty defending their positions, given the findings from the evaluations. On the other hand, the importance of existing programs was reinforced by the investment of time and energy in the Base Evaluation, although in few instances did the evaluations call for increased funding for existing programs. Equally rare were suggestions that programs be terminated. But then neither approach would have been well received within the transactive/exchange environment of the urban policy development process.

As it was, the final draft of the policy was constantly being criticized for being too confrontational. A memorandum from the assistant to the Secretary of Commerce pointed this out:

> The February...draft presents a more thoughtful and balanced statement than earlier versions of the importance of cities and the factors which have led to their growth and decline. You and your staff are to be commended for the progress made in articulating the nature and causes of the urban problem. Moreover, the need to shift to a "conservation ethic" which recognizes that our cities

> are "valuable national resources"...deserves major public attention.
>
> (However) I have already indicated to you a few examples of language in the report which tend to promote a specific program or to emphasize a particular approach at the expense of another, e.g., community development vs. economic development. These should be eliminated from the draft.[6]

This memo was comparatively complimentary to URPG, HUD, and the policy draft. Therefore, consistent with the interdepartmental tensions about leaks to the press of internal documents, there was a note to me, attached to the memo (Figure 7.2), asking: "Do you want to handle the leak this time?"

Selling the National Urban Policy to the President

By the end of February, decisions had been made with regard to the analysis of the urban problem, the principles and objectives already approved by the President, the outcome of the base evaluation, and the formulation of the actual policies. A formal briefing of the President in the Cabinet Room of the White House was scheduled for March 15, 1978. URPG staff prepared flip chart exhibits, and document-size handout replicas of the flip charts. The briefing was conducted by Secretary Harris and Stu Eizenstat, although all federal staff who had been directly instrumental in developing the policy were present, down to the level of HUD's urban policy office director, as well as some of the task force coordinators. Bob Embry backed up the secretary for the briefing. I was to be staff support to Embry if he needed it during the presentation. Some of the consultants we used heavily also were present.[7]

The briefing included a discussion of URPG's response to the various directives that Carter had sent through the personal memos to Harris and Eizenstat. With regard to the Base Evaluation, URPG had reduced the reams of paper generated by the analysis of existing programs to a few graphic and dramatic charts. The best of these, an "Analysis of Base—Past and Present Urban Performance of Key Federal Programs," is Figure 7.3.

Using a matrix of key programs in the rows and critical policy measures in the columns, thirteen massive federal program initiatives were measured according to four impact categories: Positive, negative, mixed, or irrelevant. The policy measures in the columns were those favored by the URPG staff, although a few other deputies and their agencies also supported these policy measures, for example Ernest Green at Labor, Chester Davenport at Transportation, Dennis Green at OMB, and Lester Solomon of EPA.

The "Urban Program Scoreboard" (Figure 7.4) translated the major innovative urban programs of four federal agencies into a similar matrix: The Community Services Agency (CSA), which funded community action and neighborhood efforts; Job Training under the Department of Labor; Title XX under Health, Education and Welfare; and HUD's Urban Development Action Grants (UDAG). The President felt informed by these charts, but ultimately expressed concern that they created controversy by singling out certain agencies for criticism through the four impact categories used. However, he felt the URPG participants had "done a good job at self-analysis."[8]

At the briefing, the full language of the policies was not presented to President Carter. Rather, cryptic categories were outlined along with bullets indicating the strategies suggested. There was a very blunt summary of the problem, and a set of policy responses that were the remedies being proposed to implement the policy. The President was concerned about the order in which the policies appeared. He thought that some should be moved up in the hierarchy. Even though there had been an attempt to have the policies appear to be of equal importance and not in rank-order, our presentation of "policies numbers 1 through 10" automatically created an appearance of priority.[9]

The President's briefing charts showed the abbreviated policies in the following order:

1) Federal Coordination/Urban Impact
2) Federal/State Partnership
3) Strengthen Local Government Capacity
4) Revitalize Neighborhoods
5) Promote City Economic Health
6) Help Cities' Fiscal Condition
7) Make Cities Attractive Places to Live and Work
8) Help Reduce Sprawl
9) Reduce Racism and Discrimination
10) Expand Job Opportunities for Urban Poor, Minorities, and Women

The President's view was that since the policies were going to be viewed by the public and press in terms of priorities, they should reflect the priorities that he supported. Carter was much more of a political strategist than he has been given credit for by those who are casual and superficial observers. He was keenly aware of the relationship between such efforts as the national urban policy process and his 1979 Presidential re-election aspirations. The final order and content of the ten national urban policies, as they were adjusted after their presentation to the President, was as follows:[10]

1) The federal government will administer existing and new programs in a coordinated, efficient, and fair manner. Before approval, all key federal activities will be evaluated to make sure they are as consistent as possible with the administration's urban policy.
2) The federal government will develop a firm partnership with state governments to solve urban problems. Federal incentives will be provided for states to implement comprehensive urban policy and strategies.
3) The federal government will encourage and support efforts to improve local planning and management capacity. Federal programs will support local efforts to develop economic, social service, and community development policies and strategies. Local government will play a major role in coordinating the use of federal funds within borders.
4) The federal government will encourage and support the efforts of neighborhood groups in revitalizing their communities.
5) The federal government will carry out strong measures to eliminate discrimination and racism from all aspects of urban life.
6) The federal government will help expand business and job opportunities for the urban poor and minority men and women. Federal programs will seek ways to increase the mobility of the growing number of men and women trapped in poverty or dead-end jobs.
7) The federal government will offer strong incentives for businesses and industry to remain, expand, or locate in economically troubled central cities. To the extent possible, disincentives for locating in troubled central cities will be ended.
8) The federal government will help troubled central cities address their critical short-term fiscal problems. The federal government, working with states and local government, will make

efforts to strengthen the long-term fiscal condition of cities and reform the current chaotic system of intergovernmental aids.

9) The federal government will help make troubled central cities attractive places to live and work. It will help improve the range and quality of decent social services available to their residents. Federal efforts will help make decent housing available to the poor and remove barriers to their choice of neighborhoods. Federal programs will encourage the middle class to remain in or return to central cities.
10) The federal government will help cities develop efficient land settlement patterns. Federal laws and programs will be amended to discourage sprawl and encourage energy efficient and environmentally sound settlement patterns in urban areas.

Some of the President's comments regarding his overall approach to the urban policy were revealing:

> We need to target both to person and to place.... The questions remains regarding the Urban Development Bank: (should it be) rural *and* urban and where is the bank to be located?
>
> Countercyclical [fiscal assistance should] be available only on a local basis, not national. [Also], take the states out of the formula.
>
> [With regard to] minority procurement, we already have increased this and I will propose to double the government set-aside again. [This is a] very exciting way to increase opportunities.
>
> [I] want programs to be seen as programs for people who live in cities and who want to return to cities....the middle income (people).
>
> [This is] the first experience in developing a national urban policy. [We] recruited private citizens and set out goals.... During my campaign, I made several definitive statements in 100-plus city halls.... Thus, I have a history of concern about cities.
>
> ...There are two purposes which the policy document should serve. ...[First] the presentation [must be in] an accurate and clear form, about what we have done.
>
> Second, the publication should be in reference book form, by sections [with] problems, recommendations of actions which different groups

can take. Not really as simple as a comic book, but almost that simple. How we present to the public will be important.

There should be a clear assignment of responsibilities. Maybe some nongovernmental entities should take some roles.
I will set aside an hour to look at a page which will set out the problem, what already has been done, what difference this has made, and so forth.... A lot that we have done has not reached the consciousness of the public. [We need to let the] press, blacks, older people, ghetto [residents] know what are we spending additionally [and] what doesn't need spending.

Success [of the policy] will depend on format used—from the public presentations to the hand book to be used by reporters.... We must put time in on this.[11]

The Final Decision Memorandum

Much of the adjustment to include all cities, as the President wanted, hinged upon changes in the language. The first such change was made to the title of the national urban policy report. After much deliberation, largely within Embry's and my office, with multiple unsolicited suggestions from across the country, it was decided to suggest to the President a renamed document: *The President's Urban and Regional Policy Group Report: A New Partnership to Conserve America's Communities: A National Urban Policy.* So it was out with "distress," whether cities, people, or both, and in with communities and neighborhoods.

Following the final decision cycle, involving President Carter, Stu Eizenstat, and White House political guru Jack Watson, suburbs were released from their symbiotic and semantic linkage of earlier drafts. For example, the word *suburbs* was eliminated from "economically troubled cities *and older suburbs,*" the original language in Policy No. 7; and "to strengthen the long term fiscal condition of older central cities *and suburbs,*" the original language in Policy No. 8.

This title suggestion and a series of decision options were presented to the President in a second decision memorandum on urban policy from Harris, McIntyre, and Eizenstat on Friday, March 17, 1978. Transmitting a huge document of more than two hundred pages, the President's urban policy principals indicated:

This memorandum outlines the key elements of an urban policy. It suggests broad policy principles, improvements in existing programs and new programs and initiatives. This memorandum is the result of months of intensive work by all of the agencies involved in the Urban and Regional Policy Group. If...these (... recommendations are approved, they) will be the basis for your urban policy message later this month."[12]

The decision memo covered the following issues:

- A strategy for the urban policy message
- A brief description of the problems of urban areas
- A concise statement of the principles that Carter agreed should guide the urban policy
- A description and analysis of the existing federal programs
- A listing and explanation of the improvements in existing programs that were being made or could be made
- A discussion of the most viable new initiatives that the departments had proposed

Additionally, the President was advised:

> The urban policy message also should contain one central theme which characterizes the Administration's efforts. Johnson, of course, had the "Great Society" and Nixon, the "New Federalism." We would like to suggest that the most appropriate theme for your policy would be "A New Partnership to Conserve America's Communities." This theme dramatizes the real commitments of the Administration to urban conservation, but also recognizes that any successful policy must be a partnership—involving all levels of government, the private sector and neighborhood and voluntary groups. It is the same theme which you stressed in your urban policy speeches during the campaign.[13]

The President Alone Decides Alone

No discussion of the final days of policy development and of the President's choices for the national urban policy's content is complete without a reflection on how the final decisions actually were made. The story is an inside one, perhaps more intriguing than informing.

On March 17, the date when the Harris/McIntyre/Eizenstat memo was officially delivered to President Carter, we all had kept close enough track of the President's schedule to know that he was going to spend the weekend at Camp David. Given the girth and volume of the decision memo, Carter would have to devote considerable time to reading, choosing among the options, and making comments as he wished.

In late afternoon, I received a telephone call from Stu Eizenstat on some urban policy–related matter. In the course of our conversation, I asked whether the memo had been given to the President yet, and when he and the President would be leaving for Camp David. Stu informed me that the President already had the memo and had also already left for Camp David. I then asked when Stu would be leaving to join the President, fully expecting that such a complicated set of decision options certainly should need some senior, urban-literate staff to offer additional clarification, and otherwise to brief the President as he proceeded.

Eizenstat informed me that he would not be going to Camp David and that, as far as he knew, no urban policy expert was going to be with the President while he made his choices. In short, the President would consider more than two hundred situations in solitude, many with multiple pages of pro and con analysis, and would then decide to approve or disapprove various options; to accept or reject suggested funding levels or specify alternative funding levels; to accept recommended agencies to carry out recommended federal activities; to reject these recommendations or choose some other agency; to continue or discontinue certain existing public programs or to amend these; and so forth in solitude throughout the length of the memorandum. I was stunned and filled with foreboding. Eizenstat seemed resigned.

Carter treated the decision instrument with an efficiency characteristic of his style. Here and there words were circled in the pro or con columns, which had been arranged in a side-by-side format so that there was some semblance of comparability. There were checks for approval and disapproval, some revisions of funding levels, but relatively few elaborative comments.

In the transmittal memorandum, the President was asked to decide on the strategy and theme of his upcoming urban policy. He approved of the five suggested elements for his national urban policy message, through which he would:

1) Outline a comprehensive urban policy by defining broad policy principles and objectives. While the new initiatives should respond to selected priorities, it is essential that the policy itself is perceived as fulfilling your campaign commitment to a "comprehensive urban policy."
2) Dramatize the long-term commitment that your administration will make to addressing urban problems. It is important that the message make clear that this administration's urban policy will

not end on March 27, 1978, when the policy is announced, but will continue to evolve, based on the principles and policies enunciated.

3) Summarize the administration's earlier initiatives (enacted and pending) that assist cities and their residents. The message should highlight the numerous actions that this administration already had taken in the FY 1978 budget revisions and in the FY 1979 budget.
4) Announce immediate actions to enhance the effectiveness of existing federal programs. These actions will streamline existing programs, improve coordination, refocus existing funding, and make federal policies and programs more supportive of urban areas. These actions will put a distinctive Carter administration stamp on the $85 billion of grants-in-aid currently available to states and localities in the FY 1979 budget.
5) Announce new initiatives that respond to priority short-term and long-term needs of urban areas. These new initiatives will involve organizational changes, supplemental funding for existing programs and new programs.[14]

In addition to approving strategy and theme for his national urban policy report announcement the following week, the President also rejected several proposals:

- A state incentive grant program at a $400 million level was rejected in favor of "a more modest state incentive program ($200 million)."[15]
- HEW's Califano had recommended the creation of a special representative for domestic assistance in the executive office of the president, with a new budget of $250 to $500 million. Carter chose instead the creation of the Interagency Coordinating Council and issued an executive order to that effect later in the process.[16]
- Carter made no response to the option that would have directed the Department of Defense (Defense Military Preparedness) to seek a limited waiver of Maybank (an amendment that precluded defense from establishing set-asides) for the $2.5 billion to provide employment stimulus in labor surplus areas.

- A proposal to fund metropolitan strategies for addressing older communities and surrounding suburban development was "disapproved."
- Carter opposed using any dollar figure in his announcement of welfare fiscal relief.
- While the President approved the initiation of the "modest relocation assistance program within existing resources, but not highlight as part of the urban policy," he noted in the margin that the initiative should be a "small demo (demonstration) only."
- The issues of the creation and location of the Urban Development Bank once again was not joined. Carter made no choice from the five options that he was offered: locate in HUD, locate in Commerce, create an interagency bank; announce bank, defer legislation; do not approve bank.
- The option of "do nothing" was chosen for the proposed interest subsidies for HUD's section 108 local bonding authority.
- Air quality technical assistance, a sore point in the nascent environmental equity debate, was rejected for funding. Carter directed that the program be folded into EPA as a capacity-building initiative.
- Although Carter approved "selective goals for minority set-asides in major construction grant programs," he rejected the proposal for a comprehensive minority enterprise program that would have strengthened Commerce's minority business enterprise (MBE) program by creating an Office of Minority Business Enterprise as a permanent statutory administration.
- While the President raised some funding levels for HUD in the area of housing rehabilitation, he rejected a proposal for assistance for the working poor, to raise the rental assistance subsidy, which the memo described as "HUD's highest priority for serving low- and moderate-income families." He also disapproved an expended Section 8 initiative and disapproved lowering the interest rates for HUD's home ownership (235) program.
- A proposal to provide assistance to troubled schools was rejected (with a very large, forceful check!)

In spite of the insularity of Carter's decision process and the absence of information on the dynamics of his choices from a staff person who advised him, some preferences seemed clear. In the decision section on communities, neighborhoods, and voluntary associations, in addition to checking the options offered (i.e., approve, disapprove), the President also checked the self-help development program proposed by HUD, drawing brackets around the description itself. He did the same with the proposed community development credit unions. Both of these proposals were consistent with his earlier memo to Harris and Eizenstat, in which he directed: "encompass federal, state, local govts + private and neighborhood groups + volunteers."

A Role for States

Throughout the policy-drafting process, the Task Force on States and Metropolitan Regions was the venue where state representatives advanced their concerns that a national cities' policy not bypass the states. Moreover, many federal departments and agencies had important relationships with states and metropolitan regional organizations, that bore on the problems of central cities and declining suburbs.

As the former governor of Georgia, the President held a special respect for the capacity of state government to affect the quality of urban life, and this sensitivity reinforced the National Governor's Association's (NGA) active role in the urban policy debate. Toward the end of 1977, NGA held a special forum on the national urban policy, at which Secretary Harris was the keynote speaker.

> We admit our past failures and the failures of other federal agencies to involve the states and local governments in this kind of process. But we also recognize that something must be done now to improve this situation.

Massachusetts Governor and NGA President Michael Dukakis wrote:

> A central question in the debate on national urban policy is still...what role will state government play? As an increasing number of people have come to recognize, the states have both money and power that can be marshalled in the battle to bring stability and vitality back to our cities.
>
> ...what we need now are federal incentives for the states to reverse their old investment mistakes and undertake new measures to aid urban areas.[17]

In an interview that the President gave just prior to announcing the national urban policy, he echoed Dukakis' theme:

> We want to have as much as possible authority and responsibility at the local level of government. We realize in the broad scope of things a relatively small portion of any future budget within a city's boundary will come from the federal government. The overwhelming portion of it has got to come from (many other sectors including) regional authorities, (and) State authorities have got to play a major role.[18]

The corrections that the urban policy process recommended for states were either structural or fiscal. The fiscal remedies were self-evident. As Dukakis had observed, states could reverse their largely rural perspectives, prevalent in all but a few urban states in the Northeast (primarily, New Jersey, Massachusetts, and Connecticut) and target larger portions of their dollar resources to urban communities to assist in revitalization.

But of equal importance, the structural realities of many states—their laws, regulations, agency and legislative practices, and service-delivery mechanisms—were unfavorable to cities, often inadvertently rather than through punitive intent. These conditions were thought by many to be the most destructive to cities and needed to be corrected also.

The policy process recommended that the federal government provide cash incentives to states to encourage their review of existing structural impediments to cities—in effect, to conduct an urban impact assessment of state policies. In his comments during the White House briefing, the President pointed out that, while he did "not want to turn away from the direct federal-city relationship (which has so long characterized national urban policy), I want to provide others with incentives and opportunities to contribute to the concerns of urban America...such as states and other entities."[19] At that same briefing, Jack Watson proposed a demonstration program involving "fifteen to twenty states (which would)...require states to develop a plan for rechanneling existing resources, (with the help of) incentive funding."[20] As stated above, in his decision memorandum, the President confirmed a funding level of $200 million for incentive grants to selected states, half of what URPG proposed, but significantly more than had existed prior to the national urban policy process, which had been nothing. In the President's briefing, he had agreed that "state participation must be meaningful."[21]

Announcing the National Urban Policy

On a parallel track, while the President deliberated, several activities gathered momentum, culminating in the March 27, 1978, announcement. The policy document was finalized, based on a number of important but different sets of recommendations. At the top of the list of comments, of course, were the President's directives, provided during the White House briefing and in his three personal directives indicating what he wanted in the policy. Also, the leadership from Stu Eizenstat and his White House staff augmented the President's direct specifications. By mid-March of 1978, we all had learned whose claim that "the President would like to have the policy say..." to take seriously and whose to take with a grain of salt. The authentic Presidential messages were welcomed and helpful.[22]

Written comments from more than one-hundred national figures, who had either volunteered their observations or who had been a part of the process as it unfolded, also contributed to the final draft. The latter group were requested to send their comments in response to a review copy of the final draft that I sent on March 17, 1978. (See Appendix D.) The invitation to comment was enhanced by some admissions:

> I hope that you have not been overly dismayed by the reports in the press on the status of the urban policy statement. While it is true that the President has not yet approved a final package, nor has he approved new program initiatives, he has reviewed the proposed policies and strategies and has accepted these.
>
> I enclose also for your information a copy of the note from the President to Secretary Harris and Stuart Eizenstat following his review of an Executive Summary of the Urban Policies.... We would very much appreciate receiving comments which you might have on this version of the policy...no later than March 22.[23]

The most important part of this letter, which was replicated in similar correspondence that went to other groups also, was the following account of the policy process:

> We who have worked on developing an Urban Policy Statement are encouraged to recognize that finally we have on paper—and so identified—a statement of normative expectations about urban places, particularly those which are in various stages of distress. This effort remains unique in that it is collaborative. It represents interagency participation, rather than isolated development and super-imposition by either an elitist internal group or an external group of consultants—the models which have characterized previous policy-making efforts. In that regard, therefore, I feel that we have accomplished much. I feel also that there still remains a great deal to be done.[24]

Comments on the final draft, from black leaders, neighborhood advocates, local elected leaders and governors, and interest groups, all were sought through the task force structure that had involved these groups from the beginning. Almost all comments were supportive, in part because advocates for a national urban policy were fearful of sabotaging the effort with their criticism, no matter how well intended. For example, the Congressional Black Caucus (CBC) and the Joint Center for Political Studies both expressed positively: "(We are) encouraged by the substance of the urban policy statements and the process which was used in the development stages. There are, however some concerns in the following areas." The CBC then transmitted twenty pages of suggested reconsiderations.[25]

On the other hand, the National Black Caucus of Local Elected Officials passed a resolution that stated:

> Now , therefore, be it resolved that the National Black Caucus of Local Elected Officials endorses the concept and thrust of a National Urban Policy and urges the President to use the power of his office to assure the effective implementation of the National Urban Policy with due regard to the varied impact of such a policy on all segments of the population.[26]

Briefings

The most important briefings, in my view, were those held by the principal White House staff, mostly in the White House's Roosevelt Room. Both Stu Eizenstat and Jack Watson assembled waves of assistant secretary–level members of the Carter administration to review with them the elements of the national urban policy most likely to affect their responsibility areas. Many of these briefings were scheduled for the weekends leading up to the announcement date, and as a sample letter of invitation indicated:

> I would like to meet with you on Saturday, March 4, 1978, in the Roosevelt Room, at 11:00 AM to discuss your recommendations concerning the (.................) component of the urban policy. During the meeting we will discuss several proposed new initiatives which will finance (.............).
>
> Copies of these proposals are attached. *I hope that we can use this meeting to approach a consensus on the (....................) component of the urban policy.* (Emphasis added.)[27]

Similarly, Jack Watson and his staff briefed members of Congress, as often on Capitol Hill as in the White House. A March 20 memorandum from Jack Watson's office polled the top White House staff and Pat Harris, concerning *additional* individuals and organizations that needed to be invited to pre-announcement briefings and to the President's announcement press conference.[28]

Taking into account the individual briefings of selected groups that each of the principals held—Secretary Harris, Bob Embry, Stu Eizenstat, Jack Watson, Jim McIntyre and other OMB staff, the White House Office of Congressional Liaison, and at least six members of my immediate staff including myself—more than one hundred briefings were held during the seven days preceding March 27, 1978. In fact, on March 27, ten briefings were held in advance of the afternoon presidential press conference, largely with members of Congress, selected reporters who specialized in urban affairs, and other important local elected officials.

The President's Urban and Regional Policy Group had met the deadline I had set seven months earlier, when I developed the URPG-2 planning work program. This fact was a part of the miracle of the policy's announcement, more fascinating to me than to anyone else, given my intimate knowledge of the process by which that deadline had been chosen. As the character in the Neil Simon play, *Biloxi Blues*, observes: If you want people to believe that something is true, just write it down.

President Carter Announces a National Urban Policy

The President's announcement press conference was held in the East Room of the White House and met every expectation of pomp, circumstance, and excitement. In attendance were governors, congress people, mayors, heads of urban advocacy groups, as well as suburbanists, small town and county advocates, all of whom were nearly outnumbered by the media.

The press coverage that followed for many weeks was appropriate to the announcement of the country's first urban policy. The types of trade-offs, the final arrival by the administration at consensus, the President's compromise decisions, and the President's themes of very limited spending, greater efficiency in existing programs and partnership with states, volunteers and private organizations were emphasized by the press as the primary innovations of the policy.

A sample of the press reports reveals, however, a wide variance in the understanding of how much money would be available, and also in the perception of who benefitted most from the policy proposals. That is not a surprise. The urban policy itself did not directly address funding issues. The press materials, the President's message, and the message to Congress all contributed to the picture of the urban policy budget. Thus, as was observed earlier, the amounts differed depending on who was counting.

Figures 7.6 and 7.7 reflect two versions of the proposed federal dollars to support the urban policy initiatives. Figure 7.6 shows URPG's recommended budgeted items, prepared before the policy was announced. To some extent, this was referred to as the "HUD Wish List," which had inspired OMB's briefing of the President earlier in the process. Figure 7.7 is the list of items to which President Carter referred in his various assessments of the urban policy process as, in the main, having already been done or proposed. It is this list that most press people consulted and that was leaked just prior to the President's announcement.

Thus, the premier far-right column of the *Washington Post*'s front page, with a two-column head, read "President Unveils $8.3 Billion Plan to Aid U.S. Cities,"with a subhead, "Urban Policy: Shifting Focus of Programs."[29] Yet, the *Chicago Tribune*'s headline much more modestly read "Carter Unveils $2.4 Billion Plan for Cities," on page 6, in the "NATION" box.[30] The *Wall Street Journal*, consistent in its understatement, announced in a one-column head: "New Urban Plan Seeks Better Use of Current Funds: Carter Policy Also Includes Modest Added Spending, Some Changes in Taxes."[31] It seemed to be a matter of journalistic perspective.

The policy document, as noted, did not reveal any dollar figures, largely because approvals from the President for exact spending initiatives were not available until the last minute. In some cases, in fact, while the range of budget outlays was fairly certain, actual dollar amounts were negotiated as a part of the larger, ongoing congressional and OMB budget process. One newspaper pointed out, "Last Minute Criticism by President Shocks His Urban Policy Writers," and detailed:

> [T]he Carter Administration's much-publicized urban policy statement, all marked up, was back on the desk of his chief domestic policy adviser, Stuart Eizenstat.
>
> And the shock waves went out from there through the federal bureaucracy. Jimmy Carter did not like what he had been given.

> ...All told, about half of the total package had been blue-penciled by the President. ...One aide said privately, "We ended up with more than we thought we'd get—more than $3 billion."[32]

In addition to the policies, principles, program revisions, and new initiatives, four executive orders completed the package of URPG recommendations that the President accepted and eventually signed.[33] These were:

> *Urban Impact Analysis*—In order to establish an internal management procedure for identifying aspects of proposed federal policies that may adversely impact cities, counties and other communities.
>
> *Interagency Coordinating Council*—In order to provide for interagency coordination of the implementation of federal urban and regional policy.
>
> *Federal Procurement in Labor Surplus Areas*—In order to strengthen the economic base of our nation; and,
>
> *Federal Space Management*—In accordance with Section 205(a) of the Federal Property and Administrative Services Act of 1949 and in order to prescribe appropriate policies and directives, not inconsistent with that Act and other applicable provisions of law, for the planning, acquisition, utilization, and management of federal space facilities.

Transition

Immediately upon announcement of *A New Partnership to Conserve America's Communities: A National Urban Policy,* the Urban and Regional Policy Group was disbanded and never met again. The official coordination of urban policy implementation passed to the domestic policy council in the White House and to Stuart Eizenstat's oversight. Pat Harris, on Bob Embry's recommendation, agreed to create a new deputy assistant secretary for urban policy to serve as the HUD liaison to the domestic policy staff and to the Interagency Coordinating Council. The HUD staff responsible for preparation of the biennial growth report, now the biennial urban policy report, remained imbedded in my department under my supervision, but worked in coordination with the new urban policy deputy. Most of the URPG coordinators, who were permanent HUD staff, returned to their original assignments within HUD. The consultants returned to their normal lives, in the main. However, a few consultants continued to work on urban policy matters for HUD until just before or just after the 1980 presidential election. In August 1979, I returned to my professorship in the Department of City and Regional Planning at Howard University in time for the beginning of the 1979–80 fall semester.

Figure 7.1
Presidential Memorandum

THE WHITE HOUSE
WASHINGTON

2-16-78

To Pat Harris
Stu Eizenstat

Be sure to get written suggestions re urban policy from black leaders & other groups so as to derive good ideas & to minimize the inevitable criticisms later on

J. C.

February 16, 1978

Figure 7.2
Note from Assistant Secretary of Commerce

U.S. DEPARTMENT OF COMMERCE

13

To: Yvonne

From: Lawrence O. Houstoun, Jr.

Do you want to handle the leak this time?

Love 'n' Kisses

Larry

TRANSMITTAL FORM CD-82A (10-67)
PRESCRIBED BY DAO 214-2

USCOMM-DC 337-P77

Figure 7.3
Analysis of Base—Past and Present Urban Performance of Key Federal Programs

Key Programs	A	B	C	D	E	F	G	H	I	J	K	L	M	N	O
CETA (Title I) —DOL	✔	✔	–	✔	✔	–	○	✔	–	✔	–	○	○	✔	–
CDBG—HUD	✚	✚	✔	–	✚	✔	✔	✔	✔	○	✚	✚	○	✚	✔
Revenue Sharing	–	–	–	✔	✚	–	○	○	○	✔	✚	–	○	–	○
Countercyclical—EDA, DOL, Treasury	✔	✔	–	–	✚	–	✔	✚	✔	✚	–	○	○	○	✔
Wastewater Treatment—EPA	–	–	✔	✚	✔	○	–	✔	–	○	○	✔	–	✔	○
CETA (Title II&VI-Public Services)—DOL	✚	✔	✔	✔	✔	–	○	✔	–	✚	–	○	○	✔	–
Public Works, Title II, IX—EDA	–	–	✔	✔	✔	–	✔	✔	✔	–	✔	✔	✔	✔	✚
Mass Transit—DOT	✔	–	–	–	✚	–	✔	✚	✔	–	○	✚	✚	✔	✔

Figure 7.3
Analysis of Base—Past and Present Urban Performance of Key Federal Programs

Key Programs	A	B	C	D	E	F	G	H	I	J	K	L	M	N	O
CSA	✚	✚	✔	✔	✔	✔	○	✔	○	○	○	✔	○	✚	✔
Other Job Training—DOL	✔	✔	–	✔	✔	–	–	✔	–	✔	–	○	○	✔	–
Title XX—HEW	✔	✔	–	✚	–	–	○	○	○	○	○	✔	○	✚	–
ESEA—HEW	✔	✔	–	✔	–	–	○	○	○	○	○	✔	○	✔	○
UDAG—HUD	✚	✚	○	✔	✚	✔	✚	✔	✔	✔	○	✚	✔	○	✔

Key: Positive ✚ , Negative –, Mixed ✔, Not relevant ○

A = Targeting to distressed cities
B = Targeting to people and neighborhoods
C = Federal coordination impact
D = Incentive to states
E = Role of City Hall
F = Role of neighborhood
G = Economic development—Tax base
H = Economic development—Jobs

I = Economic development—Restructure economy
J = Fiscal condition—Immediate relief
K = Fiscal condition—Reform
L = Attractive, liveable communities, housing
M = Sprawl, efficient land settlement patterns
N = Racism/Discrimination
O = Job mobility

Figure 7.4
Urban Program Score Board

	A	B	C	D	E	F	G	H	I	J	K	L	M	N	O
CSA	✚	✚	✔	✔	✔	✔	○	✔	○	○	○	✔	○	✚	✔
Other Job Training—DOL	✔	✔	–	✔	✔	–	–	✔	–	✔	–	○	○	✔	–
Title XX—HEW	✔	✔	–	✚	–	–	○	○	○	○	○	✔	○	✚	–
UDAG—HUD	✚	✚	○	✔	✚	✔	✚	✔	✔	✔	○	✚	✔	○	✔

Key: Positive ✚ , Negative –, Mixed ✔, Not relevant ○

A = Targeting to distressed cities
B = Targeting to people and neighborhoods
C = Federal coordination impact
D = Incentive to states
E = Role of City Hall
F = Role of neighborhood
G = Economic development—Tax base
H = Economic development—Jobs
I = Economic development—Restructure economy
J = Fiscal condition—Immediate relief
K = Fiscal condition—Reform
L = Attractive, liveable communities, housing
M = Sprawl, efficient land settlement patterns
N = Racism/Discrimination
O = Job mobility

Figure 7.5
URPG's Recommended Budgeted Items ("HUD Wish List")

<u>URBAN POLICY ITEMS FOR FISCAL YEAR 1979 BUDGET PROPOSALS</u>

Urban Bank	2,000 million
CETA Improvements	1,000 million
DOL Built up, acceleration	
expanded youth programs	1,500 million
CETA Targeting Proposal (HUD)	1,000 million
Targeted Tandem	(GNMA Budget Authority)
Health, Education and Welfare	
Innercity Health Initiatives	452 million
Compensatory Programs	200 million
Headstart	200 million
Neighborhood/School Proposal	400 million
EASE Program	1,000 million
	2,052 million
Rehabilitation loans	800 million
Neighborhood Task Force Proposals	100.5 million
Urban Extension	25 million
Transportation	
Young Amendment	450 million
Transportation modernization	
Acceleration for Transportation Programs	
Major Housing Initiatives	
Section 248 - 50,000 units of new construction	3,690 million
for low and moderate income families, aided working poor in urban areas; includes mortgage insurance, rental assistance an GNMA purchase at 6-7-1/2% interest	1,500 million (Tandem Assist.)
Section 8 - home ownership (10,000 units)	346.5 million
Section 8 - existing (50,000 units)	1,700 million
Public Housing (50,000 units)	4,500 million (approx)
Section 8 - moderate rehab 165,000 units	6,800 million

Figure 7.6
Proposed Federal Dollars to Support Urban Policy Initiatives

	Initiative	Amount	
	~~EDA — Local Government capacity to implement development~~	~~10.0~~	~~(10.0)~~
2.	Soft Public Works	1000.0	(300.0)
*	CSA Youth Employment Initiative	67.5	
3	Development Bank -- Grants, losses, interest subsidy	308.0	
4	Development Bank -- Capital resources, reserves		
5.	UDAG	500.0	(50.0)
6.	EDA Title IX	400.0	(50.0)
7.	Interest Subsidies -- Section 108	90.0	
8.	Differential Tax Incentive -- HUD	[1.5 billion revenue loss]	
9.	Differential Tax Incentive -- DPS	[200.0 million loss]	
10.	Targeted Employment Tax Credit	[unclear revenue loss]	
25	Housing Assistance for Blue Collar -- 50,000 units	5200.0	(0)
29	Housing Assistance for Homeowners -- 10,000 units	346.0	(1)
30	Increased Section 8 -- 32,000 units	3200.0	(0)
26	Expanded Section 312	800.0	(350.0)
27	Section 235 homeownership	0.0	(12.0)
24	Targeted Tandem	0.0	( )
15	Urban Research and Evaluation Center	15.0	(10.0)
1.	State Role	400.0	(250.0)
28	Liveable Cities -- NEA	35.0	(35.0)
25	Urban Park -- Interior	1085.0	
24	Urban Park -- OMB	[4]00.0	
16	Expand Neighborhood Business Revitalization Program	9.0	(9.0)
12.	Comprehensive Minority Enterprise Program	30.0	(20.0)
18	Air Quality Planning Grants	75.0	(25.0)
11	Air Quality Technical Assistance	10.0	(10.0)
	Additional Title XX Funds	200.0	(200.0)
17	Assistance to Troubled Schools	1.5	(1.5)
18	Inner City Health Initiative	301.0	
23	Community Crime Initiative	50.0	(35.0)
19	Increase UMTA	450.0	(45.0)
13	New Towns-In-Town	80.0	(76.0)
*	Resources Recovery Planning	15.0	
*	Self-Help Development Fund	30.0	(20.0)
*	Community Development Credit Unions	12.4	
*	Urban Volunteer Corps	65.0	(45.0)
*	Additional Assistance for CDCs	20.0	(12.0)
4.	Metro Strategies	20.0	

TOTAL B.A. $14,805.4 million
OUTLAY

* Duplicate one or more [illegible] programs.

Notes

1. Memo from Harris to Hamilton Jordan (see Chapter 6).
2. See Figure 6.1. Handwritten memorandum from "Jimmy" to Pat Harris and Stu Eizenstat, January 25, 1978. This note from the President generated untold sniping and snickering. In addition to the substantive concerns, the "My whole family will help" line offered yet another chance for the press and other critics to make fun of the role played in the Carter Administration by the President's mother Miss Lillian, First Lady Rosalynn Carter, First Daughter Amy Carter, and even Amy's cat, Misty Melarky Ying Yang.
3. Handwritten note, signed J.C., dated 2-16-78.
4. See Chapter Six for list of White House meeting attendees.
5. Testimony by Dr. Herrington J. Bryce, Director of Research, Joint Center for Political Studies, before the U.S. House of Representatives' Committee on Banking, Currency and Housing, September 29, 1976, 9–10.
6. Memorandum from Lawrence O. Houstoun, Jr., Assistant to the Secretary (Department of Commerce), February 21, 1978, 1.
7. Also from HUD/URPG staff were Bob Duckworth, who, by that time, was the urban policy office director; Franklin James, who had become a permanent staff person and was no longer a consultant. Also present was Marshall Kaplan, who was still a consultant at that time, but had appealed to Embry, in a letter of January 5, 1978, in effect to create a new position (it was ultimately called deputy assistant secretary for urban policy) to "forge the...good staff under a tight working situation into a legitimate (urban policy) team" with Kaplan in charge. Embry was considering this request, which I was not lobbying against since I (a) was not interested in such a position; (b) was concluding my two-year leave of absence to return to my tenured professorship at Howard University at the beginning of the next academic year, August 1978, and (c) knew that, as soon as the policy was announced and legitimated, the White House staff would take over the process. This eventuality was not attractive to me, based upon my original reservations about working in an appointed position within the bureaucracy.

   White House staff who had been assigned to the urban policy exercise were present, although Jack Watson, distracted by a crisis with some governors, was in and out. Stu Eizenstat was a full briefing participant, along with Secretary Harris. OMB was represented also, although the principals from other major domestic agencies who had served on the deputies group of URPG largely were not present.
8. Yvonne Scruggs Perry's notes from March 15, 1978, White House briefing of President Carter, chronological archival materials, 5.
9. The President's sensitivity to the rank order appearance of the policies resulted in on-the-spot adjustments to the abbreviated list of policies on the briefing chart. Policies numbered one through four would remain as presented, with further elaboration of the strategies and language. Policy No.

5 was to be replaced by proposed Policy No. 9 on racism. Proposed Policy No. 10 was to become Policy No. 6. Proposed Policy No. 5 would become Policy No. 7, and 6 moved to replace proposal 8. Seven became 9, and 8 was moved to Policy No. 10.

10. As a result of the President's comments, both in the briefing and later in his second decision memorandum, these policies are verbatim from the national urban policy document, dated March 23, 1978, pp. III-3 through III-42.
11. Scruggs-Perry archival notes, Ibid., passim.
12. Memorandum for the President, signed Pat, Jim, and Stu, delivered by Stuart Eizenstat by hand on Friday, March 17, 1978, 1.
13. Memo March 17, 1978, 2–3.
14. Memo March 17, 1978, 2.
15. President's memorandum, "State Role" Part I.
16. After the transmittal memorandum and the first eight pages of part I of the attachment, pages are not numbered in the decision document. All citations will read "passim," therefore, and can be found in the memorandum, which is archival material.
17. For Harris quote, see Rochelle L. Stanfield, "Development of Carter's Urban Policy: One Small Step for Federalism," *Publius, the Journal of Federalism* (Winter, 1978): 52; Michael Dukakis, " A Role for the States in Urban Policy," (Op-Ed) *Washington Post*, December 25, 1977, A-17.
18. Carter interview, transcribed, with Sue Reisinger from the *Dayton Daily News*, mid-March 1978, 9, archival materials.
19. Scruggs-Perry, March 15, 1978, 3
20. Scruggs-Perry, March 15, 1978, 3.
21. Scruggs-Perry, March 15, 1978, 8.
22. I commented earlier about the White House staff's inclination to give the impression of constant contact with the President. In fact, few of us had such contact, even the more junior staff whose offices were actually in the White House rather than in the EOB. Among those whose comments were reliable were Eizenstat; his assistant Bert Carp; Jack Watson; Louis Martin, the President's assistant and the only substantive continuous link between the President and the African American community; and, of course, Secretary Harris who saw the President regularly in Cabinet meetings. Andrew Young was also initially close to Carter, but tensions had begun developing between Carter and Young, in part because of Young's outspoken style, particularly with regard to U.S. relations with third world nations.

    The role of African Americans in the White House is of some importance and invites examination at a later date. However, it should be noted that several black staff with whom I worked closely—Kurt Schmoke, assistant director of the domestic council (Eizenstat's staff); Lawrence Bailey, deputy assistant for intergovernmental affairs (Jack Watson's staff); Dennis Green, associate director in the Office of Management and Budget (McIntyre's staff); and

Amelia Parker, assistant to Hamilton Jordon—all African Americans—left the White House, either by choice or through reorganization moves, within a month of the urban policy's announcement. The *New York Times* announced, "White House Losing 7 Blacks From Staff: Many Leaving for Better Jobs but Some Cite Frustration with the Administration," May 14, 1978, p.1.

23. Letter sent to all academic critics, as well as, in an amended version, to a number of other private-sector participants in the policy process.
24. Above letter, 2.
25. Memorandum from Malachi Knowles (special assistant to Yvonne Perry) to Robert P. Duckworth and Marshall Kaplan, "Minority Groups Responses to the National Urban Policy," August 4, 1978, with attachments from seven groups.
26. Knowles, memo, attachment 4, 1.
27. Stu Eizenstat's memos began arriving on March 1, 1978. A series followed to all domestic departments. The subject was appropriate to the focus of each cluster of assistant secretaries.
28. Memorandum from Jack Watson, White House, to Patricia Harris, Midge Costanza, Stuart Eizenstat, Hamilton Jordan, Tim Kraft, Frank Moore, and Jody Powell, "Urban Policy Announcement: Proposed Invitees," March 18, 1978.
29. *Washington Post*, March 28, 1978, A-1.
30. *Chicago Tribune*, March 28, 1978, 6
31. *Wall Street Journal*, March 28, 1978, 3.
32. David S. Broder and Susanna McBee, *Washington Post*, Saturday, March 25, 1978, A2.
33. Archival materials; also, *Presidential Papers, Fourth Quarter, 1978*, (Washington, D.C.: U.S. Government Printing Office).

Chapter Eight

Reflecting on a Theoretical Context

> *Within the policy community, as in any other group, participants develop a shared memory of how the world has been and how they acted....This mobilization of memory usually begins with short-term and self-reflective histories of the community's deliberations and the immediate context of a policy debate.*[1]

The commitment of the Carter administration to a national urban policy was largely the result of the personal strategy of one individual, HUD's Secretary Patricia Roberts Harris. This is not to say that the obsession actually began with her, but because of her ideology and zeal, she was an effective vehicle for advancing the urban policy obsession. And one White House aide complained that Harris, who worried about issues with which Carter's people did not wish to deal, "would not believe that the federal government could not turn things around."[2]

This assessment has been echoed by many others who felt that an urban policy existed at all because Pat Harris focused with laser-beam precision on cities and their problems. A critic commented: "If she has an open mind, she would not give you that impression. She has a singleness of purpose which is awesome to behold." In fact, Harris had skillfully exploited the political debt that Carter owed to blacks, the urban poor and labor, to effectively overcome the White House's natural resistance to just the type of governmental intervention that the national urban policy represented.[3]

Harris was a powerful black woman who came to the Carter cabinet with exceptional accomplishments. A Phi Beta Kappa lawyer, she earlier had become the first African American woman ambassador, serving in that post to Luxembourg. She had further distinguished herself during her secretarial confirmation hearings as a person whose loyalties were defined by her own childhood urban experiences. A native of Chicago, she told Senator William Proxmire in her now legendary rejoinder:

> Senator...you do not seem to understand who I am. I'm a black woman, the daughter of a dining car waiter. I'm a black woman who even eight years ago could not buy a house in some parts of the District of Columbia. Senator, to say I'm not by and of and for the people is to show a lack of understanding of who I am and where I came from.
>
> I started, Senator, not as a lawyer in a prestigious law firm, but as a woman who needed a scholarship to go to college.... I started as an advocate for a civil rights agency...that had to come before this body to ask for access to housing by members of minority groups. If you think I have forgotten that, Senator, you're wrong.
>
> I have been a defender of women, of minorities, of those who are the outcasts of this society, throughout my life, and if my life has any meaning at all, it is that those who start as outcasts may end up being part of the system.[4]

It was that terrier tenacity that characterized Harris' stewardship of HUD and that served as a model for those of us assigned the responsibility of advancing her initiatives, including urban policy. Yet, she assumed the leadership of an organization—once distinguished in its urban advocacy—that had gained a tarnished reputation during the Nixon-Ford Administrations, for doing nothing remarkable to validate its urban development mandate.[5] Harris' lieutenants within HUD, therefore, had at least two separate but compatible agendas: to help their own prestige within the administration by helping Harris' power position within the Cabinet; and to advance their own broader, national celebrity as urbanists, by pursuing high-profile initiatives, which would be validated by Harris' already established image. As Bauer has pointed out:

> The focus of our concern is first of all to understand the behavior of the individual—and if not the individual, the smallest meaningful unit of analysis confronted with manifestations of public policy problems."[6]

As has been observed throughout this study, the force of individual actions, driven by individual value systems and behavioral traits growing out of professional standards and training, in large measure determined the outcomes of the process, that is, the production of a national urban policy. Thus, the positions taken by both the principal actors within HUD during the policy development process (Harris, Embry, Shalala, and Perry), as well as by HUD as an institution, were significant determinants of the policy process outcomes.[7]

Even though Embry frequently expressed the desire to have the urban policy developed within the White House, in point of fact, neither he nor the other HUD actors made a conscious effort to transfer the process. After the President's announcement, when major implementation initiatives originated in and were orchestrated by the White House, HUD still created a deputy assistant secretary position to maintain the agency's involvement with the national urban policy efforts.

The legislative amendments of 1976 had empowered HUD to produce a biennial national urban policy report, formerly the biennial growth report. There existed a division within HUD that traditionally had carried out this responsibility, in 1972, 1974, and 1976, under direction of the deputy assistant secretary for planning, the position that I held. One could argue, therefore, that the addition of a deputy exclusively for urban policy was superfluous and redundant. The advocacy of the individual who would ultimately occupy this position, however—the consultant Marshall Kaplan—influenced the decision. His leverage was the "fire in the belly" to keep HUD involved with the White House's urban policy implementation, no matter how arms-length that involvement ultimately might have to be.

Bauer also has pointed out that any political system in which policy-making is central has leverage points that include actors, roles, and institutions, interacting to produce system outcomes. Thus, within the larger political system, this configuration of the smaller system promotes its own objectives. In the case of the national urban policy process, the stated expectations and commitments of the President during his election campaign became the operative objective of HUD's institutional system, and the White House was the focal institution within the larger political system.[8]

Lasswell and Lerner, Dahl and Lindblom, Braybrooke and Lindblom, and Lindblom have all addressed the parallel and interactive effects of individual behavior with the dynamics within a policy-making system. The Braybrooke and Lindblom model, which is of particular interest in the case under review, offers a system for retrospective analysis of the events that took place.[9]

Retrospective analysis, rather than process evaluation, is at issue here. The first of these permits an examination of events that already have occurred and invites a search for reasons that may explain choices made and decisions taken, associated with these events. The latter requires a system of conscious assumptions and a testing of these assumptions against both their real and anticipated outcomes. As will be discussed later, the politics of the environment and of the venue foreclosed the luxury of tests on assumptions. Instead, actions were required, no matter how rationally inspired or how politically motivated, regardless of "complexity and apparent disorder."[10]

In the early stages of URPG-2, certain efforts were made to rationalize the planning process as it got underway—for example, the creation of a planning work program (Figure 5.1), with tasks, milestones, and a time-phased statement, was one such effort at order and rationality. Another was the engagement of several advisors from the academic community and also the continuation of consultation from PD&R's experts. However, these efforts were isolated, narrow in scope, and discontinuous.

Moreover, the values that these efforts represented were not shared across the participants and primary decision makers within URPG. Thus, as Davidoff and Reiner observe, the relationship of facts and values did hold in the abstract, but was rarely a conscious dynamic of the policy-making process. Often, choices were made that were inconsistent with the facts but represented values that continued to shift for political reasons.[11]

One example of this behavior was evident in the power struggle over welfare reform and cashing out of HUD programs. While many arguments were advanced for maintaining HUD's involvement in the provision of shelter to poor people, the decisions about welfare reform ultimately were driven by forces unrelated to the facts about the costs and benefits of the proposals. Another more dramatic example of departure from the choice theory was the decision to exclude education, welfare, health, environmental concerns, and energy reform from the national urban policy dialogue, in spite of the obvious synergy between these issues and the quality of urban life.

Another general observation about individual behavior and its effects on the larger system is relevant. Jimmy Carter has been characterized, consistent with research on presidential executive style, as having varied responses to leadership demands, depending on his perception of the stakes of a given issue. In the case of the urban policy process, Carter was unwilling to delegate sufficiently to provide himself with the distance required for consistent executive leadership. Additionally, as was mentioned earlier, Carter's political acumen was viewed by some as weak. Joseph Califano was one who was underwhelmed by Carter as politician:

> During 1977, Carter rarely discussed partisan politics with the Cabinet. Even his private conversations with those of us in politically sensitive departments...were so focused on substantive issues that we exchanged concerns among ourselves about his failure to pay enough attention to the political ramifications of what he was doing. Carter had so compartmentalized policy and politics that the annual budget process seemed to take place in an apolitical vacuum.[12]

It appears in retrospect that he saw the policy development process in terms of domestic political power, or to use other words, in terms of his electoral base. Given this practical political stake, Carter was unwilling to fully delegate responsibility for preliminary urban policy decisions, even to Stuart Eizenstat, his domestic policy chief.

Jack Watson has pointed out:

> [T]he President's attempt to be his own chief of staff, with eight or ten White House lieutenants reporting directly to him, pulled him in too many competing directions. It results in a lack of cohesion, lack of organization and cutting in on decision making before it reaches the Oval Office, the presidential level.
>
> This was in my judgment, a mistake that President Carter made in the first two years of his administration. He didn't actually appoint a chief of staff until late in the summer of 1979. I think that many of our problems on the Hill, many of our...difficulties...would have been solved had we started from the very beginning with a strong chief of staff.[13]

While this circumstance worked to the advantage of URPG in as much as Carter, a President with rural roots, as the *New York Times* noted, devoted personal attention to the urban policy process, it also resulted in mixed public and media messages about what URPG was or was not doing. It was not helpful, for example, for the meeting with OMB to occur prematurely in the URPG process, or for the President to personally "blue-pencil the policy report" one day before the announcement was scheduled. Another executive style would have avoided these appearances of criticism and contretemps.[14]

Watson's most interesting insight is the claim that lack of explicit coordinating functions made for disjointed policy as well as for a disjointed decision process. He and other critics of Carter's style of managing policy formation, clearly believed that policies would have been more coherent, consistent, and long term if the president had used custodians to help him formulate his choices. Such lieutenants would have been buffers to keep the president one step removed from the details, the exploration of suboptions, and the blame.

> (However,) the difficulty with this argument is that Carter did not want it that way. He was clear at the outset that it was not his nature to have aides report to assistants who then reported to him. He wanted the information directly.[15]

On the other hand, given the fundamental lack of continuing rapport between Carter and the cities, had he possessed a different executive style, the national urban policy might have been delegated out of existence altogether. A reflection on the Reagan/Bush years is instructive in this regard and is discussed in the following chapter.

"Muddling Through" the Policy-Making Process

It is fair to say that, to my knowledge, there was no conscious reference to policymaking theory throughout most of the URPG process, except in the deliberations of the academic critics advisory group and on the part of the resident scholars who served as long-term consultants to me. Also, the Academy for Contemporary Problems was engaged as consultant halfway through the URPG-2 effort, in part to prepare the text for the biennial urban policy report mandated by Congress. There is ample evidence that these consultants constantly referred to prevailing or appropriate theories as they evaluated the URPG products on which they were asked to comment.[16]

However, even when URPG staff leadership may have been inclined toward abstractions during the process, memory of URPG-1's demise on the crucible of "overly academic rhetoric" was a sufficient reality check to discourage, at least publicly, indulgence in such intellectual trips. Thus, speculation about the forces that were driving various URPG behaviors were silent and reflective. Additionally, given the highly charged political environment of the Carter White House, such exercises would have been suicidal.[17]

Therefore, this process of analysis is one of a few such retrospective efforts, including papers by Reiner, Warren, Stanfield, and Glickman, as well as selected monographs in the volume edited by Kaplan and Cuciti.[18] And, as mentioned above, Braybrooke and Lindblom offer a comfortable model for organizing such a post-hoc assessment, first, "because (the model) demands that any theory about the process stress attributes of the individual policy maker and the system in which (he/she) operates.

Second, (the model) requires that the theory relate variables that intervene between the individual and the system, such as interest group behavior, to the operation of these two basic variables, i.e., the individual and the contextual system."[19]

In their chapter on the "Strategy of Disjointed Incrementalism," the authors discuss eight interrelated attributes that characterize the design of policy remedies, or a "useful description of how the policy-making process operates in a democratic political system (like) the United States":[20]

1) Only those policies are considered whose known or expected consequent social states differ from each other incrementally; i.e., choices are made in a given political universe, at the margin of the status quo.
2) Only those policies are considered whose known or expected consequences differ incrementally from the status quo.
3) Examination of policies proceeds through comparative analysis of no more than the marginal or incremental differences in the consequent social states rather than through an attempt at more comprehensive analysis of the social states.
4) Choice among policies is made by ranking in order of preference the increments by which social states differ.
5) Problems are reconstructed, or transformed, in the course of exploring relevant data.
6) Analysis and evaluation occur sequentially, with the result that policy consists of a long chain of amended choices.
7) Analysis and evaluation are oriented toward remedying a negatively perceived situation, rather than toward reaching preconceived goals.
8) Analysis and evaluation are undertaken throughout society, i.e., the locus of these activities is fragmented or disjointed.[21]

A Context for Choosing: The Great Society

The decision to have a national urban policy at all reflected the influence of earlier experiences and a desire of Carter administration leaders to return to a status-quo-ante condition. After the vigor of the Kennedy-Johnson initiatives, the intervening Nixon-Ford years had been so fraught with recisions, freezes, and benign neglect that in effect, there was no urban status quo around the edges of which to make changes. The most relevant status quo history for the Democratic administration of Jimmy Carter was the Johnson White House, and Harris and Eizenstat reminded the President of this fact in their first decision memorandum: "Johnson had the 'Great Society' and Nixon, the 'New Federalism.' We recommend to you...'A New Partnership...'"[22]

Even when the proposals moved significantly beyond the scope of status quo ante familiarity, such as Califano's welfare reform proposals that cashed out HUD programs, or the tension between Commerce and HUD to capture the dollars for economic and community development, there was no tolerance in the administration for these extremes. Califano ultimately was fired by Carter, largely because of his dramatic and revolutionary reform proposals.[23] Moreover, Carter was never able to resolve the Commerce/HUD standoff because he failed to decide on the location of the Urban Development Bank (Ur-Bank). Instead, he chose to give a little piece of the budget action to HUD and an equally small piece to Commerce. Consequently, Ur-Bank died a-borning.

An examination of the ten final policies actually yields no surprises. Even in the more controversial areas—such as racism, disincentives to urban locational decisions, and state initiative—proposed changes were around the edges only. In the case of racism, for example, the only explicit reference was in the policy itself (Policy No. 5). There were no strategies in the expanded materials at the announcement, nor were there proposals for legislation or impact assessments. There was no executive order.

Emphasizing the Similarity Between Old and New

The serial analysis of options and proposals produced a set of policies that were familiar to everyone. Even in the case of an enlarged role for states, which was most revolutionary considering how long the federal-city axis had operated,[24] the proposal covered only fifteen to twenty states, that would receive planning grants to conduct studies of how they might propose to approach the problem. There was no provision for revolution, or even for immediate action.

The President, moreover, rejected the more unpredictable but innovative "Metropolitan Strategy," largely because the metropolitan regions were more aligned with counties than with cities or state capitals. Thus, they were considered by governors and the feds alike, to be mavericks with regard to cooperation and power-grabbing. In fact, the disjointed incrementalism of the entire urban policy process, through the vehicles of public forums and task forces, had permitted the intrusion of a county voice into the debate at a much higher decibel level than was comfortable for the White House and Washington politicians.[25]

Suboptimizing Analysis

The experiences of URPG-1, along with comments from Houstoun at Commerce and Kramer in the White House, effectively discouraged the introduction of analytical reports to the URPG deputies' group. While the task forces used a full range of analytic constructs and exercises, most of this cost-benefit discourse was left on the cutting room floor when final task forces' products were completed. In fact, the Red-Lining Task Force became so steeped in its analysis that it never issued a report and never generated any adaptable recommendations during the life of URPG-2. Consequently, one of the arenas in which strength and substance might have been generated for Policy No. 5 on racism, that is, a set of strategies to reduce or eliminate red lining, was totally unequal to the challenge.

Comments frequently heard informally during the URPG process, and substantiated by interviews after March 1978, concerned the analyses and assessments that occurred in PD&R. Since there was general lack of receptivity to the academic approach, although the analyses continued to be done, they were not evident to the final decision makers—the President or Congress—that considered the legislative proposals. More perplexing, the prestigious and elaborately planned White House Conference on Balanced National Growth and Economic Development, held February 2, 1978, at the height of the URPG deliberations, had limited influence on URPG. The timing for full integration was poor, and the primary channel through which the growth conference's recommendations were funneled was the Task Force on States and Metropolitan Regions.[26]

Reconstructing and Transforming the Problem

The most glaring example of problem transformation existed with regard to the notion of "cities in distress." Early in the first URPG process, the emphasis on root causes of the cities' condition—economic disinvestment, abandonment, concentration of the economically and racially disadvantaged, discriminatory fiscal policies, discriminatory regional barriers to mobility, job loss, and physical decline—had pointed to absolute disparities between cities.

These disparities were evident in several measures: regional location, with the more severe conditions existing in the rust-belt Northeast and Midwest; size of city, with smaller communities having less severe conditions than larger communities; and the much greater decline of metropolitan areas' central cities and near-in suburbs than was true for other localities.

With each iteration of the policy document, however, and with each successive wave of comments and evaluations through the disjointed incrementalistic process—task forces, White House focus groups, and multiple solicited and unsolicited critics, not to mention federal and local elected officials, and the press—the problem of "cities in distress" was reconstructed and transformed. Not only did "distress" virtually disappear from the lexicon of urban policy remedies, but also, additional and expanded research was conducted across the country and within federal agencies, besides Treasury, to establish an expanded and very long list of distressed places.[27]

The new "distress" victims were urban *and* rural; large *and* small; states *and* regions. Finally, to paraphrase Eugene O'Neil, distressed conditions "lost their true meaning" and the targeting that was intended to relieve their problems was diffused.[28] The disjointed incrementalism of the process reinforced and maintained approximately the same pattern of resource distribution that had existed before URPG and the national urban policy. Some of the triggers for certain pre-existing fiscal relief were modified (e.g., states were removed from the countercyclical formula). Otherwise, the substantive changes were imperceptible, in the main.

"A Long Chain of Amended Choices": Fragmented and Disjointed

Secretary Harris and Stuart Eizenstat pointed out to President Carter in the seminal decision memorandum that many forums had been held across the country and that thousands of Americans had been solicited for their views about a national urban policy. Moreover, through the task force processes, thousands more citizens had participated in the policy deliberations and had their views considered.

The refinements to the policy report were a function of Presidential fiat, and White House negotiations with the principal assistant secretaries throughout March 1978. Additionally, as Bob Embry and I moved around the country giving speeches and making appearances consistent with our basic job responsibilities as assistant secretary and deputy assistant secretary, respectively, we also wore the ancillary hats of the secretary's urban policy principal deputy and the URPG executive director, respectively. We constantly prepared written comments on the policy drafts as the result of these encounters.[29]

These written documents—notes and memos—were infused with our values also, about what we thought was good for cities. Our views usually were reflected in subsequent revisions of the policy report, and although their inclusion was not arbitrary, our proximity to the process permitted us a constant monitoring of how the policy document was developing. We were able to keep it on track according to our own standards.

Thus, the disjointed, incremental process maintained its interactive nature with individual actions and value systems. Choices were continuously amended, both at the systemwide policy planning level, as well as at the level of the "smallest meaningful unit," as Bauer has observed.[30]

Notes

1. Seymour J. Mandelbaum, "Urban Pasts and Urban Policies, " mimeograph, Department of City and Regional Planning, University of Pennsylvania, October 1979, 2.
2. Robert Reinhold,"City Limits: How Urban Policy Gets Made—Very Carefully" April 2, 1978, section 4, 1, asserts that the urban policy owed its existence largely to the lobbying of elected officials and federal bureaucrats, Reinhold called the process that produced the urban process "so complex, so uncertain at times, that important decisions were still being made 75 minutes before the package was disclosed at a briefing for reporters."
3. Susanna McBee, "Forceful HUD Secretary is Turning Her Critics Around," *Washington Post*, Saturday, March 18, 1978, A-6, contains quote from Bernard Hillenbrand, Executive Director, National Association of Counties.
4. McBee, "Forceful HUD Secretary," A-6.
5. Former HUD Secretary Robert Wood was to observe after Harris' death: "Since its inception the department (HUD) has always exhibited a split personality, carrying out the highly technical, almost arcane economic tasks of granting money subsidies to the volatile housing industry while purporting to speak for the urban poor and dispossessed. On the one hand, the constituencies that cluster around HUD are well-to-do mortgage bankers, prosperous homebuilders, affluent real estate developers, and politically powerful mayors. On the other, the claimants are the homeless, the public housing tenants, hard-pressed community-based organizations in ghetto neighborhoods, and churches struggling to learn the intricacies of designing, funding, and building low-income housing. Pat Harris understood both (constituencies)...but she never forgot what the department's main mission was—decent, affordable housing for everyone—and she persisted in that goal." In Marshall Kaplan and Franklin James, eds., *The Future of National Urban Policy* (Durham, NC: Duke University Press), v-vi.
6. R. Bauer, "Position Papers for NPA Information Project," mimeo, Harvard Business School, June 1, 1964.
7. Throughout this document, references to several of HUD's institutional issues have appeared, especially with regard to Califano's proposal for "cashing out" public housing programs to HEW, and with regard to challenges to HUD's Community Development Block Grant (CDBG) authority by the Department of Commerce in the battle over the Urban Development Bank. Harris took aggressive positions in opposition to both of these ideas. Moreover, HUD moved consistently to protect a number of existing programs, in conjunction with, as well as independent of, the URPG process. Figure 7.6, Chapter Seven. lists some of these programs.
8. Bauer, "Position Papers for NPA Information Project."
9. Harold Lasswell and David Lerner, eds., *The Policy Sciences* (Stanford, CA.: Stanford University Press, 1951); Robert A. Dahl and Charles E. Lindblom, *Politics, Economics and Welfare* (New York: Harper & Row, 1953). 349ff.;

David Braybrooke and Charles E. Lindblom, *A Strategy of Decision: Policy Evaluation as a Social Process* (New York: The Free Press) 1970; Charles E. Lindblom, "The Science of `Muddling Through'" *Public Administration Review* (1959):79.

10. Charles E. Lindblom, *The Policy Making Process,* Foundations of Modern Political Science Series (Englewood Cliffs, New Jersey: Prentice-Hall), 3.
11. Paul Davidoff and Thomas A. Reiner, "A Choice Theory of Planning," *Journal of the American Institute of Planners* XXVII (2, May 1962).
12. Edwin C. Hargrove, *Jimmy Carter as President: Leadership and the Politics of the Public Good* (Baton Rouge: Louisiana State University Press, 1982), 184. Also Joseph A. Califano, Jr., *Governing America: An Insider's Report from the White House and the Cabinet* (New York: Simon and Schuster, 1981), 418.
13. Hargrove, *Jimmy Carter as President,* 185.
14. Robert Reinhold, in a *New York Times,* March 26, 1978, 1, article, discussed the Carter urban policy decision process in terms of a "$3.7 Billion Cost" and a "Frenzy in the Administration," which was attributed by Reinhold to an anonymous insider, who characterized the President's decision session: "He just scared the _______ out of everybody. People began to jump out of windows and call their mothers at home. It was right interesting for awhile."
15. Hargrove, *Jimmy Carter as President,* 185.
16. Reference a series of correspondence from Ralph R. Widner, President, the Academy for Contemporary Problems, to Robert C. Embry, January 5, 1978; Yvonne Perry, February 14, 1978; and Robert Duckworth, February 24, 1978; presenting "a framework draft of the 1978 Urban Policy Report that we can use next week to produce a final draft." Also, memoranda from Dr. Thomas A. Reiner and R. Joyce Whitley raised concepts and theory-based issues: "...shouldn't there be something about building up the capacities—of institutions such as governments and neighborhoods;" as well as practical concerns for various communities that were left out of the policy documents: "...Chicago not on list...showed declining population...San Francisco somehow doesn't feel as though it should be there (on the list)." See archival materials, letter from Reiner to Perry, March 21, 1978.
17. Dom Bonafede quotes Arthur M. Schlesinger Jr., in the "White House Report," *National Journal,* April 15, 1978, 584: "...in remarks obviously aimed at Carter, (he) said ...'The White House when Franklin Roosevelt was President not only welcomed but sought and stimulated fresh thinking about national problems. His predecessor had been an engineer, who for all his intelligence, saw society abstractly, as a matter of organizing the properties of matter and energy. Once something is clear and tidy in an engineer's mind, that is it; and the obligation of the political process is to conform to the blueprint.'"
18. Thomas A. Reiner, ed., "Towards a National Urban Policy—Critical Reviews," *Journal of Regional Science* 19 (1, 1979); Robert Warren,

"National Urban Policy and the Local State: Paradoxes of Meanings, Action and Consequences," *Urban Affairs Quarterly* 25 (June 1990):541–561; Rochelle L. Stanfield, "The Development of Carter's Urban Policy: One Small Step for Federalism," *Publius, The Journal of Federalism* (Winter, 1978):39-53; Norman J. Glickman, ed., *The Urban Impacts of Federal Policies* (Baltimore: Johns Hopkins University Press, 1980); and Marshall Kaplan and Peggy L. Cuciti, eds., *The Great Society and Its Legacy: Twenty Years of U.S. Social Policy* (Durham: Duke University Press, 1986).

19. I have been greatly aided in this study by the persuasive analysis of the theories of Lindblom and others, by Enid Curtis Bok Schoettle's "The State of the Art in Policy Studies," in *The Study of Policy Formation*, Chapter 4, Raymond A. Bauer and Kenneth J. Gergen, eds. (New York: The Free Press, 1986), 149–179. In this passage, from page 151, Schoettle explores the theory of disjointed incrementalism found in Braybrooke and Lindblom, "The Strategy of Disjointed Incrementalism," 81-110.
20. Schoettle, "The State of the Art in Policy Studies," 150.
21. Schoettle, "The State of the Art in Policy Studies," 151.
22. Stuart Eizenstat and Patricia Roberts Harris, decision memorandum to Carter, January 9, 1978.
23. Califano, *Governing America*, 420 ff.
24. Roscoe C. Martin, *The Cities and the Federal System* (New York: Atherton Press, 1965) traces a self-conscious shift, for political as well as economic reasons, in the historic relationship between Washington and the cities. Beginning with the Depression, because of punitive state attitudes toward cities and a lack of state funds to address urban joblessness and disorganization, the federal government continued to reinforce this bilateral coalition for several decades.
25. County leaders, represented largely through the National Association of Counties (NACo), were quite aware of their step-child status in the eyes of federal and statewide officials. Often quarrelsome and paranoid about having equal time and participation in the URPG process, they were also proprietary about the concept of metropolitan planning and the associated metropolitan strategy. Their posture in dealing with URPG staff, as well as with Embry and me, was typical of "outsiders" who expect to be taken advantage of and, therefore, are untrusting.
26. Interviews conducted by the author with Donna E. Shalala, Robert C. Embry, and Robert Duckworth, contained in archival materials. With regard to the growth conference, its recommendations included: 1) Targeting on established high density areas; 2) Fiscal relief for hard-pressed cities; 3) Emphasis on problems of urban unemployment and particularly youth and minority unemployment; 4) Private-sector jobs initiatives; 5) Partnership of federal-state and local governments and private sector; 6) Support for federal subsidies (tax incentives, loans, grants) to encourage central city economic development; 7) Federal incentives for greater state responsibility for cities;

and 8) Federal programs and procedures administrative reforms. The full report on the growth conference is a part of archival materials.

27. Discussions earlier in this report refer to various lists of distressed cities produced by the Brookings Institution, Rand Corporation/Kettering Foundation studies, and the Committee for Economic Development (CED), in addition to the studies by the U.S. Department of the Treasury's Office of State and Local Finance.
28. From that author's play, *Long Day's Journey Into Night*, the full passage is: "None of us can help the things which life has done to us. They're done before you realize it, and once they're done, they make you do other things, until at last, everything comes between you and what you'd like to be...and you've lost your true self forever."
29. Two memoranda from Embry stand out as examples of these kinds of amendments. A three-page memo of January 5, 1978, states:

    > As I have discussed with you, I am concerned that our draft to date does not adequately or clearly express certain concerns. Please articulate these clearly in the third draft unless you disagree. If you do (and please do not hesitate to do so) please discuss the points with me.

    The memo continued with 14 points, including "A peroration indicating the importance of cities to our society," and ending with:

    > Stressing that the Administration is adopting a conservation ethic as opposed to a waste ethic. Related to this should be a much greater emphasis on conservation of energy as it relates to urban policy.

    This was followed by an equally detailed memo addressed to the principals and URPG staff, on January 5, 1978, reiterating the same 14 points, more forcefully. Archival materials.
30. Bauer, "Position Papers for NPA Information Project."

Chapter Nine

Reflections in The Mirror

If today—a decade and a half later—one were to undertake such an exercise as the Carter administration's national urban policy process, there probably would be very little support for the venture, inside or outside the White House, and even less support outside the boundaries of Washington, DC. The era of grand national policies has passed, many believe. Today, in the present environment of "What about my own issues," it is difficult even to build a consensus regarding international strategies, where once the common American good and the notion of a collective public interest prevailed.

The belief that there is a collective public interest, dense and massive enough to engender a constituency and support for a universal national policy effort, meets with cynicism. This is especially true as people increasingly are isolated by electronic interaction with their environment. As a consequence of supercharged technologies, communicators could just as easily be on the other side of the world from each other, as around the corner. For those who still live in inner-cities and in impacted metropolitan places, the preference appears to be for the interactive environment that *is* on the other side of the world, rather than around some of the more typically urban corners.

While there is general agreement that urban places are far worse off than ever—and anyone who was unsure got an object lesson from Los Angeles in 1993—there is almost no consensus about why, and more important, about whose responsibility it is to try to address this condition and to fix it.[1] Schisms and balkanization have developed, even within interest groups that have a relatively obvious and permanent profile, such as race or ethnicity, and therefore, for whom there is an expected association of shared values. Tensions rage as fully among black Americans about costs and benefits of solutions, as they do between blacks and whites.

More important, past experiences have discouraged all but the most optimistic urban advocates from seeking a national-scale fix. The feeling is that so far as urban remedies are concerned, each successive wave of massive interventive efforts—some have always referred to these initiatives as "liberal social engineering"—suboptimizes more and falls shorter of the stated goal of a decent quality of urban life.

In the current national environment, where it appears that few have first-hand information about the actual scope and shape of the urban problem, cavalier pronouncements prevail and conventional wisdom is the accepted litmus test for the validity of proposals. Recently, a member of Congress expressed consternation upon hearing that one out of every four black youth, in an elementary school classroom that he was visiting, would be killed or wounded by gunfire within the next eight years. This is not a new statistic, but the Congressman is not alone among contemporary opinion leaders who find such figures surprising. This may explain why orphanages, as depicted in the 1940s movie "Boys'Town" look like acceptable solutions to juvenile crime and violence.

Through the Glass, Darkly

In part, of course, the disappointing culmination of the Urban and Regional Policy Group' national urban policy process, and of the Carter presidency as well, which failed in its re-election attempt in 1980, are not politically encouraging to aggressive urban agendas. And there are several conventional wisdom parallels between the Carter presidency and the Clinton presidency, beyond their regional similarities and the surprise win of the election from an entrenched Republican incumbency. One similarity that bears mentioning concerns the campaign promises each made to cities during their respective presidential election bids and how each fared in fulfilling those promises.

The Carter due bill has been fully explored above. Clinton, on the other hand, after a circumspect campaign in which he promised only that "It's the economy, stupid," announced during the first ninety days of his presidency that, in effect, "It's the cities, stupid." Advancing an agenda for "rebuilding America's cities," Clinton called for:

- Investing in communities
- Empowerment through economic opportunity
- A national crime strategy
- Rebuilding our urban infrastructure
- New hope for affordable housing

- Fighting homelessness
- Empowerment through education
- Quality, affordable health care[2]

Time will tell if empowerment zones and enterprise communities are to be the sum and substance of the Clinton urban agenda, or if other items in the President's list will gain ascendancy. Clearly, in the present cynical climate, small replications of strategies that clearly work seem preferable to another try at the abortive national urban policy effort of so many years ago. The empowerment zones, being initiated in six large urban communities, three supplemental urban communities, and three rural communities, along with ninety-two enterprise locations, offer such an opportunity for smaller scale, locally inspired experimentation with remedies that are likely to work. Most of these ideas, anyway, are residuals of the thirty-year American experimentation with intended and unintended urban policies.

During the years since URPG faded away, there has been another hiatus in serious national concern for cities. In fact, while researching current aspects of urban policy for this study, it became clear that, after 1986, there were not enough popular news and journal articles on urban policy to justify continuing the urban policy heading in the *Reader's Guide to Periodical Literature*. The Reagan/Bush administration had promised little to cities and had managed to deliver less. The window looking back into policies for cities during the recent past is dark indeed.

Industry has continued to abandon cities for nonurban locations at an alarming rate. Drug abuse and associated social disorganization, along with steadily increasing perceptions of violent crime against persons and property, characterize these communities.

Yet, in spite of these indications, cities are the primary repository for newly arrived immigrants, most of whom are Spanish-speaking non-whites, followed closely in numbers by Asians. Between 1980 and 1990, immigrants accounted for 39 percent of America's total population growth, and they caused a raw population increase of 11.5 percent in the nation's ten largest cities.[3] Metropolitan areas also are the primary residence for three out of four black Americans, in whose eyes cities still appear to be the surest promise of a ladder up out of poverty into the American main stream. In view of the still unyielding attitudes against diversity that pit whites against nonwhites, well-to-do against poor, cities are the only real alternative for those who are neither white nor well-to-do.

Recent events have suggested that because urban conditions are so bad, even this alternative sets the city against itself.

Some observers feel that it is artificial to distinguish the Bush years from the Reagan years when it comes to federal policy toward cities during the last decade. In a very real sense, the impression of a seamless policy about cities is well earned. The Reagan/Bush administration succeeded in cutting the entrenched umbilical cord that some claimed stretched from the White House directly into the demanding bellies of city halls across the country.

Federal assistance programs and economic aid to cities and their residents were dismantled. Between the high point in 1978 when the national urban policy was announced, and ten years later when George Bush began his term as president, direct aid to cities fell by almost one-third: from 28 percent of the total aid distributed in 1978, to 17 percent of the 1988 total. Conversely, overall aid from the federal government to states and noncity localities (counties, suburbs, and rural districts) increased almost 100 percent in that same period, from $69 billion to over $114 billion.[4]

The Reagan/Bush team, moreover, owed substantial ideological debts to their supporters who were mostly suburban and rural, and in the main, conservatives and self-styled New Federalists. They believed that the best government was the one that governed least. And President Reagan's anti-urban attitudes lasted into and throughout the Bush presidency. Ronald Reagan "danced" with the mainly nonurban constituents who brought him to the presidency. George Bush, Reagan's Vice President for two terms and his successor, inherited and continued to fill out Reagan's nonurban "dance card."

Through the Urban Policy Looking Glass

The process of developing the national urban policy was an Alice-in-Wonderland experience, given the intensity of the time and the sense of being a part of change. Yet, the effects were fleeting and ephemeral, much like Alice's adventure. In fact, few know much in detail or remember much about the era at all. Fewer still are inclined to recall the events or to freely admit that they do.

In retrospect, the changes from the national urban policy exercise were so incremental that with the exception of the four executive orders that were signed and announced by August 1978, there was little that could be pointed to as an urban policy product. In the Great Society programs, there was CAP, the Job Corps, Head Start, and a number of other landmark initiatives, which, like them or not, were distinctive and strongly associated with the larger effort. There were no such outcomes from URPG and the Carter policy.

Disjointed incrementalism is a realistic approach to, and an intellectual framework for understanding the ongoing policymaking process in a democracy such as the United States, but it does not take into account the effects of changes in political and ideological leadership with regard to maintenance of effort. Fifteen years later, most of the urban policy modifications have disappeared. Those that do remain lack clear identity as national urban policy initiatives; others are thought to be new ideas, such as current Community Development Bank proposals, which have a striking similarity to Ur-Bank.

Even the slogan, "Partnership to Conserve America's Communities," urged upon the President by Patricia Harris and Stu Eizenstat as a talisman for the Carter White House's urban effort, has long since fallen into disuse. The opposite has been the case with the Great Society, a term whose visibility—and alleged disrepute—increases daily.

Conclusion

Within this book, we have looked at questions about the competing tensions of necessary political leadership for developing policy and the concomitant indispensable bureaucratic investment in seeing that policy is implemented. The relative speed with which the impact of the national urban policy was neutralized by changes in national political leadership, and the lack of durability thereafter of a public mentality receptive to nationally generated urban remedies, strongly suggests that there probably were serious weaknesses in any nationally directed urban policy development process.

Revisionists today energetically re-cast the results of the Great Society's programs in contemporary contexts. In so doing, they downgrade the importance of initiatives once thought to have significant value. This rewriting of history also has resulted in the elimination altogether from collective memory of efforts such as the Carter national urban policy process. One is encouraged, therefore, to look for alternatives to nationally designed solutions, when seeking lasting remedies to urban problems, which seem to be so enduring.

And, contrary to Senator Sam Erving's observation that both human beings and lightning bugs carry their illumination behind them, retrospective assessments can seriously distort, rather than illuminate, reality. Consider the current assertions, enjoying currency in some high-profile political quarters, that huge sums of money were frittered away, during the Johnson and Carter administrations, by the federal government's obsession with cities. In fact, a calculation of the most liberal annual per capita expenditure of federal funds on the urban poor at the height of so-called federal largess was $2.37.

More research needs to be conducted on the simultaneous actions that took place at the local levels—in cities and urban towns—when the federal government *was* providing a city-friendly context and strong national leadership. The solutions do not always have to come from the top. In fact, there is evidence that those that continue had their genesis at the bottom. More must be known, however, about how much national help is too much, and how little national help is still sufficient.

Notes

1. Jewelle Taylor Gibbs writes in "After the L.A. Riots: Social Work's Role in Healing Cities," Zellerback Family Fund Professor's Occasional Paper, (Berkeley: University of California, 1992), 4:

> The 1992 riots did not cause the economic dislocation of South Central Los Angeles—they merely accelerated it by contributing directly to the loss of thousands of jobs, further weakening the economic base of the area by destroying the small business sector, further eroding property values in the low-to-moderate-income neighborhoods, and discouraging potential capital investment to revitalize the area. About 20,000 workers became unemployed immediately after the riots. Although half returned to work by the end of May, 10,000 remained jobless.

2. "Bill Clinton on Rebuilding America's Cities," Democratic National Committee, 1993, Xerox.
3. "Cover Story: The Immigrants: How They're Helping to revitalize the U.S. Economy," *Business Week*, July 13, 1992, 118.
4. Richard Nathan and John Logo, "Intergovernmental Fiscal Roles and Relations," *Annals of the American Academy of Political and Social Science* (509, May 5, 1990):42.

Appendix A

National Policy and New Community Development Act of 1970

TITLE VII—NATIONAL POLICY AND NEW COMMUNITY DEVELOPMENT

Short Title and Statement of Purpose

Sec. 701 (a) This title may be cited as the "National Urban Policy and New Community Development Act of 1970."

(b) It is the policy of the Congress and the purpose of this title to provide for the development of a national urban policy and to encourage the rational, orderly, efficient and economic growth, development and redevelopment of our States, metropolitan areas, cities, counties, towns and communities in predominantly rural areas which demonstrate a special potential for accelerated growth; to encourage the prudent use and conservation of energy and our natural resources; and to encourage and support development which will assure our communities of and their residents adequate tax bases, community services, job opportunities, and good housing in well-balanced neighborhoods in socially, economically, and physically attractive living environments.

Part A—Development of a National Urban Policy

Findings and Declaration of Policy

Sec. 702. (a) The Congress finds that rapid changes in patterns of urban settlement, including change in population distribution and economic bases of urban areas, have created an imbalance between the Nation's needs and resources and seriously threaten our physical and social environment, and the financial viability of our cities, and that the economic and social development of the Nation, the proper conservation of our energy and other natural resources, and the achievement of satisfactory living standards depend upon the sound, orderly and more balanced development of all areas of the Nation.

(b) The Congress further finds that Federal programs affect the location of population, economic growth, and the character of urban development; that such programs frequently conflict and result in undesirable and costly patterns of urban development and redevelopment which adversely affect the environment and wastefully use energy and other natural resources; and that existing and future programs must be interrelated and coordinated within a system of orderly development and established priorities consistent with a national urban policy.

(c) To promote the general welfare and properly apply the resources of the Federal Government in strengthening the economic and social health of all areas of the Nation and more adequately protect the physical environment and conserve energy and other natural resources, the Congress declares that the Federal Government, consistent with the responsibilities of State and local government and the private sector, must assume responsibility for the development of a national urban policy which shall incorporate social, economic and other appropriate factors. Such policy shall serve as a guide in making specific decisions at the national level which affect the pattern of urban development and redevelopment and shall provide a framework for development of interstate, State, and local urban policy.

(d) The Congress further declares that the national urban policy should–

(1) favor patterns of urbanization and economic development and stabilization which offer a range of alternative locations and encourage the wise and balanced use of physical and human resources in metropolitan and urban regions as well as in smaller urban places which have a potential for accelerated growth;

(2) foster the continued economic strength of all parts of the United States, including central cities, suburbs, smaller communities, local neighborhoods, and rural areas;

(3) encourage patterns of development and redevelopment which minimize disparities among States, regions, and cities;

(4) treat comprehensively the problems of poverty and employment (including the erosion of tax bases, and the need for better community services and job opportunities) which are associated with disorderly urbanization and rural decline;

(5) develop means to encourage good housing for all Americans without regard to race or creed;

(6) refine the role of the Federal Government in revitalizing existing communities and encouraging planned, large-scale urban and new community development;

(7) strengthen the capacity of general governmental institutions to contribute to balanced urban growth and stabilization; and

(8) facilitate increased coordination in the administration of Federal programs so as to encourage desirable patterns of urban development and redevelopment, encourage the prudent use of energy and other natural resources, and protect the physical environment.

National Urban Policy Report

Sec. 703. (a) The President shall transmit to the Congress during February 1978, and during February of every even-numbered year thereafter, a Report on National Urban Policy which shall contribute to the formulation of such a policy, and in addition shall include—

(1) information statistics and significant trends relating to the pattern of urban development for the preceding two years;

(2) a summary of significant problems facing the United States as a result of urban trends and developments affecting the well-being of urban areas;

(3) an examination of the housing and related community development problems experienced by cities undergoing a growth rate which equals or exceeds the national average;

(4) an evaluation of the progress and effectiveness of Federal efforts designed to meet such problems and to carry out the national urban policy;

(5) an assessment of the policies and structure of existing and proposed interstate planning and developments affecting such policy;

(6) a review of State, local, and private policies, plans, and programs relevant to such policy;

(7) current and foreseeable needs in the areas served by policies, plans, and programs designed to carry out such policy, and the steps being taken to meet such needs; and

(8) recommendations for programs and policies for carrying out such policy, including such legislation and administrative actions as may be deemed necessary and desirable.

(b) The President may transmit from time to time to the Congress supplementary reports on urban policy which shall include such supplementary and revised recommendations as may be appropriate.

Appendix B

Urban and Regional Policy Group Principals and Deputies

Housing and Urban Development
Patricia Roberts Harris, URPG Convenor
Secretary for Housing and Urban Development
Personal Secretary: Catherine Burton

Robert C. Embry, Jr., URPG Deputy
Assistant Secretary for Community Planning and Development
Personal Secretary: Yvonne Emerson

Yvonne S. Perry, URPG Executive Director
Deputy Assistant Secretary Designate
Community Planning and Development
Personal Secretary: Trophelia Ajala

White House
Stuart E. Eizenstat, Principal
Assistant to the President for Domestic Affairs and Policy
Personal Secretary: Joann Hurley

Bert Carp, Deputy
Domestic Policy Staff
Personal Secretary: Sandy Dockery

Department of the Treasury
W. Michael Blumenthal, Principal
Secretary of the Treasury

Roger C. Altman, Deputy
Assistant Secretary for Domestic Finance
Personal Secretary: Nancy Fiester

Department of Commerce
Juanita M. Kreps, Principal
Secretary of Commerce

Jerry J. Jasinowski, Deputy
Assistant Secretary for Policy
Personal Secretary: Robin Stein

Department of Labor
Ray Marshall, Principal
Secretary of Labor

Arnold Packer, Deputy
Assistant Secretary for Policy, Evaluation and Research
Personal Secretary: Rene McKinney

Department of Health, Education and Welfare
Joseph A. Califano, Jr., Principal
Secretary of Health, Education and Welfare
Personal Secretary: Donna Dorgan

Appendix C

Outline of Action Required To Implement Base Recommendations (URPG)*

I. Economic and Community Development

	Type of Action	Comment
HUD - CDBG		
Consolidated HAP and CDP	Administrative	Guideline change
3 yr. pl. period-—HAP & CDP	Administrative	Guideline change
Neighborhood strategy areas—targeting	Administrative/ legislation	Targeting of respective program funds may require legislation
Enforce citizen participation requirements	Administrative	Guideline change
Amend regs to foster spatial deconcentration	Administrative/ legislative	Guideline change
Extend Econ. Devel. activities	Administrative	Guideline change
Change regs.—local govts. & business sector	Administrative	Guideline change

* This outline is based on the base evaluation memo submitted by Robert C. Embry, Jr., to Stuart Eisenstat. It should be read in the context of the memo.

	Type of Action	Comment
HUD - UDAG		
Joint EDA review of UDAG applications	Administrative	Guideline change
Standardized program requirements	Administrative	Interagency agreement/ guideline change
Simplified program requirements—EDA	Administrative	Interagency agreement/ guideline change
Joint training	Administrative	Interagency agreement
Joint technical assistance	Administrative	Interagency agreement
HUD - 701		
Refine objectives	Administrative/ legislation	Guideline changes; legislation changes may be required depending on extent of change
Require states and Metro areas to initiate planning changes	Administrative/ legislation	Guideline change; legislation may be needed depending on extent of revision of requirements
Strengthen management objectives of 701	Administrative/ legislation	Guideline change; legislation will be needed if new program required (see proposal)

	Type of Action	**Comment**
OMB Executive Order; single Metro area organization	Presidential—OMB; administrative; legislation	Amended Executive Order; guideline change; new legislation may be needed depending on final structural changes
Amend OMB A-95 review; urban impact indicators	Presidential—OMB; administrative	Amended Executive Order; guideline change
Require A-95 reviewing agencies to inform HUD of auto urban impact of Federally assisted action	Presidential—OMB; administrative	Amended Executive Order; guideline change
HUD - New Towns		
Reorient program to New town-in-town	Administrative/ Presidential	Guideline change (need Presidential action to reopen program)
Simplify procedures concerning application, funding and monitoring	Administrative	Guideline change
Flexible guidelines given changes in orientation	Administrative	Guideline changes
Clarification concerning program coverage	Administrative/ legislation	Guideline changes; legislation needed to refine program coverage
EDA - Title I and Title II - Public Works/Development		

	Type of Action	Comment
Target more assistance on communities in distressed cities	Legislation/ administrative	Legislation may be needed depending on extent of targeting, otherwise guideline changes
Revise guidelines—25,000 to 250,000 eligible	Administrative	Guideline changes
Tie program to community plans and strategies	Administrative	Guideline changes
Joint use of various EDA programs	Administrative	Guideline changes
EDA - Title II - Business Development Loans		
Tougher OEDP guidelines	Administrative	Guideline changes
Target program on communities in distress	Legislation/ administrative	Legislation may be needed depending on extent of targeting, guideline changes
Streamline and decentralize administration	Administrative	Guideline/ reorganization changes
Tighten and enforce project selection system; benefit long-term unemployment	Administrative/ legislation	Guideline changes; legislation amendments possible in relation to targeting

	Type of Action	Comment
Linkages with other agencies	Administrative	Guideline changes; interagency agreement
EDA - Title III		
Flexible State use of funds rather than project-by-project approval	Legislation	(?)
Local capacity - shift resources	Administrative	Guideline changes
Coordinate 304 assistance with EDA's economic development assistance	Administrative	Guideline changes
Evaluate EDA incentives to increase State plans and economic development	Administrative	Guideline changes
Change planning prerequisites to require work programs for expenditure of investment dollars	Administrative	Guideline changes
Close formal and informal links with either agency	Administrative	Guideline changes; interagency agreement
EDA - Title III - Section 301/302		

	Type of Action	Comment
Target funds to improve city development capacity	Legislation/ administrative	Legislation may be needed depending on extent of targeting; guideline changes
Tougher OEDP prerequisites; local capacity	Administrative	Guideline changes
Work with other agencies; coordinated planning guidelines	Administrative	Guideline changes
Improved public investment strategies to leverage private investment	Administrative	Guideline changes
Use program to strengthen policy making at local level	Administrative	Guideline changes
DOT—Urban System Highway		
Consolidate FHWA & UMTA planning funds	Legislation	
Make planning grants directly to designated MPOs	Legislation	
Make funds eligible for all transportation plan activities	Legislation	
Require statewide planning process after October 1, 1980	Legislation	

	Type of Action	Comment
Require long-range land use plans, devel. objectives	Legislation	
Emphasis on greater use of existing systems	Administrative	Guideline changes
Greater flexibility in use of funds/ transferability	Legislation	
Some Federal share of highways and public transportation	Legislation	
Allow urbanized areas to use highway funds for any road or street not on primary/ interstate	Legislation	
DOT - Interstate Highway Transfers		
Increase Federal share of Interstate Transfer projects	Legislation	
DOT - Section 3 Mass Transit Capital Grant		
Direct the discretionary transit grant to major bus fleet expansion	Capital grant	
Require governors, local officials, transit operators to designate recipient for each project	Legislation	

	Type of Action	Comment
Coordinated packaging—HUD, EDA, etc.	Administrative	Guideline change; interagency agreement
Require careful analysis of alternative prior to investment commitment	Administrative	Guideline change
DOT - Section 5 Transit Assistance		
Adjust transit apportionment formula; more sensitive to large urban area needs	Legislation	
Amend matching and maintenance of effort requirements	Legislation	
Make transit formula funds source of assistance for routine capital activities, as well as operating assistance	Legislation	
Monitoring and evaluation	Administrative	Guideline change
SBA 7(a) - Business Loans		
Streamline loan processing procedures	Administrative	Guideline change
Establish uniform risk definitions	Administrative	Guideline change

	Type of Action	Comment
Evaluate option - private lenders approve loan guarantee	Administrative	Guideline change
Negotiate with bonds in order to give greater discretion in handling SBA guaranteed loan problems	Legislation/ Administrative	Guideline change
SBA - SBIC's & MESCIB's		
Restructure SBIC's & MESCIB's to encourage higher private risk	Legislation/ Administrative	Legislation authorization; guideline change
Establish specialized venture capital SBBIC	Legislation/ Administrative	Legislation authorization; guideline change
SBA - LDC		
Provide SBA technical assistance to LDCs	Administrative	Guideline change
Strengthen staff capacity	Administrative	
Streamline applications procedure to eliminate delays	Administrative	Guideline change
Grant LDCs greater loan approval ...	Legislation/ Administrative	Legislation clarification; guideline change

	Type of Action	Comment
Help equip and train non-SBA people to assist in financial packaging	Administrative	Guideline change
CSA Community Economic Development (CDC)		
Better management and technical backup	Administrative	Shift in personnel; guideline change
Technical assistance to existing CDCs	Administrative	Guideline change
Use well managed CDCs as a focus for neighborhood demonstration	Administrative	Demonstration
Develop formal arrangements between Federal agencies linking CDCs as to range of economic/community development aids	Administrative	Guideline change; interagency agreement

II. Improving Local Social Services

	Type of Action	Comment
HEW - Social Services (Title XX)		
Pass thru funds to city hall	Legislation	
State maintenance of effort & collaborative strategies with cities	Administrative	Guideline change

	Type of Action	Comment
HEWS - Health Service Delivery		
Expanding existing health services	Legislation/ Administrative	Fund authorizations; guideline changes
Simplify program submissions	Administrative	Guideline changes
Better coordination of adolescent pregnancy programs	Administrative	Guideline change
HEW - ESEA		
Supplemental ESEA/ local educational agencies with larger numbers of low income children	Legislation	
Secure increase State role thru incentives	Legislation	
Provide school-based program to improve employability of youth	Legislation	
Demonstrate alternatives for high schools in distressed cities	Legislation	
Toughen monitoring of expenditure (ESEA) & improve evaluation	Administrative	Guideline change

	Type of Action	Comment
Toughen enforcement of public school responsibilities re-private school	Administrative	Guideline change
CSA - Community Action Program		
Free CSA support funds to respond to local needs (e.g., additional funding/ allowance of overhead)	Legislation/ administrative	Funding and guideline change
Amend authorizing statute to make salary and administrative limits more flexible	Legislation	
Direct CSA to shift emphasis from gap filling services to resource mobility	Administrative	Guideline change
Closer linkages with other agencies	Administrative	Guideline change

III. Improving the Environment

	Type of Action	Comment
EPA - Air Quality Grants		
Planning grants to local air quality agencies	Legislation/ Administrative	Authorization and guideline change

	Type of Action	Comment
Establish emission reduction program which allows room for future growth	Legislation/ Administrative	Authorization and guideline change
Closely link EPA's efforts with economic assistance grants	Administrative	Guideline change; interagency agreement
Coordinate EPA air quality efforts with community, transportation and economic development activities	Administrative	Guideline change, interagency agreement
EPA - Wastewater Facility Construction		
Coordinate facility const. function with strengthened 208 water resources	Legislation/ Administrative	Statutory authorization, guideline change
Strengthen role of regional agencies in dealing with city & suburban wastewater needs	Legislation/ Administrative	Statutory authorization, guideline change
Reduce urban sprawl potential (e.g., design certain changes, determining cost effectiveness	Administrative	Guideline change
EPA - Areawide Waste Treatment (208)		

	Type of Action	Comment
Focus more on water pollution problems of existing urban areas	Administrative	Guideline change
Changing guidelines so as to not promote sprawl	Administrative	Guideline change
Focus on urban-generated wastewater problems	Administrative	Guideline change
Assure closer links with other Federal assisted planning groups	Administrative	Guideline change
Already in statute	Administrative	Guideline change, interagency agreement
Link 201 facilities to 208 plans	Legislation/ Administrative	Statutory authorization, guideline change

IV. Fiscal Assistance/Condition

	Type of Action	Comment
Department of Treasury (GRS)		
Comprehensive zero-based budgeting evaluation	Administrative	
Department of Treasury (ARFA)		

	Type of Action	Comment
Increasingly target program	Legislation	
Eliminate current restrictions on operating/ capital expenditures	Legislation	
Eliminate requirements that funds be spent within six months	Legislation	
DOL - CETA Title I		
Re-evaluate formula to improve targeting on distressed cities and structurally unemployed	Administrative/ Legislation	Evaluation of current formula and guidelines; preparation of legislation; amend existing guidelines
Develop improved monitoring and information systems	Administrative	Guideline changes
Develop close links with other agency's community development programs through providing improved technical assistance and incentives to prime sponsors	Administrative	Guideline changes, interagency agreement
DOL - CETA, Title II and VI		

	Type of Action	Comment
Improve the targeting of funds upon States and prime sponsors within States by taking into account undercounting of the unemployed and underemployed and duration of unemployment	Administrative/ Legislation	CETA reauthorization legislation; guideline changes
Establish a permanent public service employment program that automatically provides assistance to local governments when designated unemployment levels are reached	legislation	CETA reauthorization; guideline changes
Improve targeting upon disadvantaged groups by tightening eligibility criteria, including family income and duration of unemployment	Legislation/ Administrative	CETA reauthorization; guideline changes
Improve placement by establishing placement goals, improved monitoring and limiting duration of employment in a PSE position	Legislation/ Administrative	CETA reauthorization legislation; guideline changes

	Type of Action	Comment
Discourage substitution by tightening eligibility requirements, limiting the duration of employment in a PSE position, mandating equal pay for equal work by PSE and non-PSE workers, limiting salaries and limiting salary supplementation by local governments	Legislation/ Administrative	CETA reauthorization legislation; guideline changes
Emphasize manpower development and structural targeting as CETA's countercyclical objectives become less prominent by continuing to allocate funds to areas of substantial unemployment and by creating programs to target assistance upon population groups with special needs, such as youth, older workers, and the handicapped	Legislation/ Administrative	CETA reauthorization legislation; guideline changes
Improve links with other agencies' development programs which can create jobs	Administrative	Guideline changes, interagency agreements

	Type of Action	**Comment**
DOL - CETA, Titles III and IV: Youth Employment and Demonstration Projects Act of 1977		
Improve efforts to meet needs of targeted population groups under titles I, III, and IV while continuing special programs under Titles III and IV	Administrative	Regulations and guidelines
Improve monitoring and evaluation	Administrative	Guideline change; improve monitoring and evaluation
EDA - Local Public Works		
Enforce set asides for minority contractors	Administrative	Guideline changes and enforcement
Oversee contractors to assure allocation of jobs to long term unemployed and minority workers	Administrative	Guideline changes and enforcement
Increase use of training programs in association with projects	Administrative	Guideline changes and enforcement
Manage "lowest bidder requirements, so that firms can pay extra costs of hiring, training, etc.	Administrative	Guideline changes and enforcement

	Type of Action	Comment
Continue to see that projects are expeditiously completed	Administrative	Guideline changes and enforcement

V. Improved Housing

	Type of Action	Comment
HUD - Direct Housing Loans for Elderly and Handicapped Persons (Section 202)		
Simplify handbook and development process to speed up development, reduce cost, and assist minority applicants	Administrative	Guideline changes
Provide technical assistance to minority developers to broaden the reach of the program	Administrative	Allocate staff, guideline changes
Expand portion of program targeted upon the handicapped; encourage deinstitution by providing more small group homes	Administrative	Allocate resources, guideline changes
HUD Public Housing		

	Type of Action	Comment
Revise modernization formula to encourage modernization of older projects in central cities	Legislation/ Administrative	Clarify statutory language; guideline changes
Target special allocation of modernization funds on 60 most troubled projects	Administrative	Guideline change
Continue demonstration program using tenants and neighborhood residents in the repair and management of HUD-owned projects	Administrative	Program implementation
Continue to use CETA funds and CETA funded projects for training local residents and tenants in the repair and management of HUD-owned projects	Administrative	Program implementation
Initiate the same type of management reviews and standards for public housing as for HUD/FHA-insured projects	Administrative	Guideline change

	Type of Action	Comment
Offer additional operating funds to public housing authorities which have demonstrated improved management capacity	Administrative	Allocate funds, guideline change
Housing Assistance to Low and Moderate Income Households (Section 8)		
Implement Neighborhood Services Program providing additional housing assistance funds for substantial rehabilitation of existing housing in designated areas	Administrative	Guideline change; program implementation
Grant additional housing assistance funds to metropolitan areas with areawide housing opportunity plans	Administrative	Guideline change, program implementation
Assure that 5 % of units built with assisted funds be accessible to the handicapped	Administrative	Guideline change
Require owners of buildings which qualify for Section 8 assistance to undertake modernization work	Legislation	Legislation and guideline change

	Type of Action	Comment
HUD - Single-Family Housing Subsidies (Section 235 and Tandem) GNMA Targeted		
Use 4% interest rate and 3% down-payment to create new housing opportunities for families earning up to 95% of median income	Administrative	Guideline change
Target Section 235 on low and moderate income urban areas	Administrative	Guideline change
Target tandem financing on middle-income housing in central city neighborhoods in need of revitalization	Legislation/ Administrative	Legislation and guideline change
Use GNMA targeted tandem to encourage active participation of private housing industry in central cities	Administrative	Guideline change
HUD - Mortgage Insurance		
Provide young people the opportunity to pay reduced mortgage payments for the first 5 years of their mortgage	Administrative	Guideline change

	Type of Action	Comment
Eliminate requirement for HUD inspections for single-family homes in those jurisdictions with qualified inspectors and local building codes	Administrative	Guideline change
Use local building codes in place of Federal minimum property standards (MPS) in those jurisdictions that have qualified local codes	Administrative	Guideline change
Permit new home purchasers with FGA insured mortgages to use private home warranty programs	Administrative	Guideline change
HUD - Multifamily Mortgage Insurance		
Simplify and combine processing for multifamily mortgage insurance or coinsurance with local lending institutions	Administrative	Guideline change
Develop insurance for existing multi-family structures using	Administrative	Guideline change

	Type of Action	Comment
Install computerized management monitoring system for FHA multifamily projects	Administrative	Guidelines and program implementation
Conduct management reviews for project management in all insured multifamily projects	Administrative	Guideline change
Use CETA funds and CETA-funded projects to train local residents in the repair and management of HUD-owned projects	Administrative	Guideline change, possible interagency agreement
HUD - Section 312 Rehabilitation Loan Program		
Encourage use of Section 312 funds for multifamily housing rehabilitation	Legislation/ Administrative	Prepare legislation (fund availability) and guideline change
Permit deviation from codes if the end result protects the occupant and the government's loan by meeting essential	Administrative	Guideline change
Target funds on low-income and distressed neighborhoods	Legislation/ Administrative	Clarify statute; guideline change

	Type of Action	Comment
Earmark funds for cities to improve their planning and use of staff	Administrative	Guideline change and fund allocations
Reduce restrictions and increase local discretion and responsibility for administering program	Administrative	Guideline change

Appendix D
Letter to Reviewers, March 17, 1978

DEPARTMENT OF HOUSING AND URBAN DEVELOPMENT
WASHINGTON, D.C. 20410

OFFICE OF THE ASSISTANT SECRETARY
FOR COMMUNITY PLANNING AND DEVELOPMENT

IN REPLY REFER TO:

March 17, 1978

I apologize for having taken so long to express my deep appreciation for your participation and assistance in reviewing the Urban Policy Draft in November.

As you know, your expertise and opinions are greatly respected. Therefore, I was very gratified that you were willing to take time from your busy schedule to come into Washington to help us in this very complex and challenging task.

I note regretfully that we were so very fortunate to have the late Bill Wheaton join in this effort with us. His death stresses for me the significance of our loss of him as a friend and also as a colleague, who would have been pleased that our effort has come even this far.

I hope that you have not been overly dismayed by the reports in the press on the status of the Urban Policy Statement. While it is true that the President has not yet approved a final package, nor has he approved new program initiatives, he has reviewed the proposed policies and strategies and has accepted these. I have attached for your information a list of 14 principles to which the President subscribes and which have governed our most recent efforts at redrafting the Urban Policy Statement.

I enclose also for your information a copy of the note from the President to Secretary Harris and Stuart Eizenstat following his review of an Executive Summary of the Urban Policies. I stress that this Executive Summary did not include recommended program initiatives. We are, at this time, carrying out one of his assignments; to analyze existing programs in terms of their effectiveness and effect on urban communities. Following

2.

that analysis, the new program initiatives which have been recommended by participating agencies will be reviewed by the Urban and Regional Policy staff and the White House Domestic Policy staff in the context of strengths and weaknesses found in existing programs. Finally, a decision memorandum will be presented to the President which will relate existing programs as well as new program initiatives to the Principles for an Urban Policy, to which the President already has given his approval.

We who have worked on developing an Urban Policy Statement are encouraged to recognize that finally we have on paper - and so identified - a statement of normative expectations about urban places, particularly those which are in various stages of distress. This effort remains unique in that it is collaborative. It represents interagency participation, rather than isolated development and super-imposition by either an elitist internal group, or an external group of consultants - the models which have characterized previous policy-making efforts. In that regard, therefore, I feel that we have accomplished much. I feel also that there still remains a great deal to be done.

We are grateful that you have been willing to participate, to lend your status and prestige to the effort, and to be identified with a difficult but worthwhile attempt to formulate a standard against which present and future behavior toward urban places ought to be judged. Attached is a copy of the Third Revised Draft, now entitled: National Urban Policy: Conserving Americas' Cities and Neighborhoods. We would very much appreciate receiving comments which you might have on this version of the policy. It will be very helpful to have your comments no later than March 22. I shall be happy to provide typing capability if you send your comments in draft form. We look forward to hearing from you.

Sincerely,

Yvonne Scruggs Perry
Deputy Assistant Secretary (Designate)

Attachments

Glossary

ACIR—American Center for Intergovernmental Research
BLF—Black Leadership Forum
CBC—Congressional Black Caucus
CBD—Central Business District
CED—Committee for Economic Development
CETA—Comprehensive Employment and Training Act
CDBG—Community Development Block Grant
CPD—Community Planning and Development
COSCAA—Council of State Community Affairs Agencies
CSA—Community Services Agency
DOL—U.S. Department of Labor
DOT—U.S. Department of Transportation
EDA—Economic Development Administration (Department of Commerce)
HARYOU—Harlem Youth Opportunities Unlimited, Inc.
HEW—U.S. Department of Health, Education, and Welfare, now called
HHS, the Department of Health and Human Services
HUD—U.S. Department of Housing and Urban Development
MBE—Minority Business Enterprise
MDTA—Manpower Development and Training Administration
Maybank—Aan amendment that precluded the U.S. Department of Defense from establishing set-asides in contracts
NACo—National Association of Counties
NARC—National Association of Regional Councils
NASPAA—National Association of Schools of Public Affairs and Administration
NCSL—National Council of State Legislatures
NIMH—National Institute of Mental Health
NGA—National Governors Association
NGP—National Growth Policy
OEO—Office of Economic Opportunity
OMB—Office of Management and Budget

OPEC—Organization of Petroleum Exporting Countries
PD&R—Office of Policy Development and Research
SBA—Small Business Administration
SDF—Secretary's Discretionary Fund
SMSA—Standard Metropolitan Statistical Areas
UDAG—Urban Development Action Grant Program
Ur-Bank—Urban Development Bank
URPG—Urban and Regional Policy Group

Bibliography

Archival Materials

Urban and Regional Policy Group. Internal memoranda, correspondence, working papers, policy drafts, presidential and secretarial correspondence, and personal logs and notes. January 1977 through June 1978. Specific documents cited in the text are listed below:

Altman, Roger C. "Interim Work Requirements for Members of the Public Finance Task Force." Memorandum for Public Finance Task Force, August 22, 1977.

Altman, Roger C. "Evaluation of Counter-Cyclical Revenue Sharing: Recommendation for Modification of the Program." Memorandum to URPG, September 15, 1977.

Anderson, Bernard. "Employment Policy for Urban Areas." Memorandum to Yvonne Scruggs Perry, October 17, 1977.

Carter, Jimmy. Handwritten note, February 16, 1978.

Carter, Jimmy, Memorandum, January 31, 1978.

Carter, Jimmy. Memorandum, March 21, 1977.

Champion, Hale (Deputy Secretary, Department of Health, Education, and Welfare). Memorandum to Embry, November 17, 1977.

Chollar, Robert G. (Chairman of the Board and President, Charles F. Kettering Foundation) Letter to Patricia Roberts Harris, November 28, 1977.

Curtis, Lynn. Memorandum to Harris, July 1977.

Curtis, Lynn. Memorandum to principal staff, April 25, 1977.

Curtis, Lynn and PD&R Staff. "A New Approach to a National Urban Policy." Unpublished mimeo, March 29, 1977.

Downs, Anthony. Memorandum to Robert C. Embry, Jr., December 4, 1977.

Draft Progress Report, URPG, July/August 1977.

Duckworth, Robert P. Memorandum for Embry. Undated draft, June 1977.

Eizenstat, Stuart. Series of memoranda to all domestic departments, beginning March 1, 1978.

Eizenstat, Stuart and Patricia Roberts Harris. Decision memorandum to Jimmy Carter, January 9, 1978.

Embry, Robert C., Jr., Draft memorandum to Office of Management and Budget, April 1978.

Embry, Robert C., Jr. Handwritten note to Perry, on face of Carter Campaign, "Cities,"August 1977.

Embry, Robert C., Jr. Memorandum to Eizenstat, no subject, March 1, 1978.

Embry, Robert C., Jr. Memoranda to Perry, January 5, 1978.

Embry, Robert C., Jr. Memorandum to Perry, November 7, 1977.

Embry, Robert C., Jr. Memorandum to Perry, September 1977.

Embry, Robert C., Jr. Memorandum to principals and URPG staff, January 5, 1978.

Embry, Robert C., Jr. Speech to annual conference. National Association of Regional Councils, San Antonio, TX, May 3, 1977.

Embry, Robert C., Jr. Yvonne Scruggs Perry, and several staff. "Some Assumptions Underlying a National Urban Policy." Draft collaborative paper, September 15, 1977.

Frieden, Bernard. "Report of Review Panel on Draft URPG Policy Statement." Memorandum to Embry, December 6, 1977.

Grigsby, William. Letter to Perry and Kaplan. University of Pennsylvania, Department of City and Regional Planning, November 29, 1977.

Harman, Sidney (Under Secretary of Commerce). "Comments and Recommendations on 'Cities and People in Distress'." Memorandum, December 2, 1977.

Harris, Patricia Roberts. "Chronology of National Urban Policy Development." Memorandum to Hamilton Jordan, with 10 appendices, March 2 1978 and March 8, 1978.

Harris, Patricia Roberts. Memorandum to principal staff, March 29, 1977.

Harris, Patricia Roberts, Stuart Eizenstat, and Robert McIntyre. Decision memorandum to President, March 21,1978

Harris, Patricia Roberts, James McIntyre, and Stuart Eizenstat. Memorandum for the President, March 17, 1978.

Houstoun, Lawrence, O., Jr. Memorandum, February 21, 1978.

Houstoun, Lawrence O., Jr. "Organization of the URPG Task Force on States and Metropolitan Regions." Unpublished document, July 28, 1977.

Kaptur, Marcy. "Urban Policy Process: Draft I for Discussion." Memorandum to Eizenstat and Bert Carp.

Knowles, Malachi (Special assistant to Yvonne Perry)."Minority Groups Responses to the National Urban Policy." Memorandum to Duckworth and Kaplan, with attachments from seven groups, August 4, 1978.

Krumm, Donald (a Task Force Coordinator). "Interest Group Proposals for National Urban Policy." Memorandum to all URPG staff, December 1, 1977.

McIntyre, James T., Jr. "Concepts to Guide Our Urban Policy." Memorandum to Harris and Eizenstat. Received January 10, 1978.

McLean, John W. "Timetable of Redlining Task Force." Memorandum to Embry and Perry, September 30, 1977.

Packer, Arnold. "Department of Labor Proposed Program—Urban and Regional Policy." Memorandum to URPG, September 1977.

Perlman, Janice E. "Enhancing Neighborhoods Capacity; A Preliminary Assessment." Memorandum, URPG, September 1977, 2.

Perlman, Janice. "The Neighborhood Component of a National Urban Policy." Memorandum, September 1977.

Perlman, Janice E. "White House Neighborhood Meeting of URPG Policy Process." Memorandum to Perry, December 16, 1977.

Perry, Yvonne Scruggs. Internal memorandum to URPG Staff, November 1977.

Perry, Yvonne Scruggs. Letter sent to all academic critics, as well as, in an amended version, to a number of other private-sector participants in the policy process March 17, 1978.

Perry, Yvonne Scruggs. Notes from White House briefing of President Carter, chronological archival materials, March 15, 1978.

Perry, Yvonne Scruggs. "Transitional Considerations Involving URPG." Unpublished correspondence to Embry, August 7, 1977.

Pharis, Claudia. Memorandum to Perry and Embry, October 5, 1977.

Public Finance Task Force."Review of Fiscal Impact of Federal Urban Policy Proposals on State and Local Governments." Memorandum to URPG, September 23, 1977.

Reiner, Thomas A. Memoranda to Perry, March 21, 1978.

Shalala, Donna. "Off The Top of My Head Reactions to URPG Papers." Memorandum to Embry, October 26, 1977.

URPG staff briefing. Based on analyses in Council on Economic Development (CED) "An Approach to Federal Urban Policy," December 1977, Figures 1 and 2, 30–31. March 1978.

URPG staff. Neighborhoods Task Force Outline. Unpublished document, July 1977.

URPG staff. "Outline of November Draft—Urban Policy Report," October 6, 1977.

Watson, Jack. "Urban Policy Announcement: Proposed Invitees." Memorandum to Harris, Midge Costanza, Eizenstat, Hamilton Jordan, Tim Kraft, Frank Moore, and Jody Powell, March 18, 1978.

Whitley, Joyce. Memorandum to Perry, August 26, 1977.

Widner, Ralph R (President, the Academy for Contemporary Problems). Correspondence to Embry, January 5, 1978; correspondence to Perry, February 14, 1978; and correspondence to Duckworth, February 24, 1978.

Interviews

Author interview with Lynn Curtis, June 19, 1980.

Author interview with Donna E. Shalala, June 21, 1980.

Author interview with Robert C. Embry, June 20, 1980.

Author interview with Wyndham Clarke, July 1980.

Publications

Academy for Contemporary Problems and the Kettering Foundation, National Urban Policy Roundtable: Managing Mature Cities (Conference), June 9–10, 1977. Speakers: William B. Eddy, Stanley J. Hallett, Mark J. Kasoff, Lawrence Susskind, and Wilbur Thompson.

Advisory Commission on Intergovernmental Relations (ACIR). *American Federalism: Toward a More Effective Partnership.* Washington, DC: ACIR, August 1975.

Advisory Commission on Intergovernmental Relations (ACIR). *Improving Urban America: A Challenge to Federalism.* Washington, DC: ACIR, September 1976.

Advisory Commission on Intergovernmental Relations (ACIR). *Urban and Rural America: Policies for Future Growth.* Washington, DC: U.S. Government Printing Office, 1968.

Allman, T. D. "America is an Urban Nation." Berkeley, CA: Office of Urban Research, University of California at Berkeley, September 1977.

Allman, T. D. "The Urban Crisis Leaves Town—And Moves to the Suburbs," *Harpers Magazine* (December 1978): 5–6.

Altshuler, Alan. "Review of the Costs of Sprawl." *Journal of the American Institute of Planners* 43 (1977):207–209.

"An Erosion of Aid to the Cities," *Business Week*, August 15, 1977, 36.

"Analysis Urged of Federal Impact on Cities." *Housing and Urban Affairs Daily*, July 19, 1977, 19.

Anderson, Martin. *The Federal Bulldozer.* New York: McGraw-Hill, 1967.

Arnstein, Sherry, L. "Maximum Feasible Manipulation." *The City.* June/July 1970.

Austin, B. William. *Population Policy of the Black Community.* New York, NY: National Urban League, July 1974.

Bahl, Roy. "Perspectives on a National Urban Policy." In *How Cities Can Grow Old Gracefully*, Subcommittee on the City, Committee on Banking, Finance and Urban Affairs, House of Representatives. Washington, D.C.: U.S. Government Printing Office, 1977.

Banfield, Edward C. (Chairman, Model Cities Task Force). Letter to the President, December 16, 1969. Harvard University, Department of Government, Boston, MA.

Banfield, Edward C. *The Unheavenly City: The Nature and Future of Urban Crisis.* Boston, MA: Little, Brown, and Company, 1970.

Banfield, Edward C. *The Unheavenly City Revisited: A Revision of the Unheavenly City.* Boston, MA: Little, Brown and Company, 1974.

Barrow, Stephen M. "The Urban Impact of Federal Policies: Their Direct and Indirect Effects on the Local Public Sector." In *Small Cities in Transition: The Dynamics of Growth and Decline,* edited by Herrington J. Bryce. Cambridge, MA: Ballinger Publishing Company, 1977.

Bates, Frederick L. and Lloyd Bacon. "The Community as a Social System." *Social Forces* 50 (March 1972).

Bauer, R. "Position Papers for NPA Information Project." Mimeo. Harvard Business School, June 1, 1964.

Bennis, Warren G., Kenneth D. Benne, Robert Chin, and Kenneth E. Corey, eds. *The Planning of Change*. Third edition. New York, NY: Holt Rinehart and Winston, 1976.

Benveniste, Guy. *The Politics of Expertise.* Berkeley, CA: The Glendessary Press, 1972.

Bergh, Stephen. "The Urban Impact of Federal Policies: Their Direct and Indirect Effects on the Local Public Sector." In *Small Cities in Transition: The Dynamics of Growth and Decline*, edited by Herrington J. Bryce. Boston, MA: Ballinger Publishing Company, 1977.

"Bill Clinton on Rebuilding America's Cities" Photocopy. Washington, DC: Democratic National Committee, 1993.

Blau, Peter M. *Exchange and Power in Social Life.* New York, NY: John Wiley & Sons, 1967.

Blau, Peter M. *The Dynamics of Bureaucracy: A Study of Interpersonal Relations in Two Government Agencies.* Second edition. Chicago, IL: University of Chicago Press, 1963.

Blau, Peter M. and Marshall W. Meyer. *Bureaucracy in Modern Society.* Second edition. New York, NY: Random House, 1971.

Bolan, Richard S. "Planning and the New Federalism." *AIP Journal* (July 1973).

Bonafede, Dom. "White House Report." *National Journal* (April 15, 1978):584.

Bosworth, B. and J. Dusenberry. *Capital Needs in the Seventies.* Washington, DC: The Brookings Institution, 1975.

Braybrooke, David and Charles E. Lindblom. *A Strategy of Decision: Policy Evaluation as a Social Process.* New York, NY: Free Press, 1970.

Brimmer, Andrew F. and Henry S. Terrell. "The Economic Potential of Black Capitalism." Presented paper. American Economics Association, New York, NY, December 29, 1969.

Broder, David S. and Susanna McBee. *Washington Post*, Saturday, March 25, 1978, A2.

Bryce, Herrington J. "Priorities in the Allocation of Federal Funds to Aid the Cities." Washington, DC: Joint Center for Political Studies, September 1976. Transmitted for URPG consideration, September 1977.

Bryce, Herrington J., ed. *Small Cities in Transition: The Dynamics of Growth and Decline.* Cambridge, MA: Ballinger Publishing Co., 1977.

Bryce, Herrington J. (Director of Research, Joint Center for Political Studies). Testimony. U.S. House of Representatives' Committee on Banking, Currency and Housing, September 29, 1976.

Bryce, Herrington J., ed. *Urban Governance and Minorities.* New York, NY: Praeger Publishers, 1976.

Califano, Joseph A., Jr. *Governing America: An Insider's Report from the White House and the Cabinet.* New York, NY: Simon and Schuster, 1981.

Canty, Donald, ed. *The New City: National Commission on Urban Growth Policy.* New York, NY: Frederick A. Praeger for Urban America, Inc., 1969.

Caputo, David A. *Urban America: The Policy Alternatives.* San Francisco, CA: W.H. Freeman & Company, 1976.

"Carter Gets $7B Blueprint for the Cities." *New York Daily News,* November 9, 1977.

Carter, Jimmy. *Presidential Papers, Fourth Quarter, 1978.* Washington, DC: U.S. Government Printing Office.

Carter, Jimmy. Speech to the Conference of Mayors, Milwaukee, Wisconsin, July 29, 1976.

Carter, Jimmy. Speech. Transcript in *The Washington Post,* November 9, 1977.

Carter Presidential Campaign. "Cities: Urban Policy for the Remainder of the Twentieth Century." Mimeo. Atlanta, Georgia, April 1, 1976.

Carter Presidential Campaign. "A New Beginning." Paper presented by Jimmy Carter to the platform Committee of the Democratic Party, June 16, 1976.

Carter Presidential Campaign. "Urban Policy." Address to United States Conference of Mayors, Milwaukee, WI, June 29, 1976.

"Carter's Task Force on Cities Urges $7.7 Billion Job Program for Poor." *Philadelphia Inquirer,* November 9, 1977.

Chinitz, Benjamin. *Urban Economic Development: The Federal Role.* Binghamton, NY: SUNY, October 1977.

Clark, Kenneth B. *Youth in the Ghetto: A Study of the Consequences of Powerlessness and a Blueprint for Change.* New York: HARYOU, 1964.

Clark, Kenneth B. and Jeanette Hopkins. *A Relevant War Against Poverty: A Study of Community Action Programs and Observable Change.* New York, NY: Harper & Rowe, 1968.

Cleaveland, Frederic N. and Associates. *Congress and Urban Problems.* Washington, DC: The Brookings Institution, 1969.

Coalition of Northeast Interests. *Cities in the Middle: The Way Back to Prosperity, Trenton, New Jersey.* Washington, DC: HUD, February 1977.

Coan, Carl A.S. (Legislative Counsel, National Housing Council, Inc.). Letter to Orin Kramer, White House Domestic Council, January 6, 1978.

Congressional Quarterly. "How Carter Urban Policy Was Developed." *Urban America: Policies and Problems.* Washington, DC: CQ, August 1978.

Congressional Quarterly, Inc. "Urban America: Policies and Problems." Washington, DC: CQ, August 1978.

Cose, Ellis. *Energy and the Urban Crisis.* Washington, DC: Joint Center for Political Studies, 1978.

Cose, Ellis and Milton Morris. *Energy Policy and the Poor.* Washington, DC: Joint Center for Political Studies, 1977.

Council for Economic Development. *An Approach to Federal Urban Policy: A Statement on National Policy by the Research and Policy Committee of CED.* New York, NY: CED, December 1977.

"Cover Story: The Immigrants: How They're Helping to revitalize the U.S. Economy." *Business Week* (July 13, 1992):118.

Dahl, Robert A. and Charles E. Lindblom. *Politics, Economics and Welfare: Planning and Politics: Economics Systems Resolved into Basic Social Processes.* New York, NY: Harper & Row, 1953.

Davenport, Chester (assistant secretary for policy, plans, and international affairs). "DOT's Northeast Corridor Improvement Program." Memorandum for Perry, October 20, 1977.

Davenport, Chester. "Priority-Status Report of the Urban and Regional Policy Group." Memorandum to secretary and deputy secretary, August 31, 1977.

Davidoff, Paul and Thomas A. Reiner. "A Choice Theory of Planning." *Journal of the American Institute of Planners* XXVIII (2, May 1962):103–115.

DeGrove, Dr. John M. "The Impact of Federal Grants-in-Aid on the South and its Cities." Durham, NC: The Southern Growth Policies Board, September 1977.

Derthick, Martha. "Hearings on New Federalism, Subcommittee of the Committee on Government Operations, House of Representatives." Washington, DC: U.S. Government Printing Office, 1974.

Downs, Anthony. "Creating a National Urban Policy." Washington, DC: Brookings Institution, paper transmitted Fall 1977.

Downs, Anthony. *Opening up the Suburbs: An Urban Strategy for America.* New Haven, CT: Yale University Press, 1973.

Downs, Anthony. *Urban Problems and Prospects.* Real Estate Research Corporation. Chicago, IL: Markham Publishing Company, 1970.

Duhl, Leonard J., ed. *The Urban Condition: People and Policy in the Metropolis.* New York, NY: Basic Books, Inc., 1963.

Dukakis, Michael. "A Role for the States in Urban Policy." Op-Ed. *Washington Post*, December 25, 1977, A-17.

Easton, David. *A Systems Analysis of Political Life.* New York, NY: John Wiley & Sons, Inc., 1965.

Elbing, Alvar, ed. *Behavioral Decisions in Organizations: A Framework for Decision Making* Glenview, IL: Scott Foreman, 1970.

Evan, William M. "An Organization-Set Model of Interorganizational Relations." In *Organizational Decision Making*, edited by M.F. Tuite, M. Radnor, and R.K. Chishold. Chicago, IL: Aldine Publishing Co., 1972.

Feldstein, M.S. "The Economics of the New Unemployment."*The Public Interest* 33 (1973):3–42.

Flick, David. "Let Some Areas Die to Save Others, City Told."*Cincinnati Post*, June 10, 1977.

Frieden, Bernard J. and Marshall Kaplan. *The Politics of Neglect.* Cambridge, MA: The MIT Press, 1975.

Friedman, Lawrence M. *Government and Slum Housing: A Century of Frustration.* Chicago, IL: Rand McNally & Co., 1968.

Friedmann, John. *Retracking America: A Theory of Transactive Planning.* Garden City, NY: Anchor Press/Doubleday, 1973.

Galbraith, John Kenneth. *The Affluent Society.* Boston: Houghton Mifflin Company, 1958.

Gibbs, Jewelle Taylor. "After the L.A. Riots: Social Work's Role in Healing Cities." Zellerback Family Fund Professor's Occasional Paper. Berkeley CA: University of California, 1992.

Glickman, Norman J., ed. *The Urban Impact of Federal Policies.* Baltimore, MD: Johns Hopkins University Press, 1980.

Gorham, William and Nathan Glazer, eds. *The Urban Predicament.* Washington, DC: The Urban Institute, 1976.

Graham, Elinor. "The Politics of Poverty." PUB FACTS]

Graham, Otis L., Jr. *Toward a Planned Society.* New York, NY: Oxford University Press, 1976.

Graves, Brooke. *Federal Grant-in-Aid Programs, 1803–1958.* Washington, DC: The Library of Congress, Legislative Reference Service, June 1958.

Green, Robert L. *The Urban Challenge: Poverty and Race.* Chicago, IL: Follett Publishing Company, 1977.

Greer, Scott. *The Emerging City: Myth and Reality.* New York, NY: The Free Press, 1962.

Greer, Scott. *Urban Renewal and American Cities: The Dilemma of Democratic Intervention.* Indianapolis, IN: Bobbs-Merrill Company, Inc., 1965.

Gulick, Luther. *Problems of U.S. Economic Development.* New York, NY: Committee for Economic Development, 1958.

Gutkind, E.A. *Twilight of the Cities*. New York, NY: The Free Press of Glencoe, 1962.

Haar, Charles M. *Between the Idea and the Reality: A Study in the Origin, Fate and the Legacy of the Model Cities Program*. Boston, MA: Little, Brown & Company, 1975.

Hargrove, Edwin C. *Jimmy Carter as President: Leadership and the Politics of the Public Good*. Baton Rouge, LA: Louisiana State University Press, 1982.

Harrington, Michael. *The Other America: Poverty in the United States*. New York, NY: The Macmillan Company, 1964.

Harris, Senator Fred R. and Mayor John V. Lindsay (Co-chairmen). *The State of the Cities: Report of the Commission on the Cities in the '70's*. New York, NY: Praeger Publishers, 1972.

Harvey, David. *Social Justice and the City*. Baltimore, MD: Johns Hopkins University Press, 1973.

Haskins, Gage B.A. "The Impact of International Trade and Investment: Policy on Employment in the United States." November 1977.

Heclo, Hugh. *A Government of Strangers: Executive Politics in Washington*. Washington, DC: Brookings Institution, 1977.

Hoch, I. "City Size: Effects, Trends, and Policies." *Science* 193 (1976): 856–863.

Houstoun, Lawrence O., Jr. "City Neighborhoods and Urban Policy." *Nation's Cities*. Washington, DC: National League of Cities, 1976.

Humphrey, Hubert. "Comments on the Draft of the President's 1976 Biennial Report on National Growth." Mimeo. Washington, DC, January 19, 1976.

James, Franklin. "Private Reinvestment in Older Housing and Older Neighborhoods: Recent Trends and Forces." Mimeo. Washington, DC: The Urban Institute, June 1977.

Jenkins, Timothy L. *Final Report: National Urban Policy Statement Equity Forum Feedback*. Washington, DC: Match Institution, March 15, 1978.

Jenkins, Timothy L. "National Urban Policy Statement." Washington, DC: Match Institution, February 28, 1978.

Johnson, J. L. "To hell with the Cities. Let 'em Die: When they're Exhausted and Useless, Why Not move on to Better Places?" *Los Angeles Times*, Friday, January 7, 1977, Part II, 7.

Jordan, Vernon. E. "Keynote Address to the 67th Annual Conference of the National Urban League." Mimeo. Washington, DC: National Urban League, July 25, 1977.

Jordan, Vernon E. *The State of Black America 1977*. New York, NY: National Urban League, January 11, 1977.

Kain, John F. "Coping with Ghetto Unemployment." *AIP Journal* (March 1969).

Kaplan, Marshall. *Urban Planning in the 1960s: A Design for Irrelevancy*. Cambridge, MA: MIT Press, 1973.

Kaplan, Marshall and Franklin James, eds. *The Future of National Urban Policy*. Durham, NC: Duke University Press, 1990.

Kaplan, Marshall and Peggy L. Cuciti, eds. *The Great Society and Its Legacy: Twenty Years of U.S. Social Policy*. Durham, NC: Duke University Press, 1986.

Kaplan, Marshall and Bernard Frieden. *The Politics of Neglect: Urban Aid from Model Cities to Revenue Sharing*. Cambridge, MA: MIT Press, 1977.

Kasoff, Mark J. "The Urban Impact of Federal Policies: A Preview of a New Rand Study." *Nation's Cities*. National League of Cities, November 1977.

Kettering Foundation, "Whatever Happened to River City?"

Keyserling, Leon H. *Poverty and Deprivation in the United States*. Washington, DC: Conference on Economic Progress, April 1962.

Krause, Charles A. "Geno Baroni to Get HUD Housing Post." *The Washington Post*, March 2, 1977.

Lasswell, Harold and David Lerner, eds., *The Policy Sciences*. Stanford, CA.: Stanford University Press, 1951.

Lescaze, Lee. "Moynihan Hits Feds for NYC's Decline." *The Washington Post*, June 28, 1977.

Levitan, Sar A. *The Great Society's Poor Law: A New Approach to Poverty*. Baltimore, MD: Johns Hopkins Press, 1969.

Lindblom, Charles E. *The Policy Making Process*. Foundations of Modern Political Science Series. Englewood Cliffs, New Jersey: Prentice-Hall, 1972.

Lindblom, Charles E. "The Science of Muddling Through." *Public Administration Review* 19 (1959):79–99.

Lineberry, Robert L. "Public Services and Economic Development." Evanston, IL: Northwestern University, September 1977.

Lipsky, M. and J. Mollenkopf. "Toward a National Urban Policy Based on Neighborhood Economic Opportunity and Vitality." Report to *Action*, mimeo, December 1977.

Long, Norton E. "How to Help Cities Become Independent." Unpublished paper. St. Louis, MO: University of Missouri, August 1977.

Mandelbaum, Seymour J. "Urban Pasts and Urban Policies." Mimeo. Department of City and Regional Planning, University of Pennsylvania, October 1979.

The National Urban Coalition. "National Urban Policy Paper." Washington, DC: National Urban Coalition, March 1978.

March, James G. and Herbert A. Simon, *Organizations.* New York, NY: John Wiley & Sons, Inc., 1958.

Marris, Peter. *Loss and Change.* New York, NY: Pantheon Books, 1976.

Marris, Peter and Martin Rein, *Dilemmas of Social Reform: Poverty and Community Action in the United States.* New York, NY: Atherton Press, 1967.

Martin, Roscoe C. *The Cities and The Federal System.* New York, NY: Atherton Press, 1965.

Massachusetts Office of State Planning. *City and Town Centers: A Program for Growth.* The Massachusetts Growth Policy Report, September 1977.

McBee, Susanna. "Forceful HUD Secretary is Turning Her Critics Around." *Washington Post*, Saturday, March 18, 1978, A-6,

Milgram, Morris. *Good Neighborhood: The Challenge of Open Housing.* New York, NY: W.W. Norton & Company, 1977.

Miller, S.M. and Martin Rein. "The War on Poverty: Perspectives and Prospects." In *Poverty as a Public Issue* edited by Ben B. Seligman. New York, NY: Free Press, 1965.

Miller, T.R., R.G. Bruce, Carol B. Shapiro, and H.J. Tankin. *Strategies for Revitalizing Neighborhood Commercial Areas: The Role Application and Impact of Public and Private Resources.* Final report. National Institute for Advanced Studies, November 1, 1977.

Mitchell, Howard E., Sr. *Paradigm of the Diffusion of Social Technology Process.* Philadelphia, PA: Human Resources Center, University of Pennsylvania, 1974.

Morgan, Elaine. "Are Cities Really Worth Saving?" *Washington Star*, April 3, 1977.

Morris, Robert. *Social Policy of the American Welfare State.* New York, NY: Harper & Row, 1979.

Moynihan, Daniel P. *Maximum Feasible Misunderstanding: Community Action in the War on Poverty.* New York, NY: Free Press, 1979.

Moynihan, Daniel P., ed. *Toward A National Urban Policy.* New York, NY: Basic Books, Inc., 1970.

Muller, Peter O. *The Outer City.* Philadelphia, PA: Association of American Geographers and Temple University, 1976.

Nathan, Richard and John Logo. "Intergovernmental Fiscal Roles and Relations." *Annals of the American Academy of Political and Social Science* (509, May 5, 1990):42.

National Advisory Commission on Civil Disorders. Report (Bound Volume). Washington, DC: Government Printing Office, March 1, 1968.

National League of Cities. *National Municipal Policy.* Washington, DC: NUL, 1977. Adopted at the Annual Business Session, Congress of Cities, Denver, Colorado, December 1, 1976.

National League of Cities. *State of the Cities: 1975—A New Urban Crisis?* Washington, DC: NLC, January 1976.

National Urban League. *Population Policy and the Black Community.* New York: NUL, 1974.

National Urban League. *The State of Black America 1977.* Washington, DC: NUL, January 11, 1977.

New York Times, Editorial page, November 21, 1977

"Nixon May Divert Model Cities Aid for Schools' Use," *New York Times,* April 26, 1970.

Orlebeke, Charles. "Carter Renews the Romance with National Urban Policy." *Planning* (August 1978):2393.

O'Neill, Eugene. *Long Day's Journey Into Night.* New Haven, CT: Yale University, reissue 1989.

Parsons, K.C. and P. Clavel. *National Growth Policy: An Institutional Perspective.* Ithaca, NY: Cornell University, Program in Urban and Regional Studies, 1977.

Pechman, Joseph A., ed., *Setting National Priorities: The 1978 Budget.* Washington, DC: The Brookings Institution, 1977.

Perry, Yvonne S. "Follow the Yellow Brick Road: An Overview of the Model Cities Program." Unpublished paper presented at Orientation Conference for Model Neighborhood Residents, March 16, 1970.

Perry, James M. "Mr. Carter's Cautious Urban Plan." *The Wall Street Journal*, August 9, 1977, 14.

Peterson, George E.and Carol W. Lewis, eds., *Reagan and the Cities.* Washington, DC: The Urban Institute Press, 1986.

Piven, Frances Fox and Richard A. Cloward. *Regulating the Poor: The Functions of Public Welfare.* New York, NY: Random House, 1971.

"Plan Favors Cities, Poor." *Atlanta Constitution.* November 7, 1977.

Porter, Paul R. *The Recovery of American Cities.* New York, NY: Two Continents Publishing Group, 1976.

Rand Corporation. *The Urban Impacts of Federal Policies.* Four volumes, grant from the Charles F. Kettering Foundation, June 1977 (Santa

Monica, CA: The Rand Corporation): Vol. I: Overview, Barbara Williams, project director. Vol. II: Economic Development, Roger J. Vaughn. Vol. III: Fiscal Conditions, Stephen Barro. Vol. IV: Population and Residential Location, Roger J. Vaughn and Mary E. Vogel.

Real Estate Research Corporation. *The Costs of Sprawl.* Three volumes. Washington, DC: Government Printing Office, 1975.

Reiner, Thomas A., ed. "Towards a National Urban Policy—Critical Reviews." *Journal of Regional Science* 19 (1, 1979).

Reinhold, Robert. "An Administration with Rural Roots Now Must Address the City." *New York Times*, November 1977.

Reinhold, Robert. *New York Times*, March 26, 1978.

Reinhold, Robert. "City Limits: How Urban Policy Gets Made—Very Carefully." *New York Times*, April 2, 1978.

Reisinger, Sue. Interview with Jimmy Carter. *Dayton Daily News*, March 1978.

Reschovsky, A. and E. Knapp. "Tax Base Sharing: An Assessment of the Minnesota Experience." *Journal of the American Institute of Planners* 43 (1977):361–369.

Rossi, Peter H. and Robert A. Dentler, *The Politics of Urban Renewal: The Chicago Findings.* New York, NY: The Free Press of Glenco, Inc., 1961.

Rowan, Carl. Editorial. *Washington Star*, February 8, 1978, editorial page.

"R.S.V.P." *Nation's Cities* 15 (10, October 1977).

Ruskin, David. *Cities Without Suburbs.* Baltimore, MD: Johns Hopkins University Press, 1993.

"Sailing Directions for Urban America: Beating, Reaching and Running." *Journal of the American Institute of Planners* 44 (3, July 1978):355.

Schaefer, William Donald. *A New Federal Policy for Cities: The Baltimore Proposal.* Baltimore, MD: PUBLISHER? October 11, 1977.

Scheinider, Alvin J. "Blacks, Cities and the Energy Crisis." *Urban Affairs Quarterly* (September 1974).

Schlesinger, Jr., Arthur M. *A Thousand Days.* New York, NY: Houghton Mifflin, 1965.

Schoettle, Enid Curtis Bok. "The State of the Art in Policy Studies." In *The Study of Policy Formation*, Chapter 4, edited by Raymond A. Bauer and Kenneth J. Gergen. New York, NY: The Free Press, 1986.

Schussheim, Morton J. "The Housing Outlook." Congressional Reference Service, Library of Congress, September 1977.

Schussheim, Morton J. *The Modest Commitment to Cities.* Lexington, MA: Lexington Books, 1974.

Scott, Randall W., David J. Brower, and Dallas D. Miner. *Management & Control of Growth.* Volume. 1. Washington, DC: The Urban Land Institute, 1975.

Segal, D. "Are There Returns to Scale in City Size?" *The Review of Economics and Statistics* 58 (1976):339–350.

Shalala, Donna E. and Julia Vitullo-Martin. "Rethinking the Urban Crisis: Proposals for a National Urban Agenda." *Journal of the American Planning Association* 55 (1, Winter 1989):3–13.

Smith, Edward C. "The Coming of the Black Ghetto State." *The Yale Review* 61 (2, December 1971):176.

Simon, Herbert. "Decision-Making and Administrative Organization." *Public Administrative Review* IV (Winter 1944).

Simon, Herbert. "Theories of Decision-Making in Economic and Behavioral Science." *American Economic Review* X (June 1959): 255–257.

Simon, Herbert A., Donald W. Smithburg, and Victor A.Thompson. *Public Administration.* New York, NY: Alfred A. Knopf, 1956.

Stanfield, Rochelle L. "The Development of Carter's Urban Policy: One Small Step for Federalism." *Publius, The Journal of Federalism* (Winter, 1978):39–53.

Sternlieb, George S. "Are Big Cities Worth Saving?" In *The City in the Seventies*, edited by Robert K. Lin. New York, NY: Rand Institute, 1972.

Stone, Chuck. "Black Vote Did It Up Brown for J.C." *Philadelphia Daily News,* November 3, 1976, 2.

Sundquist, James. *Making Federalism Work.* Washington, DC: The Brookings Institution, 1969.

Sundquist, James. *Dispersing Population: What America Can Learn From Europe.* Washington, DC: The Brookings Institution, 1975.

Sundquist, James L. *Politics and Policy: The Eisenhower, Kennedy and Johnson Years.* Washington, DC: The Brookings Institution, 1968.

Thompson, Wilbur. Transcript of remarks. Managing Mature Cities Conference, National Urban Policy Roundtable, Academy for Contemporary Problems, sponsored by the Charles F. Kettering Foundation, Cincinnati, Ohio, June 1977.

U.S. Department of Housing and Urban Development, Office of Planning and Research. *An Urban Development Strategy for California.* Advisory Committee Draft for Public Review and Comment, Washington, DC, May 1977.

U.S. Department of Housing and Urban Development, *Improving the Quality of Urban Life: A Program Guide to Model Neighborhoods in Demonstration Cities.* Washington, DC: Government Printing Office, December 1966.

U.S. Department of the Treasury. "Fiscal Impact of the Economic Stimulus Package (ESP) of 48 Large Urban Governments Office of State and Local Finance." Washington, DC: Government Printing Office, January 23, 1978.

U.S. House of Representatives, House Committee on Banking, Currency, and Housing. "The Rebirth of the American City." Hearings, September 20, 1976 to October 1, 1976.

U.S. House of Representatives, Subcommittee on the City of the Committee on Banking, Finance and Urban Affairs. "How Cities Can Grow Old Gracefully." Hearings, December 1977.

U.S. House of Representatives. Subcommittee on the City of the Committee on Banking, Finance and Urban Affairs. "Impact of the Federal Budget on Cities." Hearings, July 1977.

U.S. House of Representatives, Subcommittee on the City of the Committee on Banking, Finance and Urban Affairs. "Successes Abroad: What Foreign Cities Can Teach American Cities." Hearings, April 4–6, 1977.

U.S. House of Representatives, Subcommittee on Housing and Community Development of the Committee on Banking, Currency and Housing, House of Representatives. *Evolution of the Role of the Federal Government in Housing and Community Development: A Chronology of Legislative and Selected Executive Actions, 1892-1974.* Washington, D.C.: U.S. Government Printing Office, October 1975.

"U.S. Report Urges Larger Commitment to Cities and Poor." *New York Times*, November 5, 1977.

Wall Street Journal, March 28, 1978, 3.

Warren, Robert. "National Urban Policy and the Local State: Paradoxes of Meanings, Action and Consequences." *Urban Affairs Quarterly* 25 (June 1990):541–561.

Warren, Roland L. *Love, Truth and Social Change*. Chicago, IL: Rand, McNally and Company, 1971.

Warren, Roland L., Stephen M. Rose, and Ann F. Bergunder. *The Structure of Urban Reform: Community Decision Organizations in Stability and Change.* Lexington, MA: D.C. Heath and Company, 1974.

Washington Post, March 28, 1978, A-1.

Washington Post, September 1976, Editorial Page.

Weiler, Dr. Conrad. "Urban Reinvestment and the Displacement of Low and Moderate Income People: The Emergence of an Issue." Philadelphia, PA: Temple University, November 1977.

Weiss, Robert S. and Martin Rein. "The Evaluation of Broad-Aim Programs: Experimental Design, Its Difficulties, and an Alternative." *Administrative Science Quarterly* 15 (March 1970):97–109.

"What is Henry Reuss Up To?" *Nation's Cities.* Washington, DC: National League of Cities, September 1977.

"White House Orders Urban Policy Review; Revises Study Panel." *New York Times*, August 31, 1977, 10.

"White House Losing 7 Blacks From Staff: Many Leaving for Better Jobs but Some Cite Frustration with the Administration." *New York Times.* May 14, 1978,

Whitman, Walt. *Leaves of Grass.* New York, NY: Bantam Classics, 1983.

Wildavsky, Aaron. "Jimmy Carter's Theory of Governing." *The Wilson Quarterly* 1 (2, Winter 1977).

Wilson, James Q. *Urban Renewal: The Record and the Controversy.* Cambridge, MA: M.I.T. Press, 1966.

Wingo, Lowdon. "Issues in A National Urban Development Strategy for the United States." *Urban Studies* XIII (1976):3–27.

Wolman, Harold. *Politics of Federal Housing.* New York: Dodd, Mead & Co., 1971.

Woodbury, Coleman, ed. *Urban Redevelopment: Problems and Practices.* Chicago, IL: University of Chicago Press, 1953.

Yin, Robert K., ed. *The City in the Seventies.* Itasca, IL: F.E. Peacock Publishers, Inc. 1972.

Ylvisaker, Paul N. "The Deserted City." *Journal of The American Institute of Planners* 24 (1, February 1959).

Ylvisaker, Paul N. "Opening Minds and Expanding Cities." In *Ends and Means of Urban Renewal,* Papers from the Fiftieth Anniversary Forum, Philadelphia Housing Association. Philadelphia, PA, 1961.

Index

About the Author

For more than four decades, Dr. Yvonne Scruggs-Leftwich has worked to promote the interests of the nation's urban communities—as a government official, professor, policy analyst, community activist, author, and spokesperson. Currently, she is a professor at the National Labor College, George Meany Campus, Silver Spring, Maryland. Most recently, she served as executive director and chief operating officer of the Black Leadership Forum, a coalition of the nation's top African American civil rights and service organizations. In this position, she facilitated dialogue among African American leaders and constructed opportunities for collaboration across racial lines on issues important to the African American community. She also has taught government and urban power politics at several of the nation's top universities and colleges.

Dr. Scruggs-Leftwich holds a doctorate from the University of Pennsylvania, a master's degree from the Hubert H. Humphrey School of the University of Minnesota, and a bachelor's degree from North Carolina Central University. She was a Fulbright Fellow to Germany.

Previously, Dr. Scruggs-Leftwich was deputy mayor of the City of Philadelphia; New York State Housing Commissioner; Deputy Assistant Secretary, U.S. Department of Housing and Urban Development; executive director of President Carter's Urban and Regional Policy Group, which issued the first national urban policy; and director of the Urban and National Policy Institutes for the Joint Center for Political and Economic Studies. She has also co-owned several nondepository banking corporations and served as a consultant in the municipal finance field.

With more than a hundred publications to her credit, Dr. Scruggs-Leftwich continues to write about issues germane to women, African Americans, and labor education. Her areas of expertise include urban policy, politics, public administration, governmental affairs, civil rights, women=s issues, grassroots organizing and labor union activism, city and regional planning, neighborhood and community development, strategic planning, and leadership development. In addition, she writes for the National Newspaper Publishers Association and for Women's E-News. She is the author of *Standing With My Fist: Black Women in the Political Diaspora* (2005). She is working on her next book, *Sound Bites of Protest: Race, Politics and Public Policy.*